GRAPHIC ARTISTS GUILD HANDBOOK
PRICING & ETHICAL
GUIDELINES

GRAPHIC ARTISTS GUILD HANDBOOK
PRICING & ETHICAL GUIDELINES

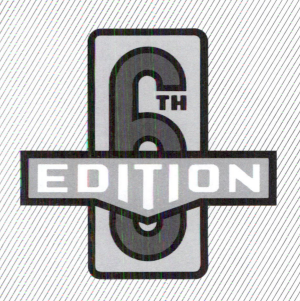

Editorial

Project committee, sixth edition:
Marsha Camera
Jerry McConnell
Jeff Seaver
Lee Stewart
Simms Taback

Project coordinator and editor:
Margi Trapani

Consultants:
Volker E. H. Antoni
Tad Crawford
Gene Eisner
Joel L. Hecker

Editorial consultant:
Susan M. Dooha

Editorial production:
Emily Tourin

Copy editor:
Rachel Burd

Editorial and Traffic:
Simms Taback

Executive Director,
Graphic Artists Guild:
Paul Basista

National President,
Graphic Artists Guild:
Kathie Abrams

Design:

Art Direction:
Simms Taback

Design:
Peter Ross
Ross Culbert Holland & Lavery, Inc.

Cover Design and Art:
Michael Doret

Production and Camera Ready:
Bob Carlson

Typography:
Marina Advani
True To Type

Printing Consultant:
Gerald McConnell

Filmwork:
H. Horsman & Co.

Printing:
Redwood Press

On Press:
Jason Taback
Michael Doret

Publisher:
Graphic Artists Guild

Distributors to the trade
in the United States and Canada:
North Light Books
A Division of F&W Publications, Inc.
1507 Dana Avenue
Cincinnati, OH 45207
1-800-543-4644
(In Ohio) 1-800-551-0884

T D E D I C A T I O N The year 1987 marks the 20th anniversary of the Graphic Artists Guild and the publication of the sixth edition of our *Guidelines*. This book has grown from a 20-page pamphlet to more than 200 pages of information on business practices and pricing ranges. The growth and depth of our book mirrors the growth in size and sophistication of our membership. It is their commitment, participation and knowledge that is the foundation of the Guild and of the *Guidelines*.

The editors of the sixth edition and the National Board of Directors of the Guild would like to take this opportunity to thank the members and consultants who have participated in the development of the *Guidelines*.

Special thanks are due to Jerry McConnell and Simms Taback, whose commitments to and work on behalf of the Guild have been critical to the success of this book and the progress of the organization.

We would also like to thank the following members and consultants whose contributions to the *Guidelines* have been invaluable.

Bill Andrews
Bob Anthony
Volker E. H. Antoni
Rick Anwyl
Arnie Arlow
Melanie Arwin
Laura Ausubel
Carol Bancroft & Friends
Brent Baylor
Noel Becker
Shelly Beckler
Ed Benguiat
Ben Benson
Sam Bernstein
Irving Bogen
Charles Boyter
Lynn Braswell
Alice Brickner
Ellen Brief
Ginger Brown
Diana Bryan
Tom Carnase
Marsha Camera
Seymour Chwast
Elizabeth Cook
Gil Cowley
D.L. Cramer
Tad Crawford
Ray Cruz
Mecca Culbert

Roland Dacombs
Zelda Dana
Stewart David
Hank De Leo
Sherry DeLeon
Joe Del Gaudio
Diane Dillon
Susan Dooha
Michael Doret
Gene Eisner
Dean Ellis
Stephanie Farago
Ron Farber
Jeff Feinen
Laura Ferguson
Larry Froehlich
Mary Galaty
David Gatti
Bob Geissman
Ruth Geniac
Dick Gill
Jan Giolito
Linda Gottfried
Susan Gray
Fred Greller
Sam Gross
Joann Grossman
Jacquie Hann
Neil Hardy
Peter Harrison

Jack Hart
Joel Hecker
Jim Heimann
Jacqui Henderson
Lynn Hertzman
Robert Heindel
Dick Hess
D.K. Holland
Walter Hortens
Gerald Huerta
Zuelia Ann Hurt
Doug Johnson
Evelyne Johnson
Shaun Johnston
M. Brooks Jones
Diane Kadah
Bernie Karlin
Ruth Katz
Deborah Kaufman
Peggy Keating
Gregory King
Jim Kingston
Alice Koeth
Arie Kopelman
Howard Koslow
Sandy Kossin
Kitty Krupat
Jane Lander
Cecily Lang
Bud Lavery
Polly Law
Donald Leake
Terry Le Blanc
Gale Litvak
Joe Lombardo
Sara Love
Shelly Lowell
Roxanne Lowit
Alvalyn Lundgren-Ellis
Richard Lyons
Linda Mancini
Susan Mayer
Mara McAfee
Kathy McCarthy
Jerry McConnell
Wilson McLean
Jim McMullan
Chuck McVicker
Carol Michelson
Wendell Minor
Rohit Modi
Paula Monroe
Vicki Morgan
Carol Morley
Dick Morrell
Nancy Moyna
Barbara Muccio

Barbara Nessim
Milton Newborn
Tom Nikosey
Regina Ortenzi
Bob Palevitz
Linwood B. Peal
Scott Pike
Maria Piscopo
Gabriel Polansky
Judith Raices
Gerald Rapp
Lawrence Ratzkin
Peter Ross
Reynold Ruffins
Craig Russell
Gerald Salvio
Dan Schuder
Jonathan Schneider
Jeff Seaver
Ed Seltzer
Deborah Shapiro
Ned Shaw
Chris Sheller
Robert Shore
Rita Sue Siegel
Joan Sigman
Chas B. Slackman
Steve Smallwood
Carol Spier
Kitty Stavros
Lee Stewart
Simms Taback
Marvin Tannenberg
Pamela Joy Trow
Frank Truglio
Sally VanDevanter
Donald Van Vort
Alfred Vitromile
Sam Viviano
Karen Watson
Anne Weinbrenner
Ricci Weinstein
Bill Westwood
Lynne Wiener
Gregory Wier-Quiton
Bob Winkler
Harry Winters
Ron Wolin
Jeahyee Wong
Josie Yee
Donald Young
Judy Yourman
Barry Zaid
Jeffrey Zeiller
Bob Ziering
Association of
Medical Illustrators
Joint Ethics Committee

PREFACE

Putting a price on a creative work is a complex process for artists and for those who purchase artwork. This sixth edition of the *Graphic Artists Guild Handbook: Pricing and Ethical Guidelines* is compiled to help both artists and art buyers determine how to arrive at fair prices; it is also a guide to acceptable and ethical business standards for our industry.

Leading members of the graphic arts profession have contributed to the *Guidelines* over the years, providing what has become the most respected single source of information for people who buy and sell creative work. But the *Guidelines* is not just a consolidation of selective wisdom and experience; it represents a universal consensus painstakingly gathered from national surveys unique in the diverse field of visual communications.

The *Guidelines* does not suggest maximum or minimum prices for artwork. Instead, it offers a solid base upon which to negotiate fair compensation for creative work. By definition, artwork differs from project to project. New artists selling designs to industry compete with experienced professionals whose reputations help sell their work. Similarly, large corporations and fledgling firms compete in the same markets for consumers' attention. And, the markets that graphic artists work in vary tremendously both in size and specialization. The *Guidelines* is an aid to both artists and art buyers who must cope with the complex *business* of visual communications.

This sixth edition contains an expanded section on computer arts, a new section on proposal/estimate forms to help determine formulas for pricing specific projects, and an expanded chapter on medical and technical illustration. All sections, including one on mastering the art of negotiation, have been updated to keep pace with the rapidly changing industries that Guild members represent.

The Graphic Artists Guild is dedicated to raising and maintaining ethical standards throughout the communications industry. We have come a long way in recent years towards our goal to eliminate abuses and establish fair and equitable artist-industry practices. The Guidelines is just one effort by the Guild that helps to achieve that goal.

Regina Ortenzi
President
National Graphic Artists Guild

Introduction: How to use the Guidelines

This book provides both graphic artists and their clients with a current compilation of pricing methods, ranges and professional business practices applied throughout the industry. The growing complexity of uses, fee arrangements, and business and financial considerations makes information of this type essential for all participants in the field.

The book is divided into six major sections: Professional Issues and Practices; Pricing and Trade Customs; Contracts; Business Management; and Reference.

Section 1: Introduction is a guide through the book that provides a detailed description of its various sections and their purposes.

Section 2: Professional Issues and Practices provides an overview of the ethical standards and practices that apply to the creation and sale of graphic artwork. Among the information included in this section is the communications industry's Code of Fair Practice and an overview of the various organizations that monitor industry practices.

The chapter on *Professional Issues* updates clients and artists on the laws, new legislative initiatives and trade practices that affect the sale of artwork. Included is the most recent information on the copyright law, moral rights and fair practices legislation, tax deductions on charitable contributions, art contests and competitions, work on speculation and cancellation fees.

Business & Legal Practices for Commissioned Artwork is a concise summary of current practices in the field. It highlights the practical details that must be considered when negotiating a commissioned work, including information on business forms, ownership of original art, credit lines, sales tax, and liability for portfolios and original art.

Finally *The Professional Relationship* gives new art buyers and beginning artists a sense of the relationships between artist and client in the communications industry. This chapter includes descriptions of various art buyers responsible for commissioning artists' work, how independent contractors operate in the market, and how artists' representatives, brokers and other sources of talent relate to both client and artist.

Section 3: Pricing & Trade Customs provides an overview of the many factors that must be taken into account by all parties who are responsible for pricing works of design or illustration. Factors that affect pricing, including such diverse elements as usage and reuses, per diem fees, royalties on merchandise for sale, billable expenses, special time demands arising out of unique style or deadline requirements, and overall size of project or print order are discussed. Various methods of pricing, including per-diem, hourly-rate and page-rate pricing as the basis for compensation, are also evaluated.

The second chapter in this section reports ranges of rates in virtually all design and illustration specialties compiled from national surveys of artists, artists' representatives and art buyers. Each trade area listed in this section includes an introduction that explains the type of work covered in the charts and factors that affect pricing in the individual areas. The pricing charts should not be read without referring to these introductions or other portions of the book that describe all factors to be taken into account when pricing a specific job.

Illustration pricing ranges cover all media in Advertising Illustration (including magazine, newspaper, brochure, catalog, mailer, point of purchase, packaging, transit-car, film, audiovisual, and motion picture and theater posters); Comps, Animatics, and TV Storyboards; Institutional and Corporate Illustration (including adult, juvenile, children's books, and textbooks); Editorial Illustration (including national, regional and trade magazines, and newspapers); Fashion Illustration; Record Album Cover Illustration; Medical Illustration; Technical Illustration; Novelty and Miscellaneous Products Illustration; and Limited Edition Prints.

A highlight of most of the specialty sections above is that the work functions and trade practices unique to that field of illustration are spelled out in detail. In this manner both art buyers and graphic artists will better comprehend the demands on time and talent necessary in each area of specialization.

Design pricing ranges cover the following areas in like manner: General Graphic Design (including corporate reports and brochures, magazine and newspaper advertising, logos, record album covers, posters, and point of purchase); Book Design (including text, trade, and juvenile books); Book Jacket Design (including hardcover, trade paperback, and mass market); Letterforms (including corporate, type houses, and publications); Textile Design (including apparel, decorative and home furnishing, wovens and knits, rugs, and special orders); and Needleart Design. Freelance Cartooning; Animation; Production; Retouching; terms and prices; and Staff Salaries in advertising, corporate, studio publishing, broadcast, textile and animation are also covered.

Since each of these areas presents ranges only, no price listed in the charts should be taken to represent a minimum or maximum price for any specific job.

Section 4: Standard Contract Forms is the most complete set of forms ever assembled for all work specialties in the industry. The forms are designed to handle most of the *basic* contract issues that arise between graphic artists and clients, although special situations (such as when royalties are involved) may require amplification or modification. These forms include model contracts for both graphic artists and art buyers.

First, there is an artist-agent model agreement form. Then, for art buyers, there is an all-purpose order form and a special purchase order form for magazine illustration.

For illustrators there is a general confirmation of assignment form (which can be made applicable to any commissioned work) and an invoice that assures that the terms agreed to on the assignment confirmation form are reinforced. For graphic designers there is a single form that covers the estimate, assignment confirmation, and invoice. Computer artists should note a separate contract to cover the special terms for artwork done on new technological equipment. For textile designer three separate forms cover confirmation of commissioned work, the invoice for work sold, and agreements with agents. Finally, for needleart designers there is a form for confirming commissioned work and an invoice to reinforce the agreed terms.

Section 5: Business Management is a guide for independent contractors in areas such as negotiation, recordkeeping, invasions and infringements of rights, copyright registration and other details of running a freelance business.

Section 6: Reference In addition to a useful glossary of terms and index, the final section of the book provides more information about the Guild and how its work serves the interests of graphic artists and art buyers everywhere. Also included is data on the population of artists in the U.S. from government and industry reports.

Ethical Standards

The Graphic Artists Guild is mandated by its constitution and its members' concern to monitor, support and foster ethical standards in all dealings between graphic artists and art buyers. This activity is accomplished in many ways: through Guild programs for members, through cooperation with related organizations, and through legislative activity on local, state and federal levels.

As part of its responsibility in this area, the Guild is a sponsor of the Joint Ethics Committee, which mediates or arbitrates disputes between graphic artists and clients in the New York area. Other sponsoring groups include: The American Institute of Graphic Arts, the American Society of Magazine Photographers, the Art Directors Club, the Society of Illustrators, and the Society of Photographers and Artists Representatives, Inc. The Joint Ethics Committee has formulated the Code of Fair Practice, which the sponsoring groups endorse.

Along with its support of the Joint Ethics Committe, the Guild has its own professional practices and grievance committees that work with members in addressing issues of professional relations between artists and buyers, and assist members in resolving violations of agreements and commonly accepted trade standards. As with all other Guild programs, these committees draw from members' experiences in the field, track industry standards and publicize any changes in the field that affect contracts and trade practices.

As part of its commitment to make information on standards and practices available throughout the industry, the Guild offers copies of standard forms and contracts to all of its members and, through the *Pricing & Ethical Guidelines*, to anyone in the industry. These forms and contracts can be used directly or can be amended to meet individual needs.

Introduction

In 1945, a group of artists and art directors in New York City, concerned with the growing abuses, misunderstanding and disregard of uniform standards of conduct in their field, met to consider possibilities for improvement. They reached the conclusion that the effort, to be successful, must start with widespread backing and be a continuing activity. On their recommendation, three major organizations (the Art Directors Club, the Society of Illustrators and the Graphic Artists Guild) established and financed an organization known as the Joint Ethics Committee.

In 1978 and again in 1985 the Committee, now representing six organizations, revised the Code to deal with increasingly complex problems in a growing communications industry.

Committee membership

The Joint Ethics Committee is composed of members from each of the following organizations: The American Institute of Graphics Arts, the American Society of Magazine Photographers, Art Directors Club, the Graphic Artists Guild, the Society of Illustrators, and the Society of Photographers and Artists Representatives. Committee members are appointed by the directing bodies of each organization with approval of the standing Joint Ethics Committee. Each organization is represented by four members who share a total of three votes.

Members of the Committee are selected with great care by their respective organizations. Their selection is based on their experience in the profession, their proven mature thinking and temperament, and their reputation for impartiality.

The operating expenses of the Committee are defrayed by the sponsoring organizations. The time and services of the members are voluntarily contributed without any form of personal gain.

Code of Fair Practice

The Code of Fair Practice, as established by the Joint Ethics Committee, was conceived with the idea of equity for those engaged in the various aspects of creating, selling, buying and using graphic arts. The Code is included in this book.

The Committee zealously upholds the ethical standards set forth in the Code and invites any and all reports of violations.

Committee procedure

The Committee meets one or more times a month to read and act upon complaints and reports of Code violations. All communications to the Committee must be made in writing. When a complaint justifies action, a copy of the complainant's letter may be sent, with the plaintiff's permission, to the alleged offender. In the exchange of correspondence that follows, matters are frequently settled by a mere clarification of the issues. Further action by the Committee becomes unnecessary and, in many instances, both sides resume friendly and profitable relationships. When, however, a continued exchange of correspondence indicates that a reconciliation of differences is improbable, the Committee may suggest mediation or arbitration.

When the Committee receives no response from the alleged offender after a reasonable length of time and adequate notice, or when the Committee receives an unacceptable response, the Committee may cite the alleged offender to the governing bodies of the parent organizations and recommend that they publicize these citations.

The proceedings and records of the Committee are held in strict confidence. In the interest of the profession, typical cases are published periodically without identification of the parties involved.

The Committee's services are not limited to members of its supporting groups. These services are available to any individual, business or professional organization in the field of visual communications.

Mediation

When the offer of mediation is accepted, both parties meet informally with a panel composed of three members of the Committee. If the dispute requires guidance in a field not represented in the Committee's membership, a specially qualified mediator with the required experience may be included. The names of the panel are submitted beforehand to both parties for their acceptance.

The function of the mediation panel is to guide, not to render any verdict. The panel convenes to direct the discussion and to bring about agreement on the questions involved.

Arbitration

When the offer of arbitration is accepted by both parties, a panel of five arbitrators is appointed. As a rule, three are selected from the Committee, and the remainder are chosen for their expertise in the particular area of the dispute. Names of the panel members are submitted beforehand to both parties for their approval. Both parties involved sign an agreement and take an oath to abide by the decision of the panel. The panel is sworn in and the proceedings are held in compliance with the Arbitration Law of the State of New York. After both sides are heard, the panel deliberates in private and renders its decision and award. The results are then formulated by the Committee's counsel for service on the parties for entry of judgment according to law.

Every award made by the Committee has been fully honored. The decisions and opinions of this Committee have become models for guidance in similar situations. The Committee's Code has been cited as legal precedent.

Committee scope

The Committee acts on matters that it defines as violations of the Code. Its judgment and decisions are supported by the professions represented in the Committee. However, it offers no legal advice on contracts, copyrights, bill collecting or similar matters.

On occasion, the Committee has settled questions not specifically covered by the Code of Fair Practice. The Committee gladly renders such aid, while not exceeding the limitations of its authority.

The Committee's influence is derived from widespread acceptance, and while it has neither judicial nor police powers, its performance has made it an effective and respected tribunal.

The Joint Ethics Committee Code of Fair Practice for the Graphics Communication Industry

Formulated in 1948 in New York City.

Relations between Artists and Buyers

The word "artist" should be understood to include creative people in the field of visual communications, including but not limited to: illustration, graphic design, photography, film and television.

This Code provides the graphic communications industry with an accepted standard of ethics and professional conduct. It presents guidelines for the voluntary conduct of persons in the industry.

ARTICLE 1
Negotiations between an artist or the artist's representative and a client should be conducted only through an authorized buyer.

ARTICLE 2
Orders or agreements between an artist or representative and buyer should be in writing and must include the specific rights which are being transferred, the fee plus expenses, delivery date, and a summarized description of the work.

ARTICLE 3
All changes or additions not due to the fault of the artist or representative should be billed to the buyer as an additional and separate charge.

ARTICLE 4
There should be no charges to the buyer, other than authorized expenses, for revisions or retakes made necessary by errors on the part of the artists or the artist's representative.

ARTICLE 5
If work commissioned by a buyer is postponed or cancelled, a "kill-fee" should be negotiated based on time allotted, effort expended, and expenses incurred. Completed work must be paid for in full. The artwork must be returned promptly to the artist.

ARTICLE 6
Alterations must not be made without consulting the artist. Where alterations or retakes are necessary, the artist must be given the opportunity of making such changes.

ARTICLE 7
The artist must notify the buyer of any anticipated delay in delivery. Should the artist fail to keep contract through unreasonable delay or nonconformance with agreed specifications, it will be considered a breach of contract by the artist.

ARTICLE 8
An artist must not be asked to work on speculation.

ARTICLE 9
There should be no secret rebates, discounts, gifts, or bonuses requested by or given to buyers by artists or representatives.

ARTICLE 10
Artwork and copyright ownership are vested in the hands of the artist.

ARTICLE 11
Original artwork remains the property of the artist unless it is specifically purchased. It is distinct from the purchase of any reproduction rights.* All transactions must be in writing.

ARTICLE 12
In cases of copyright transfers, only specified rights are transferred. All unspecified rights remain vested with the artist.* All transactions must be in writing.

ARTICLE 13
Commissioned artwork is not to be considered "work for hire."

ARTICLE 14
When the price of work is based on limited use and later such work is used more extensively, the artist must receive additional payment.

ARTICLE 15
If exploratory work, comprehensives, or preliminary photographs from an assignment are subsequently used for reproduction, the artist's prior permission must be secured and the artist must receive fair additional payment.

ARTICLE 16
If exploratory work, comprehensives, or photographs are bought from an artist with the intention or possibility that another artist will be assigned to do the finished work, this must be in writing at the time of placing the order.

ARTICLE 17

If no transfer of copyright ownership* has been executed, the publisher of any reproduction of artwork shall publish the artist's copyright notice if the artist requests so at the time of agreement.

ARTICLE 18

The right to remove the artist's name on published artwork is subject to agreement between artist and buyer.

ARTICLE 19

There must be no plagiarism of any artwork.

ARTICLE 20

If an artist is specifically requested to produce any artwork during unreasonable working hours, fair additional remuneration must be paid.

ARTICLE 21

All artwork or photography submitted as samples to a buyer should bear the name of the artist or artists responsible for the work. An artist must not claim authorship of another's work.

ARTICLE 22

All companies and their employees who receive artist portfolios, samples, etc., must be responsible for the return of the portfolio to the artist in the same condition as received.

ARTICLE 23

An artist entering into an agreement with a representative, studio, or production company for an exclusive representation must not accept an order from nor permit work to be shown by any other representative or studio. Any agreement which is not intended to be exclusive should set forth in writing the exact restrictions agreed upon between the two parties.

ARTICLE 24

No representative should continue to show an artist's sample after the termination of an association.

ARTICLE 25

After termination of an association between artist and representative, the representative should be entitled to a commission for a period of six months on accounts which the representative has secured, unless otherwise specified by contract.

ARTICLE 26

Examples of an artist's work furnished to a representative or submitted to a prospective buyer shall remain the property of the artist, should not be duplicated without the artist's consent, and must be returned promptly to the artist in good condition.

ARTICLE 27

Contests for commercial purposes are not approved of because of their speculative and exploitative character.

ARTICLE 28

Interpretation of the Code for the purposes of mediation and arbitration shall be in the hands of the Joint Ethics Committee and is subject to changes and additions at the discretion of the parent organizations through their appointed representatives on the Committee.

*Artwork ownership, copyright ownership, and ownership and rights transfers after January 1, 1978 are to be in compliance with the Federal Copyright Revision Act of 1976.

The Guild's Grievance Committee

The Graphic Artists Guild is committed to raising and maintaining ethical professional standards between graphic artists and art buyers. Most Guild chapters have a grievance committee to assist local members in resolving violations of agreements and commonly accepted trade standards. These committees provide Guild members with specific services intended as assistance in resolving individual disputes and to prevent the occurrence of grievances in general.

Monitoring industry practices

Guild grievance committees encourage artists and art buyers of all disciplines to communicate instances of unprofessional practices encountered in the field. These reports enable the committee to monitor business practices within the graphic communications industry. When such reports are not forwarded, vital information for the industry is missing and there is no opportunity to change unethical practices.

Report file

The committees maintain an ongoing record of parties reported for unethical or unfair business practices. These files serve members as central sources for checking whether prospective buyers have violated the Code of Fair Practice. Members who report abuses to the committees are thus able to forewarn fellow professionals directly and contribute to improving working conditions generally.

"Graphic Artists Beware" column

Buyers reported for flagrant, repeated or unresolved unprofessional practices are selected by the committees for citation in the "Graphic Artists Beware" column of the Guild's chapter and national newsletters. The intention of citing these companies and individuals is to keep the community of graphic artists aware of unethical or unfair practices. At the same time, the Guild puts buyers who use unethical or unprofessional practices on notice that they can no longer exploit artists with impunity.

Committee assistance

The grievance committees also provide guidance and assistance to Guild members in their personal efforts to seek resolution of grievances. The Guild is committed to seeing that its members are treated justly and fairly as professionals.

When a member's grievance is justified, the committee contacts the member to discuss the case and plan an appropriate strategy for resolution. The committee directs the member in the use of accepted business and legal procedures. Depending on the unique factors of each case, the committee's assistance generally involves: (1) guiding the member's personal efforts to resolve the grievance; (2) directing communication with the buyer on the member's behalf; and (3) mediating, if requested by both parties, to achieve a private settlement.

If further action becomes necessary, other relevant alternatives are proposed by the committee. These may include: (1) arbitration; (2) small claims court; (3) collection methods; (4) lawyer referral; or (5) litigation.

Members who wish to report unprofessional practices should forward them directly to the grievance committee at their local Guild chapter. Members requesting grievance committee assistance should also contact their Guild chapter.

The Guild's Professional Practices Committee

The Professional Practices Committee of the Guild seeks to address the issue of professional relations between artists and buyers by fostering an ongoing dialogue with all commissioning parties.

The graphic communications industry, much as any other industry, has its instances of misunderstandings and disputes. At times, these are inevitably due to the nature of interaction between people. However, a sizeable degree of contention in artist-buyer relations results from an unawareness or disregard of common standards of professional practices.

It is the Guild's position that such problems can be reduced and that mutually beneficial and productive business practices can be advanced through discussion and negotiation. Both formal and informal communication between the Guild and the industry has existed since the Guild's inception. The Guild has always acknowledged the legitimate concerns of both sides of professional issues. Through the activities of its grievance committees, the Guild seeks to contribute to a broader and fuller understanding and commitment to professional standards of practice.

Media articles

A principal means through which the committee focuses attention on professional practices is to initiate research into specific issues and produce articles for industry and Guild publications. The selection of topics results from both a monitoring of industry practices and from correspondence received by the committee.

The committee intends to expand the publication of its research and writing to reach a wider audience. These publications will take the form of individual articles, a newsletter series, (such as the recent seven-part series on dispute-resolution alternatives), and feature columns. Professional associations and trade publishers can contact the national Guild office to request articles, reprints, or reference material.

"Graphic Artists Aware" column

The Guild periodically publishes a "Graphic Artist Aware" column as a means of informing its membership of and to acknowledge advancements made in artist-buyer practices.

The column, which appears in national and local Guild newsletters, cites individual buyers and companies that have established more equitable terms for art commissions as a matter of policy. Such advance may have resulted through negotiations with the Guild, from communication with the Professional Practices Committee, or have been determined independently.

PROFESSIONAL
ISSUES

Professional Issues

I n the development of the U.S Constitution and the creation of authorship rights' protections, our nation's founders recognized the need to be able to manage the economic affairs of the country and to encourage the spread of learning and the communication of ideas. It was also clearly understood that artwork is intellectual property and is an economic resource that is traded in the marketplace. By creating protections for authors of intellectual property, the drafters of the Constitution sought to encourage and protect those who foster the dissemination of ideas to the public, while ensuring the free flow of information.

In today's world, visuals created by graphic artists are among the most important vehicles that relay messages in our society. A successful illustration can often sell a company's image as well as its products. A successful logo can help with product or company recognition, and packaging can become the key to a product's success or failure on the market.

Like other professionals, (actors, athletes, dancers, engineers, photographers, and writers) graphic artists occupy a unique place in our society and economy. They provide services that clients cannot otherwise obtain. Their special skill and style are the basis on which they sell their work. And, like other professionals, artists provide this highly skilled service and creative input within a framework of professional standards and ethics.

The Guild's intent is to help create a healthy partnership between artists and clients by encouraging adherence to fair practices. The Guild upholds the standard of a value-for-value exchange, recognizing that both client and artist contribute to a successful working relationship.

The Graphic Artists Guild is mandated by its constitution and by its members to "promote and maintain high professional standards of ethics and practices.. to establish, implement and enforce laws, policies, general and specific contracts designed to accomplish these ends." The organization's legislative agenda, therefore, is based on the needs and desires expressed by its members and its constitutionally mandated goals.

The Guild is active in creating and monitoring public policy developments including legislative initiatives at the local, state and federal levels. The issues addressed include local proposals to control escalating studio rents, state laws to encourage fair practices and to protect artists' authorship rights, federal legislation to close the work-for-hire loophole of the U.S. Copyright Law, create tax equity for artists, and develop a national standard for artists' authorship rights (moral rights).

The Guild has drafted model legislation and has lobbied locally and nationally on these issues. Early successes in California, Oregon, New York and Massachusetts created a wave of interest in artists rights' legislation. The Guild has helped create a coalition of artists', photographers' and writers' organizations representing over one-hundred thousand creators. This group is currently focusing its attention on finding a federal remedy to the work-for-hire problem.

Legislation

L ike most other professional organizations, trade associations and unions, the Graphic Artists Guild monitors and lobbies for laws that affect its members. This activity takes place with member involvement at local, state and federal levels through chapters and the national organization. Since 1976 several legislative issues have been identified by Graphic Artists Guild members: the work-for-hire provision of the federal copyright law, moral rights, fair practices, and the right to take fair market deductions for charitable contributions of art under the tax laws.

The Guild has drafted model legislation and lobbied locally and nationally on these issues. Early successes in California, Oregon and New York indicate that Guild concerns are shared widely and its legislative program is sound. In fact, the Guild has worked in tandem with a coalition of creators' organizations that has identified a community of interests encompassing the concerns of artists, photographers and writers. The Copyright Justice Coalition shares the Guild's sense of urgency for finding a federal remedy to the work-for-hire problem.

Work for hire

"Work for hire" is a provision of the U.S. copyright law, under which the employer or other commissioning party is deemed to have created the artwork for the purposes of the copyright law, leaving the artist with no rights whatsoever. And, since the artist is an independent contractor, he/she has no access to traditional employee benefits to compensate for the loss of copyright.

A work for hire can come into existence in two ways:

(1) an employee creating a copyrightable work in the course of employment; or (2) an independent contractor creating a specially ordered or commissioned work in one of several categories verified as a work for hire by a signed contract. Independent contractors can be asked to sign work for hire contracts to cover work in the following areas:

1. A contribution to a collective work, such as a magazine, newspaper, encyclopedia or anthology.

2. a contribution used as part of a motion picture or other audio-visual work;

3. A supplementary work, which includes pictorial illustrations done to supplement a work by another author; and

4. An instructional text.

If no contract is signed stating that a work will be work for hire, it will not be, unless the artist is an employee creating the work in the course of employment. However, even as an employee, an artist may request a written contract which transfers copyright ownership to the artist. In several instances, independent contractors have been found to be subject to the employee clause, in the absence of a clear written contract, and resulting from the client's contention that the work was heavily directed.

The Graphic Artists Guild opposes the use of work-for-hire contracts and has introduced legislation to close this loophole in the Copyright Law. This position is supported by a prestigious coalition of national organizations representing a broad spectrum of creators.

The Graphic Artists Guild's and the coalition's testimony before a U.S. Senate hearing in 1982 has formed the basis of a vital dialogue in creators' and copyright communities, drawing greater support with each passing year.

In 1982, California passed legislation on work for hire which states that any artist hired under a work-for-hire contract is eligible for employee benefits for the duration of the contract. This bill was supported by the Graphic Artists Guild and other creators' organizations active in the state. The intent of this legislation was to send a strong message to the U.S. Congress to provide a federal remedy for the work-for-hire problem.

Since 1982, the Guild has received support from local legislators in New York, Michigan and Rhode Island, calling on the U.S. Congress to act on the work-for-hire problem. Guild and coalition-sponsored legislation addressing the issue was introduced in 1984 in the U.S. House and Senate, and is pending introduction in 1986. The bill has broad bi-partisan support in both houses of Congress.

The Guild delivered testimony in 1985 to the Congressional Office of Technology Assessment regarding the relationship between copyright and new technology, touching on the work-for-hire issue and related authorship rights concerns.

Moral rights

The Moral Rights Act's (sometimes referred to as artists' authorship rights legislation) conceptual roots come from the French concept of *Droit Moral:* the intrinsic right of artists to protect the integrity of their creations. This concept is integral to European authorship rights systems.

Most of the cases that brought this problem to the public's attention revolve around the defacement of works of fine art, most notably the dismembering of a hanging sculpture created by Isamu Noguchi for the New York Headquarters of the Bank of Tokyo Trust Company.

However, there was a much publicized case in the graphic arts area that involved Antonio Vargas' series, the "Vargas Girls" which ran in *Esquire Magazine.* After the expiration of Vargas contract with *Esquire,* the magazine continued to run the series under the name, "The Esquire Girls," denying the original creator credit for the work. Vargas brought *Esquire* to court but lost the case. If that case were brought to court in New York State today, he would have a far better chance of winning.

Like actors, artists are judged on the basis of their last public performance. Unauthorized alterations and defacement of artwork can damage an otherwise viable career, according to members of the Graphic Artists Guild. By gathering and presenting artists' testimony about the problems that illustrators and designers face, the Graphic Artists Guild was able to broaden the legislation. The bills that have passed recognize artists' on-going relationships with the work they create.

While creators have been lobbying for the protection of their "natural rights" since the earliest days of the U.S., progress on this issue only began in the late 1970's and early 1980's when Guild-authored proposals formed the basis for legislative initiatives on the state and federal level. This legislation has had strong support from the creators' community and progress has been relatively rapid.

California enacted a moral rights law in 1979 for fine arts. The California law is based on the public interest in protecting works of art, and includes the crucial concept that artists have, at all times, the right to claim authorship of their work. The law also permits artists to seek damages and other fees when violations occur.

New York State enacted a Moral Rights law in 1983 that protects artists and photographers from unauthorized alterations, defacement and mutilation of their work. It also ensures creators the right to name credit, and the right to remove the artist's name from a piece that has been altered to its detriment by a client who has bought reproduction rights only.

New York law now protects editorial illustrators against reproductions of their work which are badly cropped, used out of the original context to the detriment of the work, recolored or otherwise negatively altered by the client. Since most editorial artists build their reputations through the dissemination of reproductions of their work, they can be severely damaged by unauthorized reproductions.

The Massachusetts moral rights law, the Art Preservation Act, signed into law in 1985 is based on the New York and California proposals. The law enables graphic and fine artists working in any medium to protect their work from unauthorized alterations and/or defacement. It also provides judicial remedies for damaged work by allowing artists to sue for damages when their work is harmed.

The Maryland state legislature introduced moral rights legislation in 1985 based on Guild-sponsored bills that have passed in other states. The Guild provided testimony regarding artists' concerns when the legislature held hearings.

The right of artists to protect the integrity of their work is so important and widely recognized that bills have been introduced repeatedly on a federal level to set a national standard in this area. As recognition of our society's interest in protecting our cultural and artistic heritage grows, more local bills will be introduced that will send messages to congress of the need for federal action on this issue.

These bills have pointed towards the need for action on a national level that would recognize artists' rights to protect their work even after the original has been sold.

In response, Guild-supported legislation on this issue has been introduced in the U.S. Congress. The bill is based on the Berne Copyright Convention and recognizes the authors' right to be given authorship credit for their work, to prevent mutilation, alteration or destruction of the work, and to recognize artists' rights to protect their reputations.

Fair practices

The Fair Practices Act, signed into law in Oregon (1979), in California, (1982); in New York, (1983); and pending in Massachusetts; clarifies who owns the original work of art when reproduction rights are sold. This legislation was drafted by Guild counsel on the basis of concerns raised by Guild members.

The Act provides that an original work of art can become the property of a client only if it is sold *in writing*. The passage of this act reinforces one of the premises of the copyright law, which is that works of art have value beyond their reproduction for a specific purpose, and that that value rightly belongs to the artist who creates them. The Fair Practices Act will prevent clients from holding on to originals unless they have written sales agreements with the creator. Where it applies, this act solves the problems that can arise when clients believe that they have obtained ownership of the original art when they have only purchased reproduction rights, or who believe that they have obtained an original through an ambiguous oral agreement.

In Oregon and California, the law provides that if there is any ambiguity as to who owns reproduction rights, the ambiguity shall be resolved in favor of the creator/artist.

For artists whose livelihoods depend on resale of reproduction rights and on sales of original works, this law is critical. It also sets a precedent for clearing up any ambiguity in ownership since a written transfer is now required.

Tax equity

There is a popular misconception that artists donating their art to a charitable organization may deduct the "fair market value" of the work. In fact, artists may deduct only the cost of producing the work, i.e. the price of the canvas, paint and other materials. If however, an artist sells the original, the buyer may donate the work and deduct the fair market value. As a result, artists have either withheld their valuable originals or sold them to private collectors, limiting public access.

Historically, artists, writers and politicians were able to donate their original art and manuscripts and receive the full market value deduction. In 1969, the situation changed dramatically. Congress sought to prevent politicians from receiving windfalls based on the donations of their papers. Broad legislation was enacted, inhibiting artists and writers as well as politicians. Since 1969, museums, which depend on artists' donations of original art to supplement their paid acquisitions have documented a sharp drop-off of donations.

Artists and writers have spoken out about this obvious inequity and have received the support of their professional organizations. They have acted in cooperation with museums, universities and libraries whose representatives believe the public access to art is in the public interest. The National Heritage Resource Act has been introduced in the U.S. Congress to answer these concerns.

New technology

In recent years computers have become a part of professional artists' day-to-day lives. Artwork is composed and enhanced on computer, stored and altered, transmitted on disc by satellite. Artwork created on computer is being used in publishing, broadcasting, advertising, textiles and a variety of other fields.

During recent years, the U.S. Congress has become concerned with the effects of new technologies on society and the marketplace. The Graphic Artists Guild and some of its members were asked to provide testimony about the impact of technology and the need for public policy development.

Artists have expressed concern that their work can be stored in "image banks," manipulated and used without their permission. While abuses of this kind already occur, artists are concerned that these problems will proliferate unless public policy is shaped to prevent them.

A public policy emphasis for research into technologies that will support the goal of protection of authorship is essential. While there is the potential for great harm to creators, the new technologies offer the potential for great creative advances. With access to training on the new computer graphics systems, artists can create a new 'graphics vernacular' to transmit society's messages in a vital and immediate way. There is also some concern that a technological training gap may emerge between those with the resources to gain access to new computer graphics systems and those without.

The Congressional Office of Technology Assessment, a study arm of the U.S. Congress, asked the Guild to comment on these and other issues during its study of new technology and intellectual property. This study will form the basis of policy-making in Congress in years to come.

Speculation: Ethical and unethical practices

The Graphic Artists Guild is unalterably opposed to any artist being asked to work "on speculation" because of the inherent risks to the artist in such circumstances. Art buyers should not ask artists to work on a project unless a fee has been agreed upon in advance.

Artists must be equitably compensated at any time they are requested to create artwork. Working on speculation places all the risks on the artist without a commitment on the buyer's part.

It is therefore considered an unethical practice, for example for a buyer to be in the position of deciding only upon completion of the art whether or not to compensate the artist. This situation occurs in agreements where payment becomes dependent on the "buyer's satisfaction" or "on publication."

In royalty arrangements for commissioned art, an advance should be provided. Payment of the advance allows the artist to recoup expenses and to manage the financial demands of the project in a more timely and realistic fashion.

Similarly, in cancellation of jobs resulting from a buyer's decision, cancellation fees must be paid at all times to compensate the artist for expended professional time, effort and expenses.

Art contests, except under special circumstances, are also opposed because of their speculative nature. For contest guidelines approved by the Guild, see pages 47 to 48.

However, when artists create artwork on their own initiative and then seek to sell it to a buyer for speculative marketing, it is considered ethical speculation and not in violation of this rule.

Where an artist in this type of situation, for example, has entered a royalty arrangement in a book contract, but artist and publisher are taking a mutual risk in their investment. The compensation to both parties is "speculative"-that is, the compensation to both being dependent on the market response to their product.

Contests and competitions

In 1980, the Graphic Artists Guild in conjunction with Designers Saturday (DS), a furniture manufacturers association, developed a competition to meet two goals: to produce high quality art for the DS annual show, and to provide a competition that was ethical and appropriate for professional artists. At the same time, the Guild was receiving complaints from artists around the country concerning the unethical nature of most contests that they were asked to enter.

The results of the experiment with DS were so successful that the Guild decided to see if other competitions and contests could be structured to accomplish the goals met by the DS model.

In an effort to gain a clearer picture of the competition scene nationwide, the Graphic Artists Guild Foundation, with a supporting grant from the National Endowment for the Arts (NEA), conducted a nationwide survey of art and design competition holders, as well as an informal poll of jurors and competition entrants.

This study resulted in the establishment of a list of guidelines for three types of art competitions: those held by art-related organizations/associations to award excellence in the field; those for which the winning entries are used for commercial purposes;

and competitions held by non-profit organizations where the winning entries are used for non-profit purposes.

Among the findings of the surveys were that:

By far, the largest and most expensive competitions are those operated by associations ancillary to the advertising industry, such as art directors' clubs and industry trade magazines. The purpose of these competitions is to honor excellence within their own communities. While these competitions do not require that original art be submitted, the sponsoring organizations generally charge high entry fees for members and non-members alike. These competitions generally attract the highest volume of entrants.

The greatest barrier to attracting professional artists as entrants in competitions is work on speculation. Most professional artists reported that they did not want or could not afford to take time from income-producing projects to create original work for a competition on a speculative basis. The most popular form of competition for this group is based on work already produced or published.

In most cases, the process for selecting a jury for competitions appears to be quite good, however, jurors noted that often the criteria or process for judging the work is poorly articulated or planned.

Another problem listed by professional artists concerning competitions is the requirement for all-rights transfers by all entrants to the competition holder.

In response to the data received from the competition study, the following guidelines were developed:

Competitions by art-related organizations/associations to award excellence.

1. The call for entry shall define clearly all rules governing competition entries, specifications for work entered, any and all fees for entry and any and all rights to be transferred by any entrants to the competition holder.

2. Jurors for the competition shall be listed on the call for entry. No juror or employee of the organization holding the competition shall be eligible to enter the competition.

3. Criteria for jurying the entries and specifications for the artwork to be submitted in all rounds shall be defined clearly in the call for entry as a guide to both entrants and jurors.

4. Deadlines for notification and proc-

ess for notification for acceptance or rejection of all entries shall be listed in the call for entry.

5. Any and all uses for any and all entries shall be listed clearly in the call for entries, with terms for any rights to be transferred.

6. For the first round, tearsheets, slides, photographs or other reproductions of existing work shall be requested in order to judge appropriateness of style, technique and proficiency of entrants. This round shall result in the choice of finalists. If samples from this round are not to be returned to the entrants, that fact shall be listed clearly in the call for entries.

7. If the competition ends in an exhibition, hanging or exhibition fees paid for by the entrants shall be listed in the call for entries.

8. After the first round, the jury may request original art for review. The competition holder shall insure all works against damage or loss until the work is returned to the artist. All original artwork shall be returned to the artist. Any fees charged to the artist for the return of artwork shall be listed in the call for entry.

9. Artwork shall not be altered in any way without the express permission of the artist.

10. All entries and rights to the artwork remain the property of the artist, unless a separate written transfer and payment for the original has been negotiated.

11. If work exhibited by the competition is for sale, any commission taken by the competition holder shall be listed in the call for entries.

Competitions where the winning entries are used for commercial purposes.

1. The call for entry shall define clearly all rules governing the competition entries, specifications for work entered, and any and all fees for entry and any and all rights to be transferred by any entrants to the competition holder.

2. Jurors for the competition should be listed on the call for entry. No juror or employee of the organization holding the competition shall be eligible to enter the competition.

3. Criteria for jurying the entries and specifications for the artwork to be submitted in all rounds shall be defined clearly in the call for entry as a guide to both jurors and entrants.

4. Deadlines for notification and process of notification for acceptance or rejection

of all entries shall be listed in the call for entry.

5. Any and all uses for any and all entries shall be listed clearly in the call for entry, with terms for any rights to be transferred.

6. For the first round, tearsheets, slides, photographs or other reproductions of existing work shall be requested in order to judge appropriateness of style, technique and proficiency of entrants. This round shall result in the choice of finalists. If samples from this round are not to be returned to the entrants, that fact shall be listed clearly in the call for entry.

7. The number of finalists chosen after the first round should be small. The finalists shall then be required to submit sketches or comprehensive drawings for final judging. All finalists shall receive some portion of the award. This eliminates the speculative nature of the competition.

8. Agreements shall be made with each artist working at the final stage, prior to the beginning of work (Graphic Artists Guild contracts or the equivalent can be used). The agreements shall include the nature of the artwork required, deadlines, credit line and copyright ownership for the artist, and the amount of the award.

9. Any work of finalists not received by the required deadline or not in the form required and agreed upon shall be disqualified. All rights to the artwork that has been disqualified shall remain with the artist.

10. The winners shall produce camera-ready or finished art according to the specifications listed in the call for entry. Artwork submitted shall not be altered in any way without the express permission of the artist.

11. The value of any award to the winners shall be at least commensurate with fair market value of the rights transferred. The first place winner shall receive an award that is signficantly greater than that of other winners.

12. The competition holder shall insure original artwork in their possession against loss or damage until it is returned to the artist.

Competitions held by non-profit organizations or where the winning entry is used for non-profit purposes.

1. The call for entry shall define clearly all rules governing competition entries, specifications for work entered, any and all fees for entry and any and all rights to be transferred by any entrants to the competition holder.

2. Jurors for the competition should be listed in the call for entry. Jurors or employees of the organization holding the competition shall not be eligible for entering the competition.

3. Criteria for jurying the entries and specifications for the final submission of artwork shall be defined clearly in the call for entry as a guide to both jurors and entrants.

4. Deadlines for notification and process of notification of acceptance or rejection of all entries shall be listed in the call for entry.

5. Any and all uses of all entries shall be listed clearly in the call for entry, with terms of any rights to be transferred.

6. For the first round, tearsheets, slides, photographs or other reproductions of existing work shall be requested in order to judge the appropriateness of style, technique and proficiency of entrants. This round shall result in the choice of finalists. If samples for this round are not to be returned to the entrants, that fact shall be stated clearly in the call for entry.

7. The number of finalists chosen after the first round shall be small. These finalists shall then be required to submit sketches or comprehensive drawings for the final judging. All finalists shall receive some portion of the award. This eliminates the speculative nature of the competition.

8. Agreements shall be made with each artist working at the final stage, prior to the beginning of work (Guild contracts or their equivalents can be used). The agreements shall include the nature of the artwork required, deadlines, credit line and copyright ownership for the artist, and the amount of the award.

9. Any work of the finalists not received by the required deadline or not in the form required and agreed upon shall be disqualified. All rights to work that has been disqualified shall remain with the artist.

10. The winner shall produce camera-ready art or finished art according to the specifications listed in the call for entry. Artwork submitted shall not be altered in any way without the express permission of the artist.

11. The value of the award should, if possible, be commensurate with the fair market price for the job. For non-profit competition holders, exceptions may be made depending on the budget and use of the artwork for the competition.

12. The competition holder shall insure any original artwork in their possession against loss or damage until it is returned to the artist.

Graphic Artists Guild Foundation Seal of Compliance.

As a service to competition holders and entrants, the Graphic Artists Guild Foundation will review calls for entry to ascertain whether they meet the minimum standards listed in the guidelines above. If a competition holder meets these standards, they are eligible to carry the Graphic Artists Guild Foundation's Seal of Compliance for ethical competition calls for entry. A sliding fee scale for the reviewing calls for entry is available to accomodate the budgets of both non-profit and profit competitions. For further information, contact the Graphic Artists Guild Foundation, 11 W. 20th Street, New York, New York 10011.

Cancellation and rejection fees

The Graphic Artists Guild strongly supports the *Code of Fair Practice* article that condemns the practice of work on speculation. All assignments should provide for a fee, even in the event of cancellation or rejection. Written agreements between artists and buyers should contain a "cancellation provision" or "rejection provision" based on the following principles:

Cancellation provision

The client agrees to pay the artist a cancellation fee if the assignment is cancelled for reasons beyond the artist's control.

1. If cancellation occurs prior to the completion of the finished art, the cancellation fee shall be no less than 50 percent of the original fee.

2. If cancellation occurs after the completion of preliminary work and prior to the completion of finished art, the cancellation fee shall be from 50 to 100 percent of the original fee, depending on the degree of completion of the finished art at the time of cancellation.

3. If cancellation occurs after the completion of finished art, the cancellation fee shall be 100 percent of the original fee.

4. All necessary and related expenses shall be paid in full.

5. In the event of cancellation, the client obtains all of the originally agreed-upon rights to the use of the artwork (except in royalty arrangements).

6. If cancelled preliminary or incomplete work is later used as finished art, the client will pay the unpaid balance of the original usage fee.

7. Both artist and client agree to submit any dispute regarding cancellation fees to the Joint Ethics Committee or other forum for binding arbitration.

Rejection provision

The client agrees to pay the artist a rejection fee if the preliminary or finished work is not found to be reasonably satisfactory and the assignment is cancelled.

1. If rejection occurs prior to the completion of finished art, the rejection fee shall be no less than 33 1/3 percent of the original fee.

2. If rejection occurs after the completion of preliminary work and prior to the completion of finished art, the rejection fee shall be from 33 1/3 to 100 percent of the original fee.

3. If rejection occurs after the completion of finished art the rejection fee shall be from 50 to 100 percent of the original fee. In no event shall a rejection fee on completed artwork be less than 50 percent of the original fee.

4. All necessary and related expenses shall be paid in full.

5. In the event of rejection, the client does not obtain any rights to the use of the artwork. Rejected work may not be used for reproduction by the client without a separate fee.

6. Both artist and client agree to submit any dispute regarding rejection fees to the Joint Ethics Committee or other forum for binding arbitration.

The cancellation and rejection fees shown in these guidelines are commonly accepted. These fees are flexible. If preliminary work is unusually complex or the assignment was required to be done on a very short deadline, the artist could reasonably expect higher cancellation or rejection fees. However, the minimums for cancellation or rejection fees is necessary to protect artists, since additional assignments from other clients may be turned away to provide time for completion of the cancelled assignment.

The Guild monitors abuses that take place with regard to cancellation fees. Even if contracts are verbal (or written but lack a cancellation provision), clients and artists should follow the accepted trade practices reflected in the Guild's cancellation guidelines. Any failure to follow these standards should be reported immediately to the Grievance Committee of the local Guild chapter.

Business and Legal Practices for Commissioned Artwork

This section is designed to give both artist and buyer an overview of the business and legal issues that constantly arise in the graphic arts field. Since copyright is the basis of transactions between artists and clients, information on copyright is essential to a full understanding of professional practices (refer also to Professional Issues section).

Negotiation

Negotiation is an art in which each party seeks to accommodate their needs as well as those of the other party. Both artist and art buyer must have goals by which to judge a negotiation. A buyer, for example, must stay within the budget and obtain satisfactory art. An artist, like any business person, must earn enough to cover overhead and make a profit. The more information each party has about the other, the more effective the negotiation. Artists who know the budget for a given job and know what other artists have been paid for similar work by the same agency or publisher will have a good idea of what they can command. Similarly, buyers who know standard ranges and contract terms will have a good idea of how to budget and what rights to buy. Of course, if either artist or buyer find that the other party will not permit them to achieve their essential goals, then the negotiation will break down and the parties will seek to fulfill their needs elsewhere.

In all negotiations, the Guild encourages artists and buyers to adhere to the standards of the Joint Ethics Committee's Code of Fair Practice. (For further information on negotiation, please refer to the chapter on Business Management.)

Business Forms

It is in the interest of artists and art buyers alike to put any agreement authorizing the use of an artist's work into writing. These agreements should be specific in naming the rights that are being transferred and in describing the disposition of the original art, cancellation fees and other terms. Written agreements should also reflect the concerns of artist and art buyer in a way that will specifically address the issues raised in negotiations.

While it is sometimes possible to enforce an oral agreement, it is wise to confirm any agreement in writing. This is the best protection against faulty memories and future conflicts. A written agreement can also be a valuable tool in helping both parties to clarify their needs. Getting it in writing is also evidence that both parties are professionals who treat the investment of their resources with care.

Formal contracts, however, are not the only way to confirm an agreement. Letters of agreement that are signed by both parties also serve as evidence of a contract. As with any legal document or form, both parties should read the entire agreement before signing. These agreements should be made and signed before work begins.

Terms

Contracts and purchase orders must contain provisions covering at least the following points:

1. The names of the artist and client, including the name of the client's authorized art buyer.

2. A complete description of the assignment.

3. The fee arrangements, including fees for usage, consultations, alterations, travel time, cancellation fees and reimbursement for billable expenses. Payment terms should be described including a schedule for advances, monthly services charges for late payment, and royalty percentages and terms, where applicable.

4. Specifications regarding when and how the original will be returned.

5. Any agreement regarding the placement of the credit line and copyright notice requirements.

6. The assignment of rights described in specific terms.

7. Responsibility for obtaining releases for the use of people's names and/or images for advertising or trade purposes should be defined.

For further information on contracts, please refer to the contracts section of this book. The *Legal Guide for the Visual Artist* by Tad Crawford, is also an excellent reference for contract information.

Copyright

The copyright law is the fundamental system of protections for artists that flow from the U.S. Constitution, Section 8, Article 1. Congress created the copyright law to protect and encourage creators and to foster the dissemination of ideas to the public by creating rewards. The copyright law that went into effect on January 1, 1978, replaced the 1909 version.

Freelance artists' livelihoods depend on their ability to claim authorship for the pieces they produce. They build their reputations, and therefore their ability to attract clients and build a career, on the basis of past performance. Indeed, artists' careers succeed or fail by their skill and style in translating the ideas and messages society needs to disseminate.

Copyright law defines artists' rights to control the usage of their original, creative art and is the basis of pricing and fair trade practices.

A bundle of rights

Since an artist's copyright is a bundle of rights, each different usage can be transferred separately and with specific limitations attached. Fees are assigned based on the value agreed upon for the specific copyright usage being transferred. Any rights not specifically transferred remain the property of the creator.

The concept of limited usage for the initial fee is one of basic fairness since no one can be certain what a copyrightable work will ultimately be worth. Negotiations regarding the price for a commissioned work, therefore, are normally based on the usage the buyer indicates will be made of the work.

Transferring rights

Transfers of exclusive rights, or all rights, by the creator of a work of art must be written and signed by the artist or the artist's agent and must specify what rights are being transferred. Nonexclusive rights, which can be transferred to more than one client at a time, can be transferred verbally.

For contributions to collective works (such as magazines, anthologies, encyclopedias, etc.) where there is no signed agreement, the law presumes the transfer of only the non-exclusive rights for use in that particular collective work. This holds true for any later collective work in the same series (such as a later issue of the same magazine), or any revision of the collective work. All other rights remain vested with the artist.

Copyright must be transferred in writing for the transfer to be valid. Because ownership of the physical art may be transferred legally without a written contract, artists in California and New York lobbied successfully to create state laws that require ownership of original art to be transferred in writing.

Some limitations

Copyright owners have the exclusive right to reproduce their work, sell it, prepare derivative works (such as a poster copied from a painting), perform their own work, and display their work (except that the owner of a copy of the work can also display it). Anyone who violates these rights is infringing on the artist's copyright and can be penalized and prevented from continuing the infringement.

There are some limitations on artists' exclusive control of their work. Fair use is one such limitation. Fair use is a copyright law concept that permits someone to use a work without the artist's permission for a purpose that does not compete with or injure the market for the work, such as using an illustration in an article about the artist's career.

Another limitation relates to the compulsory licensing provision of the law, which permits a non-commercial, educational broadcasting station to use published work without the artist's consent. Rates of payment for such use are established by the Copyright Royalty Tribunal and each station is required to publish a list of artists entitled to receive payment.

Work for hire

The work-for-hire provision of the copyright law is the limitation of artists' rights that carries the broadest implications for artists. By signing work for hire, an artist becomes an employee for the purposes of the copyright law and does not own the copyright of the work created. In addition to losing the copyright, the artist receives none of the normal employee benefits such as unemployment insurance, health insurance, sick pay, pension benefits, disability, and so on.

When a freelance artist signs a work-for-hire contract, the employer or client becomes the owner of the copyright and has all authorship rights. The artist has no further relationship to the work, cannot display it, copy it or use it for other purposes. The client can change the art and use it again without limitation.

For a commissioned work to be work for hire, the work must fall into certain categories in the law covering such uses as: magazines, newspapers, encyclopedias or anthologies, motion pictures or audiovisual works, instructional texts, atlases or charts, a collection of pre-existing materials, or a work illustrating a work by another author.

There are two kinds of work for hire. The copyright law says that copyrightable work done by an artist who is an employee (within the scope of their employment) can be a work for hire. This means that the artist is working at the employer's office during regular business hours, on a scheduled basis, is directed by the employer, and is working with tools supplied by the employer. This artist is an employee, is entitled to employee benefits and should be having taxes withheld from their paycheck.

A work created by an independent contractor can be a work for hire if the artist and client sign an agreement saying that the work is a work for hire. Some recent court cases (Aldon, Peregrine) have offered the interpretation that a work can be work for hire if the artist is sufficiently directed by the client. It is essential, therefore, that artists negotiate contract terms describing rights transferred before work begins.

The Graphic Artists Guild is emphatically opposed to the use of work-for-hire contracts by art buyers who commission work by freelance artists. Work for hire is an unfair practice that gives art buyers benefits and recognition that belong to the creative artist. These contracts devalue the integrity of artists and their work by enabling buyers to alter the work in any way without consulting the artist and by preventing artists from obtaining any payment for the future use of their work.

Original art

Well-known illustrators can command high prices for the sale of their original artwork. In fact, many artists who work in the graphic arts fields also sell their work through galleries, to collectors, and to corporations. Original art may be exhibited, used as portfolio pieces, given as gifts, or willed as part of an estate.

Concern for the protection of ownership of an original work not only flows from artists' interests in obtaining additional income based on the sale of the original, but also from their recognition that protecting the original is an essential part of protecting their reputations and careers.

Ownership of the physical art is separate from the ownership of rights. Like ownership of rights, the ownership of the original is vested with the artist from the moment that the artwork is created. Selling the physical artwork does not transfer any rights of copyright. Nor does selling a right of reproduction to a client give the client any claim to the physical artwork.

The artwork can be given to the client temporarily in order to make reproductions, but the client must take reasonable care of it and return it undamaged to the artist. For a separate fee, of course, an artist can sell the physical artwork to a client or to another party who wishes to buy it.

Registering copyright

Copyrights created after January 1, 1978, as well as those existing for work not published or registered, will last for the artist's life plus 50 years. Works copyrighted before 1978 will now run 75 years (but must be renewed on Form RE if renewal would have been necessary under the pre-1978 law).

The work does not have to be published with a copyright notice or registered with the Copyright Office in order to be copyrighted. The artist has copyright as soon as the work is created, but placing copyright notice on the work is important to avoid losing this copyright protection. All artworks can be

Price Ranges

Section 4: Standard Contracts

Section 5: Business Management

Section 6: Reference & Glossary

CONTENTS

registered, whether they are published or not.

If copyright is protected as soon as the artist creates the work, why register the copyright? There are several reasons, including the fact that registration is necessary to bring a lawsuit for infringement and to collect statutory damages and attorneys' fees. Registration also limits the ability of a defendant to claim "innocent" infringement.

Copyright notice

The copyright notice is Copyright or Copr. or ©; plus the artist's name, an abbreviation of the name or an alternate designation by which the artist is known; and the year date of first publication. For example, notice would take the form of: ©, the artist's name, 1986 (for more information, refer to the Business Management chapter).

The copyright notice can be placed on the back of an artwork or, when it is published, adjacent to the artwork. Other reasonable placements of the copyright notice for published works are specified by the regulations of the Copyright Office. Pieces in an artist's portfolio should have copyright notice on them, including published pieces, when the artist has retained the copyright.

When a work is published in a magazine, anthology or other collective work, the copyright notice in the magazine will protect the work from going into the public domain. It is better, however, for artists to have their own copyright notice appear with the contribution when it is published. This helps avoid certain risks of infringement and makes artists eligible for a group registration of published contributions.

However, if an artist omits the notice or has it in an incorrect form, the copyright may be protected under provisions of the law that save copyright despite defective notice. In such cases, the creator still has five years in which to file for copyright registration while making a reasonable effort to add the copyright notice to all copies that lack it. Only if this is not done does the work enter the public domain and become freely available to all who wish to copy it. Also, an omission of copyright notice won't affect the validity of protection, if the notice is omitted in violation of an agreement that the notice accompany the published work.

Group registration

To cut the cost of registration, the Copyright Office provides that unpublished artworks can be registered in groups. For example, five numbered drawings could be collected in a binder and registered as "Drawings by Artist, Series 1." Only one $10 fee would have to be paid and the art would not have to be registered again when published. A good reason to request copyright notice in the artist's name for contributions to periodicals is that it makes possible an inexpensive group registration of all contributions published in a one-year period with the copyright notice in the artist's name. Form GP/CP is used in addition to form VA for such a registration.

Original art does not have to be sent to the Copyright Office in order to register a work. While the copyrightable content of an artwork must be shown, this can be done with transparencies or photocopies.

Termination of rights

Transfers of copyright can be terminated by the artist during a five-year period starting 35 years after the date of publication or 40 years after the date of execution of the transfer, whichever period ends earlier. This right of termination is an important feature of the 1978 copyright law when transfers or licenses are of exceptionally long duration. The right of termination does not apply to work for hire or transfers made by a will.

Further information on copyright

For further information on copyright, artists can send for a free copy of the Copyright Information Kit (Copyright Office, Library of Congress, Washington, D.C. 20559). The kit includes a substantial packet of information on copyright and registration. Free copies of copyright registration applications can be obtained by calling the Copyright Office Hotline at (202) 287-9100.

Another excellent source of information on copyright and related issues is the *Legal Guide for the Visual Artist,* by Tad Crawford, published by Madison Square Press, 10 East 23rd Street, New York, New York, 10010.

Cancellation fees

When a commissioned assignment that has been completed is cancelled through *no fault of the artist,* the full fee must be paid. If the assignment is unfinished at the time of cancellation, artists may charge part of the original fee in proportion to the degree of completion. Such a cancellation fee should not be less than one-half of the original fee. Buyers usually, but not always, obtain all of the originally agreed upon rights to the use of the work upon full payment of the original fee.

Rejection fees

When a buyer rejects commissioned artwork as *not reasonably satisfactory,* the artist must be paid a rejection fee in compensation for time and effort expended. The fee for completed work is normally at least one-half of the original usage fee. If the assignment is unfinished at the time of rejection, the artist may charge part of the original fee in proportion to the degree of completion. Such a rejection fee should not be less than one-third of the original fee. In this situation a buyer foregoes any rights to the use of the artwork. All work and material must be returned to the artist.

When royalty arrangements have been entered into, all rights to the artwork, as well as possession of the original art, must revert to the artist upon cancellation. Since payment to the artist was to be based on a percentage of anticipated product sales rather than a fixed dollar amount, an equitable cancellation fee must be negotiated. Such arrangements often encompass an artist's retention of any advance.

In the event of cancellation, all expenses incurred by the artist todate must be reimbursed in full.

Cancellation terms should be stipulated in writing in confirmation forms and purchase orders, or these fees must be negotiated at the time cancellation occurs. Full payment of fees should be made contingent upon receipt of the artwork, and not upon publication, to cover the possibility of cancellation after acceptance. For a further discussion of Guild policy regarding cancellation fees, refer to page 26.

Expenses

Graphic designers traditionally bill their clients for all the expenses of executing an assignment. Textile designers and illustrators have usually absorbed such expenses as art supplies because, for them, the amounts tend to be quite modest. Expenses such as shipping, photostats, film, costumes, model's fees, unusual travel costs, production expenses, and consultation time should be billed to the client. These expenses should be agreed upon and set down in the original written agreement. Often a maximum amount for expenses will be indicated beyond which artists may not incur expenses without additional authorization by the client.

Credit lines

Illustrators usually incorporate their signatures on their artwork and those are typically reproduced as part of the piece. For important pieces, especially when a letter of agreement is needed to spell out the terms of usage and payment, artists are making "credit line" requirements part of the deal.

For some this may mean a printed credit line, for others merely the reproduction of the signature in the artwork. In some cases, as is traditional with magazines, both credits may be permitted.

This parallels, to a degree, a new development in magazine photography in which some photographers now require, by contract, that their fees will be doubled if an adjacent credit line is omitted. The theory is that, given the modest rates for editorial work, the value of the credit line is as important as the basic fee. This activity hardly constitutes a "trade practice," but it may grow in time and could affect designers and illustrators as well.

A copyright notice can be made part of the credit line, simply by adding © before the artist's name, and the year date of publication after the name (©Jane Artist 1981). Such a copyright notice benefits the artist without harming the client.

Reproductions

It is a courtesy for clients to provide artists with examples of the finished piece as it was reproduced. This piece can be used in an artist's portfolio and provides a view of the project in its completed form. Regardless of who owns a copyright in the artwork, artists' use of their own original art in a portfolio is permissible as fair use (that is, uses that aren't competitive with uses that the copyright owner might make).

Sales tax

Various states have different policies in regard to sales tax. In states that have sales tax, the rate usually ranges from 3 to 9 percent. The tax is levied on the sale or use of physical property within the state. A number of exemptions exist, including special rules for the sale of reproduction rights. The applicable state regulations should be consulted.

Many tax laws are unclear as they relate to the graphic communications industry. In any case in which artists are doubtful whether to collect the tax, it is safest to collect and remit it to the state sales tax bureau. If artists should collect the tax but don't, they, as well as their clients, will remain liable for the tax (but, of course, it can be difficult to try to collect the tax from clients on assignments that have been performed in the past). Artists are, in fact, tax collectors for the state.

Liability for portfolios and original art

If an artist's portfolio is lost by an art buyer, the law of "bailments" (the holding of another's property) makes the buyer liable for the reasonable value of that portfolio, if the loss arose from the buyer's carelessness. If the portfolio contained original art such as drawings, paintings or original transparencies, the amount in question could be quite substantial. The same potential liability exists with respect to commissioned artwork a client has agreed to return to the artist. A model "Holding Form" for use by textile designers appears in the contracts section of this book and can be modified for use by other disciplines.

There are two ways to minimize the risks in the loss of original work. The first is with "valuable paper" insurance. That, however, is not enough since, as with any insurance, continued claims will lead to either prohibitive premiums or a complete loss of coverage.

Buyers also need effective systems for tracking and storing all original art in their offices. They should make sure that the receipt of every portfolio is recorded and a notation is made of its destination within the organization. If possible, buyers should avoid keeping portfolios overnight and on weekends. All original art should be logged out when it goes to any supplier, such as color separators or printers, and logged in when it returns. Finally, suppliers should understand that they may be held liable for any losses they cause, as a result of the damage or disappearance of any original art.

Since the likelihood of guaranteeing protection in the handling of original art is remote, buyers should minimize legal risks through the purchase of suitable insurance and, more importantly, the installation of proper record-keeping procedures.

Speculation

The Guild is unalterably opposed to work on speculation because of the risks to artists inherent in such requests. Artists who create their own work and seek to sell it are not in violation of this rule, but art buyers should not ask artists to work on a project unless a fee has been agreed upon. Art contests, except under special circumstances, are also opposed because of their speculative nature. For contest guidelines approved by the Guild, see the chapter on professional issues.

The Professional Relationship

Our society and our economy rely on an extensive communications system, and graphic artists serve an increasingly visually sophisticated public. Economic projections for the next decade suggest that the graphic arts profession will continue to grow as fast as or faster than other professions, based on the importance of the communications industry. The field is competitive and clients can select among a wide range of artists producing diverse, original, high quality images.

Graphic artists are professionals dedicated to solving communications problems. Many run their own studios and are responsible for the day-to-day business matters that concern any entrepreneur. Those with their own studios must pay overhead, including insurance, taxes, studio space, marketing costs, assistants, and the other costs of doing business. Their rates are based on these costs, on their professional judgment, training, experience and on market forces. However, the fees that artists charge are based primarily on usage. Fees based on usage is the foundation of the U.S. copyright law.

The client

Graphic artists often specialize, focusing their talents on work in the publishing industry, for retailers and manufacturers, for broadcast companies or advertising firms. Their clients may be individuals, small companies or conglomerates. Some clients purchase art on a regular basis and some are first-time or infrequent clients.

Clients who buy art regularly, usually have staff—corporate art buyers, art directors and other representatives with expertise in that area. In a large corporation, for example, the art director, art buyer or stylist in charge of hiring artists to work on projects probably has some knowledge of professional practices and pricing issues.

Clients who buy art occasionally may rely on art directors, design firms, studios or agencies contracting with them for the project who will, in turn, hire artists.

In either event, clients are the experts in their own fields and must communicate their needs to the graphic artist in terms of the product and the market. These artists then bring their own style and expertise to bear in helping the client solve the visual communications problem posed.

The practical basis of a successful partnership between clients and artists is respect for ethical professional practices, as well as the ability to describe problems effectively and/or envision solutions.

During initial meetings, artists and clients discuss possible solutions to the design problem, fees, usage and contract terms. These discussions create a relationship that addresses the concerns of both parties.

The art director

In many organizations, art directors are assigned simultaneously to a variety of projects or accounts. They are responsible for finding the artists, negotiating the terms of the job and supervising the assignment.

Art directors draw together the individuals to complete the project on the basis of knowledge of the client's concerns and the diverse styles of the professionals available. An art director may rely on advertising directories promoting artists' work, may place ads in the papers, contact employment services or call in artists for an opportunity to review their portfolios.

When speaking with artists, art directors need to be familiar with the time schedule for the project, the project's budget, how the artwork will be used and a variety of other factors.

Freelance artists negotiate rights, terms, and fees with the art director or client. The factors described in this book are the basis of business dealings for graphic artists.

The art buyer

Many large advertising agencies hire professionals to supervise the hiring of outside talent such as illustrators and photographers. The art buyer works with the art director to select the freelance artist to be used on a commission, and is responsible for negotiating use of the work, fees, etc., on each commission. Art buyers often handle budgets, schedules, traffic and invoicing on each freelance assignment. Often an art buyer will oversee the assembling of a selection of portfolios for review by the creative group in order to select the freelance artist to be used on a commission.

How artwork is commissioned

Aside from directly commissioning a freelance artist, artwork can be secured through various intermediaries, such as agents. It is important that the ground rules for the relationship between an artist and the person ordering the work be established clearly before beginning work. This prior agreement protects both client and artist from misunderstandings about the process and expectations that can create problems later in the project. The Guild recommends that a written agreement be signed by both parties prior to the beginning of work.

Advertising agencies

Artwork for advertising agencies is usually purchased by an art buyer or art director. Artists are selected based on the style of art needed and the portfolio submitted. At the time of assignment, most agencies provide artists with a purchase order that details rights purchased, ownership of art, delivery dates for pencil and finish, prices for completed assignment, cancellation fee at pencil and finish stages, and any additional expenses such as delivery charges, or shipping.

Rights purchased may be in any or all of the following categories, which should be spelled out in the purchase order.

Complete buyout: includes the purchase of all rights and ownership of the original art.

Limited buyout: restricted uses normally within a specific market area and/or media. Ownership of original is separate.

Publication use: Includes use in newspapers, magazines, Sunday supplements, internal publications, and any material included as part of a publication such as freestanding inserts, etc.

Point of purchase: includes all point-of-sale materials such as signs, leaflets, shopping cart posters, catalogs, brochures, direct mail, etc.

Outdoor use: all posters that are not point of sale, such as painted bulletins, 30-sheet posters, transit posters, bus shelters, etc.

TV use: Television rights only.

Presentation and research use: purchased at the lowest possible rates since the material will not be used in commissionable media (the artist's order should cover an agreement for an additional fee if used extensively).

Test market use: Purchased at lower rates for use in a limited number of markets. As in *presentation and research use,* an artist's agreement should cover additional fees if use is expanded.

Representatives

Some representatives work under contract (the Guild has its own standard Artist/Agent Agreement, as well as a standard Textile Designer/Agent Agreement, which appear in the Contracts section of this book). Agents have the legal right to act on behalf of the artists they represent. They can legally obligate the artist, but only in ways agreed to in the agent-artist contact. Thus, artists should have a lawyer read any contract and make certain the terms are clearly understood before signing. If a more casual relationship is undertaken, the Guild recommends that both parties sign a memo that spells out the various responsibilities of each.

Exclusivity or nonexclusivity is a crucial issue in any contract, since artists must feel that *all* of their work will be marketed in the best manner. Representatives who ask for exclusive contracts should be willing to identify the other artists that they represent. Under this kind of an arrangement, representatives should not be free to broker unlisted talent, unless both parties agree. Some items to be considered follow.

Mounting of portfolio pieces and presentations, laminations, etc.: A clear understanding should be reached as to who pays the cost of these items and the fact that the artist ultimately owns them.

Mailing of promotion pieces, shipping of artwork, insurance, etc.: Many representatives will split or absorb these costs with the artist. The arrangement should be understood by both parties.

Billing: Whether it is wiser for agent or artist to handle the billing will depend on the circumstances. Any reputable party will supply copies of any purchase orders and invoices to the other party. If a purchase order does not exist, then a copy of the check should be supplied to the other party. One practical aspect of this procedure is that if the person handling the billing dies, goes into bankruptcy or reorganizes, the other party has proof of what is owed.

Commissions: The conventional artist-representative arrangement calls for a 25 percent commission to the representative. In the textile design field, the range for commissions is 25 to 40 percent. The rate of commission reflects the degree of responsibility assumed by the representative. (See, in particular, the section covering business practices for textile design.) A representative provides most client contact and art names, promotion of the artist, delivery, billing and other services in an effort to keep an artist in full production. Commissions should be based only on the fee paid to the artist, not on expenses normally billed to the client; the expenses should be subtracted from a flat fee before the commission is computed. Also, accounts that artists have prior to retaining a representative (i.e., *house accounts*) are usually serviced by the agent at a lower commission rate, if the agent is given these accounts.

Termination: This is a sensitive area for both agent and artist. Each party should be able to terminate on 30 days written notice, but an agent may demand a continuing right to receive commissions after the termination date. This right should not apply to house accounts. An agent might reasonably request the right to a commission on any assignments received by the artist for a period of three months after the termination date if the accounts were obtained by the agent. If an agent has represented an artist for more than six months, the right to receive commissions after termination might be increased by one month for each additional six months of representation (so that after two years of representation, the agent would receive commissions for six months after termination). The circumstances in each case will differ, but artists should rarely agree to give agents commissions on assignments obtained more than six months after the effective date

of termination. Of course, if an agent is entitled to receive a commission, it doesn't matter *when* payment is actually received.

Studios

Many studios delve into the freelance market for styles of work they cannot create. Studios may act as buyers in purchasing artwork directly or act as intermediaries in obtaining assignments for artists on a project involving several other talents. In most of these cases, artists are subcontractors, and their fees should be established in very clear terms. Some of the considerations on billing mentioned with respect to representatives should apply here. However, since studios frequently handle complete packages involving layout, illustration, lettering, type, retouching, etc., it may not be practical to supply individual copies of invoices. For this reason the working conditions should be established clearly at the outset. (Studio staff see the pricing section on salaried staff.)

Brokers

Most brokers do not represent talent on an exclusive basis, relying instead on their contacts among clients and their knowledge of various talents to put together a deal. Some of these, as with studios, can be quite complex, complete packages. Most of the points raised in the sections on representatives and studios would apply. Perhaps it cannot be emphasized too strongly that price, relative responsibilities, and working conditions should be established before accepting the assignment. In the absence of a formalized working relationship, *artists should establish a price that they consider adequate for the work,* leaving the broker free to negotiate above that price and keep the excess as a commission.

Sources of talent

There are several resources available to clients and artists to find and/or promote talent. Among the most widely known and used are the advertising directories. These directories generally showcase a specific type of work, such as illustration or graphic design. Normally artists purchase space in a directory that displays

representative work chosen by the artist and
gives a contact address for either the artist or
the artist's representative. Other directories
are compilations of juried shows. Directories
also serve the industry as references for
the types and styles of work being done in
each field.

Among the best known directories
nationally are: For illustration: American
Showcase (published in NY), Art Directors
Annual* (NY), Creative Blackbook (NY),
Chicago Talent (IL), Graphic Artists Guild
Directory (NY), Society of Illustrators
Annual* (NY), RSVP (NY), and the L.A.
Workbook (CA). For design: AIGA Annual*
(NY), American Illustration (NY), Creative
Blackbook (NY), The Graphic Artists Guild
Corporate Design Directory (NY). And for
photography: ASMP Book (NY), Creative
Blackbook (NY), and the L.A. Workbook
(CA).

Employment agencies and "freelance"
referral agencies in various cities around the
country refer artists to clients for a fee. They
operate in the same way that most employment agencies do, they simply specialize
in the arts' markets. Often these agencies
are listed in trade magazines and the
Yellow Pages.

If none of these services is accessible
in a particular area, it is recommended that a
client or artist contact the local professional
organization that services the graphic arts
industry for referrals.

*These directories are compilations of juried shows.

How Artwork Is Priced

Price determined by use

The Copyright Law establishes the premise for ownership and sale of artwork. It vests with the creator a bundle of rights that can be sold separately or in blocks.

The principle for determining the price of artwork is that the price is related to the value of the intended *use* the buyer will make of the art. The more extensive the use, therefore, the greater the compensation to the artist. Some inexperienced art buyers are surprised by this standard. They assume that they are buying a product at one flat price, which gives them the right to reuse or manipulate the art however they wish upon payment. But artists normally sell only specific rights to the *use* of their creative work. *The more rights sold, the greater the compensation required.* (For further information, please refer to *How Artwork is Priced*).

The basic standard of sale for a commissioned work of art is "first reproduction rights" or "one-time reproduction rights". Reuses, extended uses, differing uses, foreign uses, etc., should receive additional compensation. "Exclusive," "unlimited," or "all rights" agreements, therefore, should take into consideration all possible uses that can be made of the artwork.

In some cases (corporate logos, advertising, product identity, etc.), the buyer may genuinely need to acquire most, or all, rights. Buyers should be aware that artists must be adequately compensated for such extensive grants of rights to the use of their work. In other cases the buyer has no need for such extensive rights. Artists should identify what rights a buyer needs and negotiate only those rights that the buyer is willing to pay for.

If buyers are asking for 'all rights' or 'work for hire' to protect themselves from competitive or embarrassing uses of the work, a limited rights contract can be worked out that prohibits uses by the artist that are, in fact, competitive or embarrassing.

The chart "Media Usage" demonstrates how usage can be narrowed or broadened. Any usage category can be given restrictions as to duration of use or number of uses and the geographic area in which usage is permitted. Also, the usage should be specifically limited to one title or product. And within each category there are frequently subcategories too numerous to list here. The

Graphic art is commissioned in highly competitive and specialized markets—there are *no* standard prices. Prices depend upon several factors: the type of work required; the complexity of the art; the use to which it will be put; the artist's reputation and "track record"; etc. Actual prices are the result of negotiations between artist and buyer, taking into consideration all the relevant factors. Guidelines for pricing vary from discipline to discipline, so the discussion that follows should be supplemented by reading the appropriate sections on pricing for each discipline.

Accordingly, although the prices listed in our *Guidelines* are based on nationwide surveys, they are not meant to be taken literally as specific prices. The nature of the art market makes this impossible—nor is this kind of standardization necessarily desirable. Our figures are *benchmarks* that individuals may use as beginning points in establishing prices according to the particular relevant factors of the job in question.

The pricing ranges that appear in this book reflect market conditions and do not necessarily represent what the Guild considers proper compensation to an artist. Some art markets may be depressed or overcrowded and therefore provide inadequate compensation and substandard employment conditions for artists.

grant of usage rights might very well refer to the specific category or subcategory of intended use.

Media Usage

Advertising
Animation
Billboards
Brochures
Catalogs
Consumer magazines
Newspapers
Product packaging
Point of purchase
Trade magazines
Television
Other

Editorial or Journalism
Anthology
Book jackets
Consumer magazines
Encyclopedias
Film strips
Newspapers
Newspaper supplements
Television
Textbooks
Trade books
Trade magazines
Other

Industrial
Album covers
Annual reports
Brochures
Film strips
House organs
Trade slide shows
Other

Manufacturing
Apparel
Domestics
Home furnishings
Jewelry
Novelty items
Paper products
Other

Promotion
Booklets
Brochures
Calendars
Cards
Posters
Press kits
Other

Royalties

A good way of establishing price in relation to use is by a royalty arrangement. This is the accepted method of payment in the book publishing industry. A royalty is actually a percentage paid to the artist based on the total of the client's sales. Royalty arrangements must always include a basic "up-front" payment to the artist as an advance against royalties, otherwise the artist is working on speculation with no monetary commitment from the buyer. Royalties are not applicable in cases where the use of the art does not involve any resale or where a resale is difficult to determine.

Licensing

When a design or illustration is developed for resale and marketing as a product, it is usually done under a licensing agreement. B. Kliban's cats, Peanuts, the Muppets and Strawberry Shortcake are examples of products that have been licensed successfully.

Peanuts and the Muppets were already famous cartoon characters and were licensed very easily. Strawberry Shortcake was a character that was carefully developed by a major company and was marketed with a strategic and well-financed advertising campaign specifically for the purposes of licensing. These characters were sold to decorate all kinds of novelty items, clothing, dishes, calendars and posters, which are common forms of licensing.

In the fashion and textile industries, name designers like Ralph Lauren, Gloria Vanderbilt and Jack Prince market their special design collections (usually called 'marketing concepts') to mass markets under a licensing agreement. It is difficult for lesser name designers to market their designs in a similar manner, but it is becoming a more common practice.

Recently new companies have formed to specialize in representing licensed properties. They plan marketing support for these products through animated movies, TV series, publishing ventures, records and other forms of promotion.

A license is an agreement whereby an artist, designer or developer who owns the rights to the art permits another party, usually the client, to use the art for a limited specific purpose, for a specified time, in return for a fee or royalty. At the expiration of the license, the right to use the property reverts to the owner.

Payment under licensing agreements normally take the form of royalties. When the product or artwork is to be sold commercially, royalties are usually a percentage of the profit or retail price.

To provide for sufficient payment, the license should be subject to certain sales or production requirements that insure the artist or owner the royalty payment agreed to by both parties. If these requirements are not met, the license should terminate. In the event that this happens, the artist or owner is free to license the work to others for the same or similar uses.

Artists and owners should insist upon

proper quality control of the product to prevent inferior goods and to maximize sales potential. It is up to the arist, in consideration of client needs, to set those standards. In the event that the client or manufacturer fails to meet these standards, the license should terminate.

The duration of a license must be spelled out clearly. Many licenses are for relatively short, fixed terms with renewal clauses based upon successful performance. This type of agreement is fair to both parties since it provides for continued license of the art only when the artist is assured of obtaining payment and the client is satisfied with the product.

It is important to differentiate between rights granted and those retained, since there are multiple markets available and more than one license agreement for a particular piece of artwork.

The artist or owner is entitled to periodic accounting statements with details of sales made and royalties due. And, the artist should have the right to audit the appropriate books and records to verify the statements and to insure that payment is forthcoming.

Proper copyright notice must accompany the distributed art and, where possible, name credit should be given to the artist. This can be written into the licensing agreement.

Per diem rates

I n some cases artists are hired on a per diem or day-rate basis. This is a perfectly acceptable method of pricing providing that the day-rate is adequate and just compensation for the work involved and is agreed on beforehand by both artist and buyer.

Artists should establish a basic per-day rate for their work. This, together with an estimate of the number of days needed to complete the work, art direction, consultation, travel, etc., is the basis for a rough price estimate. *A word of caution:* some jobs look deceptively simple and even the most experienced artists sometimes encounter greater expenditures of time than first anticipated. Questions concerning delivery time, degree of finish, complexity, expenses and general responsibilities ought to be included in the estimate, and it should be made clear that an estimate is merely that and is not binding.

Hourly rate formula

T he hourly rate formula is another method used to figure pricing.

The hourly rate takes into account overhead factors such as rent, utilities, salaries, benefits, promotion, outside professional services, equipment, transportation, office and art supplies, business taxes and entertainment. A standard formula for figuring an hourly rate is to divide yearly overhead costs by 900 hours or whatever total billable hours you feel you will work in a year (900 hours accounts for a 35-hour week, 50 weeks per year). The number used by many accountants for a year's total work hours is 1800. However, self-employed artists often spend a great deal of time on work activities that cannot be billed to a client, like writing proposals, working on self-promotion, billing clients, etc. For example, dividing an artist's overhead figure of $100,000 by 1000 billable hours would produce an hourly-rate billing of $100 to cover expenses.

When estimating an hourly rate, a quick multiplication of the minimum number of hours a project will take by an hourly rate will verify whether the project will make money, lose money or break even. At that point, the artist has the option of negotiating for more money or paring down the project to meet a realistic time projection.

Design studios usually have two hourly rates: one for principals and one for employees. The difference is the salary level. For example, in the graphic design section, the hourly rate for a principal is, on average, $50 to $100 and for studio staff $25 to $50.

Page-rate pricing

P age-rate pricing is a method of pricing determined by a percentage of the advertising page rate of a given publication. Pricing for artists' fees, therefore, is directly related to the same pricing system used by the publication and its advertisers. The page-rate fee is also tied to inflationary increases due to the spiraling costs of paper, printing, and mailing (i.e., as the page rate rises, so will the fee).

Page rates vary according to the type and circulation of a magazine. These rates, therefore, provide a good barometer of a magazine's resources. *Reader's Digest,* for example, charges $90,500 (Jan. 1, 1986) for a one-page black-and-white advertisement. Obviously, the *Digest* delivers a potential market to the advertisers that make this cost worthwhile. A page in *Forbes* costs $23,790. A page in *Business Week* goes for $27,620. Page-rate pricing reflects these different costs in the fees paid for artwork.

This method of pricing is best suited to the so-called *higher priced markets* where a higher fee is more appropriate than otherwise recommended in the *Guidelines*. (*See Note in chart below.*)

Page rate pricing formula

Editorial   **Suggested percentages for pricing**

B&W page	B&W spread	Color cover	Color page	Color spread
PR* × .10	PR × .125	PR × .15	PR × .13	PR × .14

Advertising

PR × .125	PR × .135	–	PR × .1675	PR × .175

*PR = Page Rate.

Examples

	Business Week	Forbes	New York
Circulation	770,000	720,000	415,000
Non-bleed B&W page rate	$27,620.00	$23,790.00	$12,640.00
Editorial			
B&W page × .1	$2,762.00	$2,379.00	$1,264.00
B&W spread × .125	3,452.50	2,973.75	1,580.00
Color cover × .15	4,143.00	3,568.50	1,896.00
Color page × .13	3,590.60	3,092.70	1,643.20
Color spread × .175	4,833.50	4,163.25	2,212.00

Page-rate pricing formula applied to 1986 rates for *Business Week*, *Forbes* and *New York* magazines for a one-page, single insertion, black & white non-bleed page.

Reuse and extended use of artwork

Artwork purchased for a specific use should not be reused or adapted for purposes without additional compensation to the artist. If the possibility of reuse exists at the time of purchase, it should be so stated and the price adjusted accordingly. If reuse or adaptation occurs after purchase, the buyer should negotiate reasonable additional compensation with the artist. If adaptation of the original art is required, the artist should be given the opportunity to revise his or her own work. No original art should be altered without the artist's prior consent.

Complexity of style

Some styles and techniques require considerable time to execute even though they may appear simple. Consideration of the diversity or complexity of style for a particular work should be part of any negotiation, since the degree of complexity is reflected in artists' fees.

Print orders

The size of the print order in the case of publishing, or the contemplated space in the case of advertising, is a factor that will affect fees for artwork. Large print orders require commitments by publishers for paper, printing, binding, and distribution, and large space usage in widely circulated quality media requires substantial outlays by advertisers. The price of artwork should reflect these considerations.

Inflation

During periods of inflation, the Guild recommends that the government price index on cost of living increases for the date of publication of this edition, be added to the figures contained in the pricing charts. For example, on Jan. 1, 1984, the rate for a one-page black-and-white advertisement in *Reader's Digest* was $90,500, in *Forbes* $20,280 and in *Business Week* it was $24,120. When compared to the Jan. 1, 1986 rates, it is clear that advertising page rates have increased in the two years since the publication of this book. Prices should be reviewed yearly to gauge whether they are accounting for increases in the inflation rate.

Unusual time demands

Deadlines requiring artists to work unreasonable hours, over weekends, nights or holidays should be taken into consideration when negotiating fees. Whatever the reasons for unusual time demands, artists should not be expected to produce work at regular rates under those circumstances. Overtime rates are standard for typography, printing, and other services produced outside normal working hours. This same standard is applied to commissioned artwork.

Inordinate costs

Inordinate but necessary costs of producing a job, such as model fees, prop rental, consultation, research time and travel expenses, are negotiable items in pricing. Assemblage, for example, may require substantial outlays for rental or purchase of elements and photography fees to achieve desired results.

When artists are required to make substantial commitments of large sums for type, photostats, model fees, etc., it is customary to charge a markup in the range of 15 to 25 percent on such commitments to cover overhead and provide adequate cash flow.

Consultation

If a job requires extensive consultation, artists can estimate their hourly or day rate and add a consultation fee comparable to time away from productive work. It is not uncommon, especially for a brief consultation to solve a particular problem, for the consultation fee to be substantially in excess of a normal hourly rate.

The nature of the project, proposed usage, unusual time demands, travel requirements are factors in estimating a consultation fee.

Large projects

Large orders may carry lower per-unit prices than single or smaller orders. In such cases, lower prices are in keeping with standard business practices.

Buyer's budget

Budgets break down into different categories depending on the method of determining value: quality or price.

Clients (graphic designers as well as art directors and corporate clients) often use this book, or the *ASMP Business Practices Guide* for photography, to budget for quality. Other methods for pricing for many clients are based on the projected budgets for similar projects, or advice from colleagues who have commissioned similar jobs.

Previous budgets, however, only show what the last person hired charged for a similar project. Items such as inflation, new concepts, new talent and new expenses create too many variables to budget accurately from a previous job.

Another method of budgeting is a yearly projected arts budget, which places a value on the entire year's graphics activity. This system, while it allows for flexibility in the short run, can produce some unsatisfactory graphic prices towards the end of a fiscal year.

In any art, mechanical or printing budget, the client must consider what is generally billable. The contract section of the *Guidelines* offers a listing of most billable items (142 to 169).

Freight and sales tax are often excluded from budget estimates since they are subject to complicated sales tax law. These charges must be estimated, if appropriate, in order to calculate the full expenses that may be incurred for each project.

Research and development

After a project is commissioned, the next step is often research. Research may be as simple as opening one's files to locate relevant clips or reference material (photographs, magazines, illustrations). In some cases, however, research is a complicated process that may require such activity as corporate identity searches to verify the originality of a logo design. Clients and artists may collaborate on the research phase, depending on the resources available to both.

After the research is completed, the development stage generally begins. In the simplest cases, development is the refinement of an idea. Using the corporate identity example again, development may mean considering several ideas, exploring the applications and visual impact of those ideas, and developing a presentation.

Research and development for a corporate identity program is a substantial portion of the entire project in terms of cost and time. In this case, a thorough proposal outlining the various stages of a project is standard procedure.

Billable expenses for computer-assisted graphics and illustration

Artists who do not own computer equipment but are able to arrange access to equipment should maintain strict records of expenses in order to bill the client. In the current market, billable expenses related to the use of outside computer equipment include: rental fees, transportation to and from the equipment (especially if rental time is off peak hours when travel may be

hazardous), and any costs incurred in recording work on hardcopy, including 35mm film and processing or videotape. Also to be billed are such items as fees paid for technical assistants if they are required or included in the equipment rental fee, research and reference costs, and expenses for preparing raw art (photos, stats, line art, etc.) to be used with digitizing camera input.

There are other expenses that should be negotiated; for example, equipment or technology purchases or expenses to meet unrealistic deadline requirements (i.e., purchase of a telecommunications program to transmit a digital image to another region or city in time for an unreasonably short print deadline).

Artists should also follow basic markup considerations in instances where time is spent negotiating for rental time, or purchasing supplies and services. These items should be factored in as regular overhead, or charged as consulting fees.

The going billable rate for computer animation/paint systems is $250 to $350 per hour, and rental fees range from $100 to $200 per hour.

Any artist working in this area should be aware that the newness of this technology and the speed with which the technology changes requires a continual review of expenses and charges.

General Illustration

General illustrators are graphic artists who create visuals in many different styles and for many different markets. Most illustrators are freelance artists who maintain their own studios and work for a variety of clients, as opposed to salaried artists working for a single organization. While some artists have representatives to promote their work to art buyers, many do their own promotion and marketing along with the creation of their artwork.

Illustrators use a variety of techniques such as air brush, pastel, pen and ink, water color, mixed media, and computer-generated work. It is helpful for illustrators to have some knowledge of the various printing and separation methods in order to maintain the quality of the final printed piece.

Reference materials, including clip files and books, are among the many resources illustrators use for planning and completing a commissioned work.

Illustration is sold on the basis of usage and reproduction rights. That is, the price quoted on a project is based on the standard factors of deadline, overhead, complexity of style, *intended usage,* and *intended market.* Original artwork, unless sold separately, is the property of the illustrator.

Usage rights sold are generally based on the client's needs. Other uses for a work may be sold as long as they are non-competitive or do not compromise the commissioning client's market. In any event, it is recommended that clients only buy rights particular to the project.

The pricing ranges listed below do not constitute specific prices for particular jobs. They are guidelines which should be considered along with other factors specific to the commissioned work under consideration. Please refer to the related material in other sections of this book.

Advertising illustration

Advertising illustrators are graphic artists who work with art directors, account executives, copywriters, and/or creative-group heads of agencies to illustrate products or services for specific advertising needs. Agencies often ask illustrators to work in a specific style represented in their portfolios. Illustrators sometimes follow a sketch supplied by the agency and approved by the client. The terms and fee for the art are normally negotiated by the illustrator or the artist's representative with the agency's art buyer.

Premium prices for illustration are paid in the advertising field where the highest degree of professionalism and performance is expected from artists working within unusually strict time demands. Changes and last minute alterations are not uncommon. Indeed, illustrators may need to create work that will please several people of varying opinions, since many advertisements are created by committee. Prices are negotiated strictly on a *use* basis with extra dividends for complexity of style, tighter deadlines, residual rights sold, and "buyouts."

The three categories of magazines used in the tables are discussed in the Editorial Illustration section. Examples of each can also be found in that section.

All prices for illustration in the *Guidelines* are based on a nationwide survey that was reviewed by a group of experts through the Graphic Artists Guild. These figures are meant as a point of reference only and do not necessarily reflect such important factors as deadlines, job complexity, research, reputation and experience of a particular artist, technique or unique quality of expression, and extraordinary or extensive use of the finished illustration.

The price ranges shown represent *only the specific use for which the illustration is intended* and do not necessarily reflect any of the above considerations. The buyer and seller are free to negotiate, taking into account all the factors involved. By their nature, however, advertisements are conceived of with multiple appearances in mind . Therefore it is understood that the specific use may refer to unlimited use in a specific area, within a specified time period. This must be made clear before the project starts and the price is agreed upon.

The following standard trade practices should be adhered to:

1. The intended use of the art must be made clear in a purchase order, contract, or letter of agreement stating the price and terms of sale.

2. Normally, artists sell only first reproduction rights unless otherwise stated.

3. If a piece of art is to be used for other than its original purpose, the price should be negotiated as soon as possible. Since the secondary use may be of *greater* value than the primary use, there is no formula for reuse fees.

4. Illustrators should negotiate reuse arrangements with the original commissioning party with speed, efficiency, and all due respect to the client's position.

5. Return of original artwork to the artist should be automatic unless otherwise negotiated.

6. The use of art always influences the price. If the advertising is to be featured over an extensive area or is a buyout, fees should be significantly higher than when it is used locally or within a selected area.

7. Fees for work required in a very short period of time should be higher than the figures listed here. Regular overtime figures may be used as a rule of thumb.

8. The size of a rejection fee is negotiable, but should always be paid. The rejection fee for finished work should be upwards of 50 percent of the full price depending on the reason for rejection and complexity of the job. When the job is rejected at the sketch stage, a fee of one-third of the original price is customary. This fee may be less for quick, rough sketches and more for highly rendered, time-consuming work.

9. A cancellation fee should be agreed upon if a job is cancelled through no fault of the artist. Depending upon the stage at which the job is terminated, the fee paid should cover all work done.

10. Work done on speculation is against industry trade practices and contrary to the Joint Ethics Committee's Code of Fair Practice.

11. The Graphic Artists Guild is unalterably opposed to the use of work-for-hire contracts.

12. Unusual props, costumes, model fees, travel costs, production expenses, consultation time, etc., should be billed separately to the client. These fees should be agreed upon and set down in the original written agreement or as an amendment of the agreement.

13. The pricing ranges listed below do not constitute specific prices for particular jobs. They are guidelines that should be considered along with other factors specific to the commissioned work under consideration. Please refer to related material in other sections of this book.

Comparative fees for advertising illustration in consumer publications (magazines)

National magazines	Black and White	Color
Spread	$4000	$6000
Full page	3300	4500
Half page	2500	3000
Quarter page	1400	1600
Spot	1000	1200
Regional magazines		
Spread	3000	4000
Full page	2000	3000
Half page	1500	2000
Quarter page	1200	1500
Spot	1000	1200
Limited audience magazines		
Spread	2200	4000
Full page	1500	2500
Half page	1200	1500
Quarter page	1000	1200
Spot	800	1000

Notes:

National magazines are magazines with circulation figures of over 1,000,000.

Regional magazines have circulations of 500,000 to 1,000,000.

Limited audience magazines have circulations under 500,000.

Comparative fees for advertising illustration in consumer publications (newspaper)

Newspapers in major market area	Black and White	Color*
Full page	$3500	$–
Half page	2800	–
Quarter page	2000	–
Spot	1400	–

Newspapers in regional market area

	Black and White	Color*
Full page	2500	–
Half page	1700	–
Quarter page	1500	–
Spot	1000	–

Newspapers in local market area

	Black and White	Color*
Full page	2000	–
Half page	1500	–
Quarter page	1000	–
Spot	750	–

Supplemental magazines for newspapers in major market area

	Black and White	Color*
Spread	4000	5000
Full page	3000	4000
Half page	2250	3000
Quarter page	1200	1600
Spot	1000	1250

Supplemental magazines for newspapers in local market area

	Black and White	Color*
Spread	2800	3500
Full page	1800	2800
Half page	1450	1900
Quarter page	1000	1350
Spot	750	1000

*Add 50% for color printing in newspaper.

Notes:
Major market newspapers have circulation figures over 100,000.

Regional market newspapers have circulation figures from 10,000 to 100,000.

Local market newspapers have circulation figures under 10,000.

Comparative fees for advertising illustration in trade publications

Mass trade publications	Black and White	Color
Spread	$3000	$4000
Full page	2000	3000
Half page	1500	2000
Quarter page	1200	1500
Spot	1000	1200

Specific trade publications

Spread	1500	2500
Full page	1400	2200
Half page	1200	1500
Quarter page	1000	1200
Spot	800	1000

Notes:

Mass trade publications are publications with circulation figures of over 35,000.

Specific trade publications have circulations under 35,000.

Comparative fees for advertising illustration for promotion and direct mail

Brochures Large distribution or major corporation	Black and White	Color
Cover	$2500	$3000
Full page	1800	2000
Half page	1400	1700
Quarter page	1000	1200
Spot	800	600

Brochures
Small distribution or small corporation

Cover	1800	2200
Full page	1200	1500
Half page	800	1000
Quarter page	600	800
Spot	400	600

Mailers
Direct response

Poster	3000	4500
Full page	2000	2500
Half page	1200	1500
Quarter page	1000	1200
Spot	800	1000

Catalogues
Large distribution

Cover	2300	2800
Full page	1250	1600
Half page	1150	1400
Quarter page	700	900
Spot	400	500

Catalogues
Small distribution

Cover	2000	2500
Full page	1100	1400
Half page	1000	1200
Quarter page	600	800
Spot	350	450

Comparative fees for advertising illustration for point of purchase

Counter card	Black and White*	Color
Small campaign	$1900	$2500
Major campaign	2600	3500

Shelf Sign

	Black and White*	Color
Small campaign	2600	3500
Major campaign	3750	5000

Display

	Black and White*	Color
Small campaign	3350	4500
Major campaign	4850	6500

Notes:
"Major" and "small" campaign categories can also be taken to reflect the relative corporate size of the client, and the overall importance of impact intended for the point of purchase campaign.

Since point of purchase ads can contain lettering, many figures, product rendering and large areas, complexity is a large factor in pricing in this medium.

*Point of purchase often uses 2 and 3 color processes. Approximate 25% increase for each color overlay.

Comparative fees for advertising illustration for outdoor advertising

Transit cards	Black and White*	Color
Major campaign	$2250	$3000
Regional campaign	1500	2000
Local campaign	1125	1500

Bus posters

Major campaign	3375	4500
Regional campaign	2250	3000
Local campaign	1500	2000

Station posters

Major campaign	4500	6000
Regional campaign	3000	4000
Local campaign	1875	2500

Billboards

Major campaign	4875	6500
Regional campaign	3750	5000
Local campaign	2625	3500

*Add 25% for each cover overlay.

Comparative fees for illustration for packaging

National distribution or extended life of product	Black and White*	Color
Simple	$2700	$4000
Complex	4500	6000

Limited distribution or short life of product		
Simple	1300	2000
Complex	2500	3500

Notes:
Most purchasers of product packaging will need to purchase extensive rights for use of the artwork due to the unpredictable nature of the market. Royalty arrangements have been made, but are fairly unusual.

*Add 25% for each color overlay.

Comparative fees for illustration in theatre and film advertising

Consumer magazines	Color
Large production	$3000-5000
Small production	750-2500

Film poster
Major distribution

Comprehensive sketch	3000
Finished art unused	5000
If used in final poster	10,000 +

Film poster
Very limited distribution

Comprehensive sketch	2000-2500
Finished art unused	3500-4000
If used in final poster	5000

Note:
In most film poster assignments, the art is usually commissioned in 3 stages: *(1)* sketch, *(2)* a highly rendered comp and *(3)* the finished poster art. Separate fees are usually arranged for each stage of completion. Often the finished art is not used so a separate payment must be agreed upon.

Comparative fees for film and audiovisual illustration

Television commercial	Major National Account
Styling of a 30- or 60-second animated spot including backgrounds and key illustrations, depending on complexity of illustrations and number of key illustrations required.	$3500-12,000

Animatics

Depending on amount of illustrations and required use (animatics usually have a limited use) and size of test market	$2500-4500

Audiovisual presentation*

Per color slide	$150-175

Note:
Typically, animatics use "key frames," plus a number of additional "spare parts," such as arms, legs that are adjusted in sequence to create the effect of movement.

*Typical audiovisual presentations are meant to be quick and effective. The illustrations commissioned for this category are generally quite simple in style. More complexity would of course demand a higher fee.

Comps, animatics, and TV storyboard illustration (pre-production art)

Artists who specialize in pre-production art mainly service the advertising industry and are usually called upon to produce high caliber professional work within tight deadlines. Although some artists tend to specialize, nearly all are engaged in three areas of pre-production art: comprehensives of "comps" as they are generally called; animatics; and TV storyboards.

(1) *Comps* are visual renderings of proposed advertisements and folders (print media only) including headlines, body text, and a "visual," which is the sketch of the illustration or photo to be used in the finished piece.

Comp rendering may range from loose or rough drawings to "super comps," which are very tightly rendered and require a high level of skill, such as tight product illustrations and headlines in specific type faces as directed by the art director.

(2) *TV storyboard* is a visual presentation of a proposed commercial using a limited number of frames, usually drawn on a telepad. Storyboards are generally used in-house (within the agency) and to present the concept of the proposed commercial to the client.

A Key frame is a large single frame used in concert with other frames to establish the overall mood or to portray the highlight or key moment of the commercial. It must be given extra attention and compensation as it carries most of the narrative burden.

(3) An *animatic* is a limited, animated film using camera movements, a select number of drawings, some animation and a sound track. An animatic is usually produced to test a proposed "spot" or TV commercial. The need for animatics has risen due to the increased desireability of test marketing for advertisers. An animatic must "score" well on audience recall, etc., in order to go in to full production.

Video storyboards use storyboard art only (no moving parts) and movement is achieved with simple camera moves. Often a tighter style than normal is required and the fee should be approximately 25 percent higher than for regular storyboards.

In pricing animatics, one background illustration and one to one and a half cut-out figures comprise one frame. Two figures and their moving parts can constitute one frame when backgrounds are used for several scenes. Pre-production artists should try to get taped copies of their work from production houses so that they can compile a reel of sample commercials for their portfolios.

Fees in this field depend on job complexity including factors such as the degree of finish required, the number of subjects in a given frame, the type of background required and so on.

Artists must know ahead of time whether film or videotape will be used since each has its own special requirements. A good grasp of current TV commercial styles is crucial to success in this field. Some agencies will also request that artists work in-house and that fact should be taken into account when establishing a fee.

Rush work is billable at a minimum of 25 percent more than the regular fee. Day rates are not encouraged and flat fees should be priced carefully on a per-frame basis, which considers all factors involved in the job.

Comparative fees for pre-production art for television commercials

Animatics	Major National Account
Per frame (after 10 frames)	$200-250
Flat fee (up to 10 frames), depending on complexity	2000
Television Storyboards (per frame)	
Miniboards*	25-40
Telepad†	35-60
4x5 inches	50-75
5x7 inches	75-100
8x10 inches	150

*Miniboards are less than $2^{3}/_{4}$x$3^{3}/_{4}$ inches.

†Telepads are $2^{3}/_{4}$x$3^{3}/_{4}$ inches.

Comparative fees for comprehensive illustration for presentation

Magazine advertising	Black and White	Color
Major campaign		
Spread	$600	$750
Full page	400	500
Small campaign		
Spread	400	500
Full page	300	350
Institutional Advertising		
Major campaign		
Spread	400	500
Full page	250	375
Small campaign		
Spread	300	250
Full page	200	250

Institutional and corporate illustration

An *institutional* or *corporate illustrator* is a graphic artist who works with a graphic designer or art director to create illustrations for use in annual reports, in-house magazines or newspapers, and similar material. Often the illustrator is given responsibility for conceiving the concept and determining the style of the illustration. In annual reports particularly, illustrations are used to enhance the institution's or corporation's public image.

All the prices for illustration in the *Guidelines* are based on a nationwide survey that was reviewed by a group of experts through the Graphic Artists Guild. These ranges are meant as a point of reference only and do not necessarily reflect such important factors as job complexity, research, deadline, reputation and experience of a particular artist, technique or unique quality of expression, and extraordinary or extensive use of the finished illustration.

The prices ranges shown represent *only the specific use for which the illustration is intended* and do not necessarily reflect any of the above considerations. The buyer and seller are free to negotiate, taking into account all the factors involved. By their nature, however, advertisements are conceived of with multiple appearances in mind. Therefore, it is understood that the specific use may refer to unlimited use in a specific area, made clear before the project starts and the price is agreed upon.

The following standard trade practices should be adhered to:

1. The intended use of the art should be made clear in a purchase order, contract, or letter of agreement that states the price and terms of sale.

2. Normally, an artist sells only first reproduction rights unless otherwise stated.

3. If a piece of art is to be used for other than its original purpose, price should be negotiated as soon as possible. Since the secondary use may be of *greater* value than the primary use, there is no formula for reuse fees.

4. Illustrators should negotiate reuse arrangements with the original commissioning party with speed, efficiency, and all due respect to the client's position.

5. Return of original artwork to the artist should be automatic and timely unless otherwise negotiated.

6. The use of art always influences the price. If the illustration is to be featured over an extensive area or is a buyout, fees should be significantly higher than when it is used locally or within a selected area.

7. Fees for work required in a very short period of time should be higher than the figures listed here. Regular overtime figures may be used as a rule of thumb.

8. The size of a rejection fee is negotiable but should always be paid. The rejection fee for finished work should be upwards of 50 percent of the full price depending on the reasons for rejection and complexity of the job. When the job is rejected at the sketch stage, a fee of one-third of the original price is customary. This fee may be less for quick, rough sketches and more for highly rendered, time-consuming work.

9. A cancellation fee should be agreed upon if a job is canceled through no fault of the artist. Depending upon the stage at which the job is terminated, the fee paid should cover all work done.

10. Work on speculation is contrary to standard industry trade practices and to the Joint Ethics Committee's Code of Fair Practice.

11. The Graphic Artists Guild is unalterably opposed to the use of work-for-hire contracts.

12. Unusual props, costumes, models' fees, travel costs, production expenses, consultation time, etc. should be billed separately to the client. These fees should be agreed upon and set down in the original written agreement.

13. The pricing ranges listed below do not consititue specific prices for particular jobs. They are guidelines that should be considered along with other factors specific to the commissioned work under consideration. Please refer to related materials in other sections of this book.

Company magazines and in-house organs

In-house organs and *company magazines* have become large-scale publications and a relatively new market area for corporate illustrators. While the audience for these publications is comparatively small, their budgets can be larger than those of many consumer magazines. The company magazine does not depend on circulation and advertising-page revenues for income but rather works with a budget directly funded by the parent corporation.

Nonprofit or *not-for-profit corporations* are groups and associations that incorporate for purposes other than private profit. These corporations raise their operating contributions. The Ford Foundation, Common Cause, religious organizations, labor unions, and the Graphic Artists Guild are examples of nonprofit organizations.

Fortune double-500 companies are 1000 of the largest corporations in the world ranked by net worth in an annual survey by *Fortune* magazine. They generally have more than 100 employees, though they are ranked by net worth rather than the number of employees.

Annual reports

An *annual report* is the yearly fiscal report of a company. It usually reflects the image of the company that its board of directors and officers wish to present to the stockholders and the financial community.

In this field, illustrators are often called upon to do thoughtful, provocative, and interesting illustrations to offset the written and financial material that is being presented. Annual reports turn out to be highly effective vehicles of the companies self-promotion.

Fees for illustration are relative to the size of the corporation and the nature of the annual report and are usually negotiated on a one-time use basis only.

Corporate calendars

Prices for illustration for company calendars can vary greatly. Usually, the fee is dependent on the size of the company and the complexity of the subject.

Comparative fees for corporate illustration for employee magazines and company publications

Large corporation including Fortune 500 company	Black and White*	Color
Cover	$2200	$3000
Spread	2600	3000
Full page	1700	2500
Half page	1200	1400
Quarter page	850	1000
Spot	600	750

Small corporation

	Black and White*	Color
Cover	1500	1800
Spread	1700	2000
Full page	1000	1300
Half page	750	900
Quarter page	600	700
Spot	400	500

Nonprofit corporation

	Black and White*	Color
Cover	1000	1500
Spread	1250	1500
Full page	850	1000
Half page	600	800
Quarter page	450	650
Spot	300	450

Comparative fees for illustration for corporate annual reports

Large corporation or Fortune 500 company	Black and White*	Color
Cover	$3500	$5000
Spread	3000	4500
Full page	2000	3000
Half page	1500	1750
Quarter page	1000	1200
Spot	750	900

Small corporations, nonprofit

	Black and White*	Color
Cover	2000	2800
Spread	1850	2500
Full page	1200	1700
Half page	850	1200
Quarter page	650	800
Spot	450	650

Comparative fees for twelve illustrations for corporate calendars

	Black and White*	Color
Large corporation or Fortune 500 company	$–	$24,000– 30,000
Small corporation or publisher	$12,000	$18,000

Book jacket illustration

Book jacket illustration or design is the second most important ingredient in the promotion and sale of a book, superseded only by the fame and success of the author.

The publishing business has undergone a period of tremendous growth and change in the last decade and many of the large publishing houses have been acquired by conglomerates. Still, the publishing business is flourishing, and prices for book jacket and paperback cover illustration have risen accordingly.

It is a complex area of illustration for pricing, so strict attention should be paid to all the factors involved. For example, paperback covers generally pay better than hard covers simply because the paperback market is much larger. Also many book jacket illustrators act as both designer and illustrator and so their method of doing business is structured somewhat differently (book jacket designer/illustrators should refer to the Book Jacket Design section for further information).

It is important to note that illustrators who specialize in the book jacket field tend to receive lower fees than illustrators who do only several covers a year. Illustrators known for their painterly, highly realistic, or dramatic studies may command much higher fees than those whose styles are more graphic and design oriented. Although this practice is prevalent in the entire illustration field, it is particularly evident in publishing.

Major paperback houses sometimes put illustrators under contract to do a specified minimum number of covers per year at per-cover fees from $1,500 to $3,500 and more. In such cases, contract terms must be clearly understood or checked by an attorney. Such contracts may prohibit illustrators from working for other publishers.

Some paperback publishers give very specific instructions on assignments including the art director's rough notes from a cover conference. If an illustrator is required to read a lengthy manuscript in search of illustrative material and then produce sketches subject to approval by editors, this factor should be taken into account when negotiating the fee.

Other factors requiring additional fees include: (1) Changes in approach and direction after sketches are completed, that require new sketches, (2) Additional promotional uses that are above and beyond what is the common trade practice (when art is used separately from the cover it is considered advertising); (3) Extremely tight color comprehensives done for sales meetings and catalogs. All of these contingencies ought to be understood and negotiated by buyer and seller before the assignment is confirmed.

The pricing ranges for illustration in the *Guidelines* are based on a nationwide survey that was reviewed by a group of experts through the Graphic Artists Guild. These ranges are meant as points of reference only and do not necessarily reflect such important factors as job complexity, research, reputation and experience of a particular artist, technique or unique quality of expression, and extraordinary or extensive use of the finished illustration.

The ranges shown represent *only the specific use for which the illustration is intended* and do not necessarily reflect any of the above considerations. The buyer and seller are free to negotiate, taking into account all the factors involved. By their nature, however, advertisements are conceived of with multiple appearances in mind. Therefore, it is understood that the specific use may refer to unlimited use in a specific area, within a specified time period. This must be made clear before the project starts and the price is agreed upon.

The following standard trade practices should be adhered to:

1. The intended use of the art should be made clear in a purchase order, contract, or letter of agreement stating the price and terms of sale.

2. Normally, an artist sells only first reproduction rights unless otherwise stated.

3. If a piece of art is to be used for other than its original purpose, price should be negotiated as soon as possible. Since the secondary use may be of *greater* value than the primary use, there is no formula for reuse fees.

4. An illustrator should negotiate reuse arrangements with the original commissioning party with speed, efficiency, and all due respect to the client's position.

5. Return of original artwork to the artist should be automatic and timely unless otherwise negotiated.

6. The use of art always influences the price. If the illustration is to be featured over an extensive area or is a buyout, fees should be significantly higher than when it is used locally or within a selected area.

7. Fees for work required in a very short period of time should be higher than the figures listed here. Regular overtime figures may be used as a rule of thumb.

8. The size of a rejection fee is negotiable but should always be paid. The rejection fee for finished work should be upwards of 50 percent of the full price depending on reasons for rejection and complexity of the job. When the job is rejected at the sketch stage, a fee of one-third of the original price is customary. This fee may be less for quick, rough sketches and more for highly rendered, time-consuming work.

9. A cancellation fee should be agreed upon if a job is cancelled through no fault of the artist. Depending upon the stage at which the job is terminated, the fee paid should cover all work done.

10. Work on speculation is contrary to standard industry trade practices and to the Joint Ethics Committee's Code of Fair Practice.

11. The Graphic Artists Guild is unalterably opposed to the use of work-for-hire contracts.

12. Unusual props, costumes, models' fees, travel costs, production expenses, consultation time, etc., should be billed separately to the client. These fees should be agreed upon and set down in the original written agreement or as an amendment of the agreement.

13. The price ranges listed below do not constitute specific prices for particular jobs. They are guidelines that should be considered along with other factors specific to the commissioned work under consideration. Please refer to related material in other sections of this book.

Mass market and trade

Mass-market books are mysteries, spy stories, gothics, fantasy and science fiction, historical and modern romance novels that appeal to a wide audience. Trade books are books of poetry, serious fiction, biography, how-to books, and more scholarly works that appeal to a special audience.

Mass-market books normally pay higher fees because of the larger print runs and profitability; leading mass-market books command the prices. When pricing work in these areas, the size of the print order should be taken into account.

A hard cover assignment might also include paperback rights, for which a minimum of 50 percent of the original fee should be charged. A considerably larger paperback reprinting should amount to 100 percent of the original fee and possibly more.

Domestic book club rights are usually included in the original hard cover fee. All other residual rights, especially movie and television rights, should be negotiated separately.

Comparative fees for paperback book cover illustration

Mass market	Front cover	Wrap-around
Major distribution	$2800	$3500
Trade		
Major distribution	1500	2000
Small distribution	1000	1200
Young adult		
Major distribution	1500	1800
Small distribution	1200	1600
Textbook	Black and White*	Color
Major distribution	700	1000
Small distribution	500	750

*Add 25% for each color overlay.

Book illustration

Comparative fees for hardcover book jacket illustration

Mass market	Front cover	Wrap-around
Major distribution	$2850	$3500
Trade		
Major distribution	1500	2000
Small distribution	1000	1300
Young adult		
Major distribution	1200	1500
Small distribution	1000	1250
Textbook	Black and White*	Color
Major distribution	950	1500
Small distribution	650	1000

*Add 25% for each color overlay.

Book illustrators are graphic artists who work with editors, art directors, or book designers to create illustrations for trade or text books. This extensive field offers myriad assignments to artists.

Illustration in this area can vary from simple line drawings to full-color spread illustrations. The book and its related elements are considered a package. The importance of illustration to the package may be limited or significant depending on needs determined by the publisher. Book illustrators are sometimes authors and/or designers as well and, occasionally, one person creates the entire package.

When the art budget for a book is relatively large and the visuals are of major importance, endpapers, die cuts, pop-ups and other elements may be considered possible.

Illustrations have long been recognized as an important ingredient to the editorial and marketing value of a book.

The size of the print order, use of art in promotional material, and reprint and reuse of artwork are all legitimate points for price negotiations. Other factors affecting fees in this complex area include:

1. Extensive research, props, renderings, or model fees. In these cases, additional payment should be negotiated.

2. The type of book and the importance of the author.

3. The size of the contemplated print order, and the artist's reputation and record of commercial success.

4. Color separations (overlays). Artists should be paid *as much as or more than* the price of full-color illustrations since they are doing the engraver's work, thus reducing engraving costs.

5. Unless otherwise negotiated, original art is returned to the illustrator, who normally sells first reproduction rights only.

6. The number of reuses expected after the initial rights purchase. It is customary for illustrators to receive one-half of the original price for the reuse of their art. If the art is to be widely used in promotional material, this factor should be taken into account *when negotiating the original fee.*

7. Length of time estimated for the total project. Long projects may require payment to the illustrator as work progresses. For example, one-third the total fee should be paid upon approval of sketches, one-third upon delivery of finished art, and the remainder within thirty days of delivery of finished art.

All prices for illustration in the *Guidelines* are based on a nationwide survey which was reviewed by a group of experts through the Graphic Artists Guild. These figures are meant as points of reference only and do not necessarily reflect such important factors as job complexity, reputation and experience of a particular artist, technique or unique quality of expression, and extraordinary or extensive use of the finished illustration.

The price ranges shown represent *only the specific use for which the illustration is intended* and do not necessarily reflect any of the above considerations. The buyer and seller are free to negotiate, taking into account all the factors involved. By their nature, however, advertisements are conceived of with multiple appearances in mind. Therefore, it's understood that the specific use may refer to unlimited use in a specific area, within a specified time period. This must be made clear before the project starts and the price is agreed upon.

1. The intended use of the art should be made clear in a purchase order, contract or letter of agreement that states the price and terms of sale.

2. An illustrator should negotiate reuse arrangements with the original commissioning party with speed, efficiency, and all due respect to the client's position.

3. Fees for work required in a very short period of time should be higher than the figures listed here. Regular overtime figures may be used as a rule of thumb.

4. The size of a rejection fee is negotiable but should always be paid. The rejection fee for finished work should be upwards of 50 percent of the full price depending on reasons for rejection and complexity of the job. When the job is rejected at the sketch stage, a fee of one-third of the original price is customary. This fee may be less for quick, rough sketches and more for highly rendered, time-consuming work.

5. A cancellation fee should be agreed upon if a job is cancelled through no fault of the artist. Depending upon the stage at which the job is terminated, the fee paid should cover all work done.

6. Work on speculation is contrary to standard industry trade practices and to the Joint Ethics Committee's Code of Fair Practice.

7. The Graphic Artists Guild is unalterably opposed to the use of work-for-hire contracts.

8. The price ranges listed below do not constitute specific prices for particular jobs. They are guidelines that should be considered along with other factors specific to the commissioned work under consideration. Please refer to related material in other sections of this book.

Children's Picture Books

In this market, an advance against royalties is usually paid, one-half on signing the contract and one-half on delivery of artwork. The royalty and amount of the advance are determined by the illustrator and publisher based on the illustrator's reputation, experience, and desirability of talent rather than the number of pages to be illustrated or whether the color is to be preseparated.

The publisher usually suggests color limitations and size, but the illustrator often has a say in how the books will be produced. When doing color separations on books with a fourth color, that color should be negotiated as additional work since most preseparated books are two or three colors.

Advance against royalties are negotiable. Obviously, it is to the illustrator's advantage to obtain as large an advance as possible, since considerable time can pass before royalties are actually paid. An advance against royalties should always be paid, otherwise the work is considered speculative in nature.

Jacket art is usually wraparound, and is considered part of the total negotiated price for the book.

Publishers usually pay an author/illustrator less than they pay in total to an author and an illustrator working on a book together. While this practice is fairly common in the industry, it is a trade practice that the Guild opposes.

Paperback editions should be negotiated separately. When books are reprinted in paperback, artists are not necessarily offered an additional advance, and the royalty is less than that for the hardback edition. However, an advance for paperback rights *is a negotiable item and should be negotiated at the time of the original contract.*

The contract for a picture book can be a complicated legal agreement. The Guild recommends that an attorney look over the contract if the illustrator is unfamiliar with or is uncertain about what is being signed.

Young adult picture books

Advances or royalties normally are not paid in this category. All books are done for a straight fee. A typical book includes a full-color wraparound jacket and from 8 to 14 black-and-white interior illustrations of various sizes.

Juvenile workbooks

Most workbooks are given out through brokers or agents who work directly with the publisher on pricing for each book. Brokers and agents specializing in this field represent many illustrators who work in varied styles. Workbooks usually are priced out per page, per half-page, or per spot. Although fees are quite low, an entire workbook can add up to a considerable amount of work. Artists who are able to turn out this kind of artwork at a fast rate may find this type of assignment quite lucrative and feel secure in knowing that months of work lie ahead. Often, a single book needing a considerable amount of illustration is divided up among several illustrators in order to meet the publishing deadline.

Budgets for workbooks vary considerably depending on the size of the publisher, locality, publication schedules and experience of the artist.

Comparative fees for interior illustrations for young adult novels

Major publisher with major distribution	Black and White*
Spread	$700
Full page	500
Half page	350
Quarter page	225

*Add 25 percent for each color overlay.

Comparative fees for interior illustrations for trade and adult hardcover books

Major publisher with major distribution and large print runs	Black and White*	Color
Spread	$1200	$1750
Full page	850	1000
Half page	500	650
Quarter page	350	450
Spot	225	275

Comparative fees for interior illustrations for trade paperback and adult paperback

Major publisher with major distribution	Black and White*
Spread	$650
Full page	450
Half page	300
Quarter page	200
Spot	150

Small publisher with small distribution	
Spread	450
Full page	325
Half page	250
Quarter page	150
Spot	100

*Add 25 percent for each color overlay.

Small publisher with small distribution

Spread	600	850
Full page	450	650
Half page	300	450
Quarter page	250	300
Spot	175	200

*Add 25 percent for each color overlay.

Comparative fees for interior illustrations for college and young adult textbooks

Major publisher with major distribution	Black and White*	Color
Spread	$750	$1000
Full page	600	800
Half page	400	500
Quarter page	275	375
Spot	175	250

Small publisher with small distribution

Spread	500	750
Full page	400	600
Half page	275	400
Quarter page	200	275
Spot	150	175

*Add 25 percent for each color overlay.

Comparative fees for illustration in juvenile workbooks

	Spirit Duplicating Master* or Black and White
Full page	$225-325
Three fourths page	200-275
Half page	150-225
Quarter page	85-125
Spot	35-50

Comparative fees for illustration in juvenile textbooks

	Black and White	Color
Full page	$285-350	$380-475
Three fourths page	220-285	300-400
Half page	200-275	250-350
Quarter page	100-140	150-200
Spot	45-60	60-80

Notes:

A spot illustration is one animal, one person or one inanimate object. Add 25% for each additional color.

Necessary research should be supplied by the publisher otherwise additional compensation is warranted.

*A Spirit Duplicating Master is black and white line art.

Advances against royalties for children's picture books*

	Text and Illustrations	Illustrations Only
First book (previously unpublished)	$3500-5000	$2500-3000
Previously published	7000-8500‡	4000-6000†

*Standard royalty arrangements are 10 percent up to 15,000 copies and 12½ percent thereafter for an author/illustrator; 5 percent up to 15,000 copies and 6¼ percent thereafter for the author and illustrator separately.

†Can go as high as $8000-10,000 for an illustrator with a notable reputation or a very complex style.

‡Can go as high as $10,000 to 12,000 for an author/ illustrator with a notable reputation or a very complex style.

Editorial illustration

Editorial illustrators are graphic artists who work with editors and art directors of consumer and trade magazines and newspapers to illustrate specific stories, covers, columns or other editorial material. Editors, art directors, and illustrators discuss the use, slant, and intended impact of the piece or pieces of art before sketches are prepared. Often illustrators prepare several sketches to explore a range of approaches to the problem. Editorial art is usually commissioned under tight deadlines, especially in news publications.

Fees for editorial illustration traditionally have been lower than fees in the advertising field. This is generally true for all the creative services in the editorial area, including fees and salaries paid to writers, photographers, and editors. In fact editorial fees have changed very little in the last ten to twenty years despite inflation and ever-rising production costs (the cost of paper, printing and binding, and mailing). Current fees paid by many national magazines are sometimes lower than their fees for the same work twenty years ago. Newspapers have always paid on the low end of the scale despite the coming of age of four-color supplements, weekend magazines and special sections.

On the positive side, the editorial area always has provided a showcase for illustrators just coming into the field and an opportunity for more experienced illustrators to try new techniques and styles. In a sense, it has been a trade-off, albeit an inequitable one.

All price ranges for illustration in the *guidelines* are based on a nationwide survey which was reviewed by a group of experts through the Graphic Artists Guild. These figures are meant as points of reference only and do not necessarily reflect such important factors as job complexity, research, reputation and experience of a particular artist, technique or unique quality of expression, and extraordinary or extensive use of the finished illustration.

The price ranges shown represent *only the specific use for which the illustration is intended* and do not necessarily reflect any of the above considerations. The buyer and seller are free to negotiate, taking into account all the factors involved.

The following standard trade practices should be adhered to:

1. The intended use of the art should be made clear in a purchase order, contract or letter of agreement that states the price and terms of sale.

2. Normally, an artist sells only first reproduction rights unless otherwise stated.

3. If a piece of art is to be used for other than its original purpose, price should be negotiated as soon as possible. Since the secondary use may be of *greater* value than the primary use, there is no formula for reuse fees.

4. An illustrator should negotiate reuse arrangements with the original commissioning party with speed, efficiency and all due respect to the client's position.

5. Return of original artwork to the artist should be automatic unless otherwise negotiated.

6. The use of the art always influences the price. If the illustration is to be featured over an extensive area or is a buyout, fees should be significantly higher than when it is used locally or within a selected area.

7. Fees for work required in a very short period of time should be higher than the figures listed here. Regular overtime figures may be used as a rule of thumb.

8. The size of a rejection fee is negotiable but should always be paid. The rejection fee for finished work should be upwards of 50 percent of the full price depending on reasons for rejection and complexity of the job. When the job is rejected at the sketch stage, a fee of one-third of the original price is customary. This fee may be less for quick, rough sketches and more for highly rendered, time-consuming work.

9. A cancellation fee should be agreed upon if a job is cancelled through no fault of the artist. Depending upon the stage at which the job is terminated, the fee paid should cover all work done.

10. Work done on speculation is contrary to standard industry trade practices and to the Joint Ethics Committee's Code of Fair Practice.

11. The Graphic Artists Guild is unalterably opposed to the use of work-for-hire contracts.

12. Unusual props, costumes, model's fees, travel costs, production expenses, consultation time, etc. should be billed separately to the client. These fees should be agreed upon and set down in the original written agreement or as an amendment of the agreement.

13. The pricing ranges listed below do not constitute specific prices for particular jobs. They are guidelines that should be considered along with other factors specific to the commissioned work under consideration. Please refer to related material in other sections of this book.

Magazines

Several categories of consumer magazines are presented below. However, magazines don't always fall into one exact category. While *Time* and *Reader's Digest* are national magazines, *Forbes* is circulated nationally and yet it falls into the regional or medium circulation category because of its specialized audience and lower circulation. *New York* magazine is geared to a local readership, yet its larger circulation classifies it in the regional or medium category. *Family Circle*, on the other hand, would be classified as a national magazine because of its high circulation. *Popular Mechanics* falls into the local or small category, even though it may have national distribution.

For editorial assignments in trade publications, figures on circulation and readership are the most accepted basis for judging the proper categories for publications. Occasionally the type or readership and costs spent on production can influence the level of quality of the publication and fees paid for commissioned artwork. Circulation and distribution information is usually available from advertising and subscription departments of magazines.

Spot illustrations are usually one column in width and simple in subject matter. Although quarter-page illustrations are not spot illustrations, some magazines (particularly those with lower budgets) make no distinction between the two. If a spread illustration takes up one-half or less of each page, fees should be based on the partial page rates shown. For example, a fee for such a spread might be based on the fees for two half-page illustrations.

Newspapers

Newspaper illustrations are usually paid according to published size, which is measured in agates and column width. For example, a medium-sized illustration is approximately 65 agates.

Newspapers like the *New York Times* and *Washington Post* are considered national publications for the purpose of pricing because they are very large circulation dailies and are national in scope. A great share of the readership is outside the cities where they are published, and these newspapers also publish foreign editions. Medium circulation newspapers generally are regional in nature, sell outside the city where they are published, most often carry national news, and publish four-color supplements and weekend magazines. Local newspapers, naturally, have the lowest circulation, however, even in this category the size of readership varies widely and must always be taken into account when determining price.

It is worth repeating that this is one of the lowest-paying fields of illustration and has its value mostly as a trade-off for the excellent exposure that large daily newspapers provide. Still, the Guild maintains that the prevailing prices in this market are low and that exposure is not an equitable trade for low fees.

Comparative fees for editorial illustration for consumer magazines

Large circulation (National)	Black and White	Color
Cover	$–	$3500
Spread	–	2400
Full page	–	1500
Half page	750	900
Quarter page	600	700
Spot	400	500
Medium circulation (Regional)		
Cover	–	2500
Spread	–	2000
Full page	–	1000
Half page	600	750
Quarter page	450	600
Spot	300	400
Small circulation (Local)		
Cover	–	2000
Spread	–	1700
Full page	750	900
Half page	500	650
Quarter page	350	500
Spot	250	350

Comparative fees for editorial illustration for trade magazines

Large circulation (National)	Black and White	Color
Cover	$–	$2500
Spread	–	2000
Full page	–	1200
Half page	700	850
Quarter page	500	600
Spot	350	450
Medium circulation (Regional)		
Cover	–	2000
Spread	–	1700
Full page	–	1000
Half page	650	750
Quarter page	400	500
Spot	250	350
Small ciculation (Local)		
Cover	–	1800
Spread	–	1400
Full page	–	900
Half page	500	600
Quarter page	300	450
Spot	200	300

Comparative fees for editorial illustration for newspapers

Large circulation (National)

	Black and White
Section cover	$700
Half page	500
2 or 3 column	350
Smallest spot	175

Medium circulation (Regional)

	Black and White
Section cover	600
Half page	450
2 or 3 column	300
Smallest spot	150

Small circulation (Local)

	Black and White
Section cover	500
Half page	400
2 or 3 column	250
Smallest spot	125

Comparative fees for editorial illustration in supplemental magazines for Sunday newspapers

Large circulation (National and regional)

	Black and White*	Color
Cover	$–	$2000
Spread	–	1600
Full page	–	1400
Half page	600	750
Quarter page	400	500
Spot	250	300

Local circulation

	Black and White*	Color
Cover	–	1200
Spread	–	1300
Full page	–	1000
Half page	450	600
Quarter page	300	350
Spot	150	200

*Add 25% for each additional color

Record album illustration

The demand for engaging, forceful, and highly creative record album packaging has attracted the best of today's talented editorial and advertising illustrators, who have in turn created a new art form. Many record album covers have become collector's items. Several books have been published recently on record album cover art and an ongoing market has developed for collecting.

Commissions for record album illustration can be extremely lucrative. Fees tend to vary widely, however, depending on recording artists, particular label and recording company, and the desirability and fame of the illustrator.

For complex record packages, fees have gone higher than $10,000. This kind of assignment, however, requires many meetings, sketches, and changes.

Most recording companies produce under different labels depending on the recording artist and type of music.

The minor labels of major recording companies are usually reserverd for less commercial records and reissues of previous recordings. There is no discernable difference between fees paid by West Coast companies (Capital, Warner Bros.) and East Coast companies (Columbia, Motown, Atlantic). In all cases, only record company publication rights are transferred, and the original art is returned to the artist. Sometimes, tie-in poster rights are included.

All the prices for illustration in the *Guidelines* are based on a nationwide survey which was reviewed by a group of experts through the Graphic Artists Guild. These ranges are meant as points of reference only and do not necessarily reflect such important factors as job complexity, reputation and experience of a particular artist, technique or unique quality of expression, and extraordinary or extensive use of the finished illustration.

The following standard trade practices should be adhered to:

1. The intended use of the art should be made clear in a purchase order, contract or letter of agreement that states the price and terms of sale.

2. A purchase order or contract is recommended at the beginning of each and every project.

3. If a piece of art is to be used for other than its original purpose, price should be negotiated as soon as possible.

4. Normally, an artist sells only first reproduction rights unless otherwise stipulated.

5. Return of original artwork to the artist is automatic unless otherwise negotiated.

6. The size of a rejection fee is negotiable but should always be paid. The fee for finished work should be upwards of 50 percent of the full price depending on reasons for cancellation and complexity of job. When the job is cancelled at the sketch stage, a fee of one-third of the original price is customary. This fee may be less for quick, rough sketches and more for highly rendered, time-consuming work.

7. Work on speculation is contrary to standard industry trade practices and to the Joint Ethics Committee's Code of Fair Practice.

8. The Graphic Artists Guild is unalterably opposed to the use of work-for-hire contracts.

9. Unusual props, costumes, models' fees, travel costs, production expenses, etc., should be billed separately to the client.

10. The price ranges listed below do not constitute specific prices for particular jobs. They are guidelines that should be considered along with other factors specific to the commissioned work under consideration. Please refer to related material in other sections of this book.

Comparative fees for record album cover illustration

	Popular and Rock	Classical and Jazz
Major recording company	$3000-5000+	$2000-3000
Small recording company or new label	–	1500-2000

Fashion illustration

Fashion illustrators are graphic artists who illustrate clothed figures and accessories within a certain style or "look" for stores, agencies, or manufacturers. Occasionally, fashion illustrators work in the editorial area for fashion magazines or newspapers.

Sometimes, these artists are required to create an illustration with only the garment for reference (i.e., the illustrator must invent the model, pose, and background).

Factors affecting pricing include model fees, props, photography, research, and special materials.

The market for clothing and accessory illustration has declined in recent years, but has been offset in part by growth in the beauty and cosmetic areas, which includes product package illustration.

Most clothing illustration is paid on a per-figure basis, with an additional charge for backgrounds. *Model fees are always a billable expense.* Most accessory illustration is paid on a per-item basis. When more than one item is shown, additional items can be charged at a lower unit price. With the exception of specialized work, accessory illustration rates are generally 50 to 75 percent of per-figure prices.

The price ranges reflect rates for women's, men's, and children's illustration. These ranges do not reflect complexity of style and fees for the new, highly rendered and photographic style of fashion illustration, which commands a 50 percent premium over the high end of the range in all categories. A particular illustrator's experience and desirability is, of course, always an important factor in determining the fee.

All price ranges for illustration in the *Guidelines* are based on a nationwide survey which was reviewed by a group of experts through the Graphic Artists Guild. These ranges are meant as points of reference only and do not necessarily reflect such important factors as job, complexity, reputation and experience of a particular artist, technique or unique quality of expression, and extraordinary or extensive use of the finished illustration.

The price ranges shown represent *only the specific use for which the illustration is intended* and do not necessarily reflect any of the above considerations. The buyer and seller are free to negotiate, taking into account all the factors involved. By their nature, however, advertisements are conceived of with multiple appearances in mind. Therefore it's understood that the specific use may refer to unlimited use in a specific area, within a specified time period. This must be made clear before the project starts and the price is agreed upon.

The following standard trade practices should be adhered to:

1. The intended use of the art should be made clear in a purchase order, contract or letter of agreement that states the price and terms of sale.

2. Normally, an artist sells only first reproduction rights unless otherwise stated.

3. If a piece of art is to be used for other than its original purpose, price should be negotiated as soon as possible. Since the secondary use may be of *greater* value than the primary use, there is no formula for reuse fees.

4. An illustrator should negotiate reuse arrangements with the original commissioning party with speed, efficiency, and all due respect to the client's position.

5. Return of original artwork to the artist should be automatic unless otherwise negotiated.

6. The use of the art always influences the price. If the illustration is to be featured over an extensive area or is a buyout, fees should be significantly higher than when it is used locally or within a selected area.

7. Fees for work required in a very short period of time should be higher than the figures listed here. Regular overtime figures may be used as a rule of thumb.

8. The size of a rejection fee is negotiable but should always be paid. The rejection fee for finished work should be upwards of 50 percent of the full price depending on reasons for rejection and complexity of the job. When the job is rejected at the sketch stage, a fee of one-third of the original price is customary. This fee may be less for quick, rough sketches and more for highly rendered, time-consuming work.

9. A cancellation fee should be agreed upon if a job is cancelled through no fault of the artist. Depending upon the stage at which the job is terminated, the fee paid should cover all work done.

10. Work done on speculation is contrary to standard industry trade practices and to the Joint Ethics Committee's Code of Fair Practice.

11. The Graphic Artist Guild is unalterably opposed to the use of work-for-hire contracts.

12. Unusual props, costumes, models' fees, travel costs, production expenses, consultation time, etc. should be billed separately to the client. These fees should be agreed upon and set down in the original written agreement or as an amendment of the agreement.

13. The pricing ranges listed below do not constitute specific prices for particular jobs. They are guidelines that should be considered along with other factors specific to the commissioned work under consideration. Please refer to related material in other sections of this book.

Comparative fees for fashion illustration for advertising

Newspapers	Black and White*
Major department store, small ad	$350-500
Major department store, full page	500-800
Large specialty shop/small ad	350-500
Small specialty shop/small ad	350-500
Mat service, any size	75-100
Major advertising agency	500-1000
Small advertising agency	400-750
Trade-manufacturer	350-500

*Add 25% for each additional color.

Magazines	Black and White	Color
National, one-third page	$500-800	$–
National, full page	500-1000	750-1500
Local, one-third page	350-500	–
Local, full page	350-500	400-600
Trade-manufacturer	350-500	400-600

Other	Black and White	Color
Mailers and brochures, trade or consumer	$350-500	$400-600
Store catalog	–	200-275
Patterns	–	200-350

Note:
Prices are based on one figure. Accessories are usually 50 to 75 percent of the per-figure price, depending on complexity of the accessories.

Medical illustration

Medical illustration is one of the most demanding and highly technical areas of the graphic arts. Medical illustrators are specially trained graphic artists who combine a ready scientific knowledge of the human body with a mastery of graphic techniques, to create medical and health illustrations. The work of a medical illustrator ranges from ultra-realistic, anatomically precise pieces emphasizing instructional content, to imaginative and conceptual pieces emphasizing subjective impact.

Accuracy of content and effectiveness of visual presentation are paramount in this field. Many medical illustrators hold Master's degrees from one of six medical schools offering training in the field. Formal studies include gross anatomy, physiology, microanatomy, pathology, nueroanatomy, and surgery. Medical illustrators maintain extensive personal medical reference libraries and clip files.

Most medical illustrators work with a wide variety of rendering techniques including pen & ink, pencil, carbon dust, water color, colored pencil, acrylic and, recently, computer. Many of these artists also design and construct models, exhibits and prosthetics. Training for medical illustrators may include techniques for animation, film and video.

Until comparatively recently, the major buyer of medical illustration was the instructional market, primarily medical schools, related hospitals and clinics, scientific textbook publishers and clinical journals. During the past two decades, however, bustling editorial and advertising markets for medical illustration have been evolving.

Because of their extensive backgrounds in science and medicine, medical illustrators often work directly with clients, editors and art directors in the conceptual development of graphics projects.

Another new and growing market for medical illustration is the legal field. Medicolegal illustration is commissioned specifically for use in legal proceedings to clarify complex medical or scientific information for judges and juries.

Prices in this field are based on market use, copyright uses purchased, complexity of the project, research requirements, and the individual artist's experience and skill. For the purposes of the *Guidelines* pricing information is given for only the primary markets that commission medical art.

Pricing information in this section is based on a nationwide survey conducted by the Association of Medical Illustrators in cooperation with the Graphic Artists Guild. The ranges shown are meant as points of reference from which both buyer and seller are free to negotiate taking into account usage, copyright, complexity, research and the artist's experience, skill and reputation.

The following standard trade practices should be adhered to:

1. The intended use of the art must be made clear in a purchase order, contract, or letter of agreement that states the price and terms of sale.

2. Work for hire agreements are unalterably opposed.

3. Unless specified otherwise in writing, the artist sells first use reproduction rights only.

4. Reuse of any artwork, unless specified otherwise in writing, requires payment of an additional fee.

5. Return of original artwork to the artist should be automatic unless specified otherwise in writing.

6. Negotiated fees for a buyout or for extensive use should be significantly higher than first use fees.

7. Work required in an unreasonably short time should carry a higher fee.

8. A rejection fee should always be paid for work done in good faith, but the size of the fee is negotiable.

9. A cancellation fee should always be paid if the job is cancelled through no fault of the artist. The fee should cover expenses and all work done.

10. Work done on speculation is contrary to standard industry trade practices and to the Joint Ethics Committee's Code of Fair Practice.

11. Shipping fees, travel costs, model fees and other unusual expenses should be billed separately. Billing of expenses should be discussed with the client and agreed upon in writing at the outset of the project.

12. The pricing ranges listed below do not constitute specific prices for particular jobs. They are guidelines that should be considered along with other factors specific to the commissioned work under consideration. Please refer to related material in other sections of this book.

(Charts are on the following pages)

Comparative fees for medical illustration in advertising

	Line	Tone	Color
Conceptual	$500-1400	$875-2300	$2100-4000
Anatomical/Surgical	500-1400	800-2300	1900-3400
Product	300-1300	600-1750	1400-3000
Poster	–	–	2300-5000
Spot*	400-1000	700-1500	–
Per diem rate for special consultation and/or research			250-1000

Notes:
1. The rates shown are for the purchase of first use rights *only.*
2. A negotiable re-use fee of 25-30% is based on when, where and how the art is to be reused.
3. Reasonable expenses are charged separately.
4. Sketches or comps are ⅓ to ½ of the rates shown.

Comparative fees for medical illustration in editorial publications

Professional Publications	Line	Tone	Color
Cover	$–	$700-1000	$750-1200
Spread	600-1000	700-1000	750-1150
Full page	350-600	400-700	500-900
Spot*	100-300	200-400	250-500

Consumer health and science publications (magazines and books)			
Cover	–	–	$1500-3000
Spread	–	–	1500-3000
Full page	–	–	750-2000
Spot*	–	–	500-1000

*Because of the scientific complexity of the subject matter, reproduction size is often irrelevant in pricing. For the purpose of these charts, a spot is considered to be any illustration ¾ of a page or less.

Comparative fees for instructional illustration

	Line	Tone	Color
Simple	$ 75-150	$100-200	$200-350
Moderate	140-250	150-300	300-500
Complex	200-350	300-500	375-800

Note:
Rates shown are for limited non-commercial rights only. Reuse fees range from 25-30% of the original price and are based on the intended reuse.

Comparative fees for medicolegal illustration

	Simple	Complex
First image (per panel)	$350-700	$600-1000
Additional related image (per panel, maximum 3 images)	250-500	375-600
Overlays	100-300	125-375
Hourly rates for consultation, deposition or testimony	50-150	
Per diem for consultation, deposition or testimony	350-800	

Note:
An exhibit is comprised of one or more images on a single panel. Sizes vary from 8½"x11" to 32"x40".

Comparative fees for model construction

	Simple	Complex	Hourly rate
Construction of model	$1500	$3000	$30-50

Note:
All materials and expenses are billed to the client.

Technical illustration

Technical illustrators are graphic artists who create highly accurate renderings of machinery, charts, instruments, scientific subjects (such as biological studies, geological formations, and chemical reactions), space technology, cartography (maps), or virtually any subject that requires precision of interpretation in illustration. Technical illustrators often work directly with a scientist, engineer or technician to achieve the most explicit and accurate visualization of the subject and/or information.

Technical illustration is used in all areas of graphics communication in this age of high technology. Some of the areas most commonly requiring this specialized art are: annual reports, special interest magazines, industrial publications, package illustrations, advertising, corporate, editorial, computer graphics, and audio visuals.

These artists may work in a variety of media: ink, wash, airbrush, pencil, watercolor, gouache, computer graphics, etc., and are often trained in mechanical drafting, mathematics, diagrams, blueprints and production.

The factors affecting pricing in this field include: (1) research and consultation time, (2) travel, (3) reference materials, (4) complexity of project. All prices for illustration in the *Guidelines* are based on a nationwide survey which was reviewed by a group of experts through the Graphic Artists Guild. The price ranges shown here represent *only the specific use for which the illustration is intended* and do not necessarily reflect any of the considerations above. The buyer and seller are free to negotiate price, taking into account all the factors involved.

The following standard trade practices should be adhered to:

1. The intended use of the art should be made clear in a purchase order, contract or letter of agreement that states the price and terms of sale.

2. A purchase order or a contract is recommended at the beginning of each and every project.

3. If a piece of art is to be used for other than its original purpose, price should be negotiated as soon as possible.

4. Normally, an artist sells only first reproduction rights unless otherwise stipulated.

5. Return of original artwork to the artist should be automatic unless otherwise negotiated.

6. The use of the art always influences the price. If the editorial use is to be featured over an extensive area or is a buyout, it should pay significantly more than when it is used locally or within a selected area.

7. Work required in a very short period of time should pay more than the figures listed here. Regular overtime figures may be used as a rule of thumb.

8. The size of a rejection fee is negotiable but should always be paid. The rejection fee for finished work should be close to the full price depending on the reasons for cancellation and complexity of the job. When the job is cancelled at the sketch stage, a fee of one-third of the original price is customary. This fee may be less for quick, rough sketches and more for highly rendered, time-consuming work.

9. Work on speculation is contrary to standard industry trade practices and to the Joint Ethics Committee's Code of Fair Practice.

10. The Graphic Artists Guild is unalterably opposed to the use of work-for-hire or done-for-hire contracts.

11. Unusual props, costumes, models' fees, travel costs, production expenses, etc., should be billed separately to the client.

12. The price ranges listed below do not constitute specific prices for particular jobs. They are guidelines that should be considered along with other factors specific to the commissioned work under consideration. Please refer to related material in other sections of this book.

Comparative fees for technical illustration for advertising

National magazine	Black and White*	Color
Spread	$3500	$5000
Full page	2500	3700
Half page	1800	2500
Quarter page	1200	1500
Spot	750	1000

Regional and mass trade magazine		
Spread	2200	3500
Full page	1700	2500
Half page	1200	1700
Quarter page	750	1200
Spot	500	800

Specific trade and limited audience magazine		
Spread	1500	2000
Full page	1200	1700
Half page	1000	1500
Quarter page	750	1000
Spot	350	600

National newspaper advertising campaign†		
Spread	3000	$–
Full page	2500	–
Half page	1500	–
Two column (quarter page)	1000	–

Newspaper supplement	Black and White	Color
Spread	$–	$3500
Full page	–	3000
Half page	–	2000
Two column (quarter page)	–	750

*Add 25 percent for each color overlay.

†No specific prices are available for small town local newspapers. A broad range of fees are negotiable depending on budgets and the artist's reputation.

Comparative fees for technical illustration for editorial publications

In-house publication	Black and White	Color
Cover	$–	$1000-1500
Spread	1250	1500-1800
Full page	1000	1250

Magazines		
Cover*	–	2000-2500
Spread	1500-1800	2500-3000
Full page	1000	1500

*Complex covers with gate-folds pay $3000 +.

Brochures		
Promotion and presentation	250-700	500-1000

Packages		
"How to use"	200-800	

(Continued on next page)

Comparative fees for technical illustration for editorial publications (continued)

Books	Black and White*	Color
Full page, complex	750	1200
Full page, simple	400	500
Spots	75-200	

Presentations

Flip charts (simple)		200-450
Trade show material		500-1300

Technical materials

Product user and service manuals		20-35/hr.
Data sheets		12-25/hr.

Consultation fees

Per hour $75-125   Per diem $250-400

Novelty and miscellaneous products illustration

The greeting card and the paper novelty fields are experiencing a great business boom with unprecedented sales, new greeting card companies, and fresh card lines entering the market constantly. Since success and failure in this business is based largely on the whim of the public this area lends itself perfectly to royalty arrangements. Royalty agreements for calendars and posters are handled in the same manner as royalty agreements in the book field (see Book Illustration section for further information).

All the prices for illustration in the *Guidelines* are based on a nationwide survey which was reviewed by a group of experts through the Graphic Artists Guild. These ranges are meant as points of reference only and do not necessarily reflect such important factors as job complexity, reputation and experience of a particular artist, technique or unique quality of expression and extraordinary or extensive use of the finished illustration.

The price ranges shown represent *only the specific use for which the illustration is intended* and do not necessarily reflect any of the above considerations. The buyer and seller are free to negotiate, taking into account all the factors involved. By their nature, however, advertisements are conceived of with multiple appearances in mind. Therefore, it is understood that the specific use may refer to unlimited use in a specific area, within a specified time period. This must be made clear before the project starts and price is agreed upon.

The following standard trade practices should be adhered to:

1. The intended use of the art should be made clear in a purchase order, contract or letter of agreement that states the price and terms of sale.

12. Normally, an artist sells only first reproduction rights unless otherwise stated.

3. If a piece of art is to be used for other than its original purpose, price should be negotiated as soon as possible. Since the secondary use may be of *greater* value than the primary use, there is no formula for reuse fees.

4. An illustrator should negotiate reuse arrangements with the original commissioning party with speed, efficiency, and all due respect to the client's position.

5. Return of original artwork to the artist should be automatic and timely unless otherwise negotiated.

6. The use of the art always influences the price. If the illustration is to be featured over an extensive area or is a buyout, fees should be significantly higher than when it is used locally or within a selected area.

7. Fees for work required in a very short period of time should be higher than the figures listed here. Regular overtime figures may be used as a rule of thumb.

8. The size of a rejection fee is negotiable but should always be paid. The rejection fee for finished work should be upwards of 50 percent of the full price, depending on reasons for rejection and complexity of the job. When the job is rejected at the sketch stage, a fee of one-third of the original price is customary. This fee may be less for quick, rough sketches and more for highly rendered, time-consuming work.

9. A cancellation fee should be agreed upon if a job is cancelled through no fault of the artist. Depending upon the stage at which the job is terminated, the fee paid should cover all work done.

10. Work on speculation is contrary to standard industry trade practices and to the Joint Ethics Committee's Code of Fair Practice.

11. The Graphic Artists Guild is unalterably opposed to the use of work-for-hire contracts.

12. Unusual props, costumes, models' fees, travel costs, production expenses, consultation time, etc. should be billed separately to the client. These fees should be agreed upon and set down in the original written agreement, or as an amendment of the agreement.

13. The pricing ranges listed below do not constitute specific prices for particular jobs. They are guidelines that should be considered along with other factors specific to the commissioned work under consideration. Please refer to related material in other sections of this book.

The fees listed in this section represent nonreturnable advances figured on a projection of the first year's royalties. The average royalty is 5 percent of the retail price, and this increases to 7.5 percent after a certain number of items are sold. This number depends upon the particular item and its market costs. It is advisable to seek the advice of

an attorney before signing a royalty agreement, which is a binding contract.

Novelty merchandising

Art for T-shirts, towels, mugs, tote bags, and other such items should be sold under a royalty-type agreement called *licensing*. Spin-offs from nationally known and highly developed characters like *Peanuts* and B. Kliban's cats are sold in the same manner. Royalties for licensing rights vary from 2 to 10 percent according to the fame of a particular character, art, or artist and the type and price of the retail product. In this field of novelty merchandising a large royalty percentage is generally more desireable than smaller royalties with a larger advance. It is advised that an attorney be retained to negotiate a licensing contract. (See the discussion of royalty in the Book Illustration category for more information.)

Limited edition prints

Art for limited edition prints may be created by artists independently or under contract with a gallery or publisher. Payment is either on a commission or royalty basis, and an advance is usually included. Both the advance and the ultimate payment to the artist will vary depending on the size of the print run, the number of colors printed, the selling price, and other factors. A typical arrangement of a limited edition of prints is for advance against 50 to 67 percent of gross sales revenues (i.e., the gallery's commission is 33 to 50 percent).

If the publisher or gallery is responsible for all production costs (i.e., platemaking, etching, proofing, paper, ink, etc.) including advertising and promotion, artists will receive less. Under such agreements, artists are entitled to a limited number of "artist's proofs" to use in any way they wish. A typical edition will range from 100 to 250 prints. Each print is usually numbered and signed by the artist.

In all cases, marketing can make or break the venture. Market research should be done prior to entering into a binding agreement, making significant outlays of money or investment of time in creating the art. The market for limited edition prints is regulated by law in a number of states, including New York, California, and Illinois. Extensive disclosures or disclaimers may have to accompany limited edition prints sold in these states.

Comparative fees for illustration for greeting cards and novelty products

	Black and White*	Color
Greeting cards	$350	$500-700
Calendars for sale (approx. 12 illus.)	4000	6000
Posters for sale (litho or silkscreen, three to five colors)	–	2000

Fees listed are nonreturnable advances against royalties.

*Add $50 for each color overlay.

Animation

Animators are graphic artists whose skills entail creating the illusion of movement. Knowledge of movement and technical film details are essential for the animator. In the process of animation, the animator begins with a layout, which gives the "path" for movement. Following the model sheets of characters, which are based on the designer's concepts and are often supplied by an advertising agency (when doing a television commercial), the animator creates specific movement based on the written directions and camera instructions. These directions and instructions, along with any dialogue, music, or sound effects, are broken down frame by frame for 35-mm film. Often, the animator will physically stage the action.

Generally, animators work for a studio but there are those in the Animators Union who free-lance. There are nonunion animators, but union membership is required in order to work in unionized studios.

Animation has a range of uses such as television commercials, medical and educational films, television specials, titles, feature films, special effects, and the familiar Saturday morning cartoons. There are also independent animated films which are an entirely different art form with a broad spectrum of styles. Usually these are shown in film festivals or competitions that serve as showcases for the artist's work.

A factor affecting pricing is whether one is a free-lance or on staff. If the animator is free-lancing pricing is also affected by what category the animation falls under (e.g., the intricacy of the movement, how much movement there is, and how intricate the drawings must be). This is decided upon before work is begun.

There is a category in the union titled *graphic film artist* which involves knowledge of cameras and film. An image is taken and a computerized camera figures the movement of that image for the desired effects. The most common examples of this are the television station and network logos broadcast with movement and "glowing halo" effects.

Animation is a highly specialized field, but advancement is possible according to one's skills. There are animators who also work in other areas; some are illustrators, designers for film, and cartoonists. It does not follow that cartoonists or illustrators have the skill or patience to be animators. Most are satisfied with seeing their drawings animated by someone else's hand. Occasionally, artists who supply a design may want to try animating it.

In showing work, portfolios of storyboards, backgrounds, model sheets, and similar items are useful to animators who have expertise and seek work in these areas. The animator's samples, however, are usually condensed onto a film reel or a video cassette in order to show the true nature of one's ability in animating movement.

Most animation in this country is done with drawings that are then inked and painted onto cels. Other techniques of commercial value are cut-outs, which are moved under the cameras; flat hinged puppets, which are also moved under the camera; kinesthesis or filmographs, which require figuring camera movels to extend movement in a single piece of artwork such as a photograph; pixilation, or trick photography, in which objects are manipulated and appear to be speeding through the frame; computer animation, which can be hard edged, geometric, abstract, or figurative; and three-dimensional animation, which has clay figures or puppets or any other three-dimensional object used to narrate a story; and highly realistic miniatures used in special effects.

Pay scales of temporary animation artists

Classification	Weekly	Hourly
Director	$1,260.00	$ 36.00
Story, story sketch	905.63	25.88
Layout	905.63	25.88
Animator†	945.63	27.00
Assistant animator	590.63	16.88
Inbetweeners	511.88	14.63
Production coordinator	650.48	18.59
Preplanner/checker (animation)	590.63	16.88
Junior checker (ink and paint)	464.63	13.28
Inkers	464.63	13.28
Painters	448.88	12.82
Background	776.48	22.19
Graphic film artist I	708.75	20.25
Graphic film artist II	647.33	18.50

Animator

	Per Diem	Weekly
Limited footage, 14 ft @ $10.50	–	147.00
Light footage, 7 ft @ $26.25	–	183.75
Medium footage, 5 ft @ $42.00	–	210.00
Heavy footage, 4 ft @ $57.75	–	231.00

Assistant animator	Per Diem	Weekly
Light footage, 7 ft @ $15.75	–	$110.25
Medium footage, 5 ft @ $25.20	–	126.00
Heavy footage, 4 ft @ $34.65	–	138.60
Light footage, 7 ft @ $19.69	–	137.83
Medium footage, 5 ft @ $31.50	–	157.50
Heavy footage, 4 ft @ $43.31	–	173.24

*Temporary work scale is at time-and-one-half of regular salary. See salaried Staff section for staff salaries. All animation figures were supplied by the Animators Union, Local 841, IATSE, and represent the union pay scale.

Cartooning

Cartoonists are humorous illustrators who draw pictorial representations or caricatures, often satirical, showing action, a situation or person, of topical and humorous interest.

Because of their mass accessibility and their relative simplicity in conception and style, cartoons appear deceptively simple to create. However, cartooning is a highly demanding specialization with a long "apprentice" period required to reach the point where all the various elements involved can be brought together consistently and sharply. In fact, freelance cartooning includes work in syndicated comic strips and panels, advertising, humorous illustration for text, trade and children's books, television, public relations, and sales promotion.

Magazines

Magazine cartoons are created by freelance cartoonists who generally conceive the idea (although gag writers are used at times), draw it, and then offer it for sale to magazines. Most cartoonists market their work in order of rate paid, with higher-paying publications given first look.

Cartoonists bring a unique blend of writing and drawing skills to bear on every cartoon they create. They know how to stage a cartoon as graphic theater with setting, characters, and situation instantly communicated. A successful cartoon says it faster than a paragraph of descriptive words with more impact, and most importantly, it makes you laugh.

The magazine cartoon is probably the most popular of the graphic arts. Media surveys invariably place cartoons among readers' first preferences.

Syndication

Many freelance cartoonists develop comic strips or panels for distribution to newspapers by national and international syndicates. Since the number of newspapers using syndicated material are limited, the field is highly competitive. Very few strips or panels are introduced in any given year and then often only when an existing feature is dropped. It is therefore very tempting for cartoonists whose strips or panels are accepted by a syndicate to sign the first contract offered.

Because syndicated cartoonists' earnings are based on the number of newspapers carrying their strips or panels and the circulation level of the papers, the assumption is that syndicates use fairly standard contracts.

Syndicate contracts are complicated and vary considerably among the major firms in the field. As in all other business relationships, it is expected that each party to the contract will seek to attain the most favorable terms through negotiation. Cartoonists owe it to themselves and their creations to prepare as well as they can for this process.

Should cartoonist be offered a contract by a syndicate, it is important to get the best legal representation possible. A lawyer with expertise in cartooning, visual arts, copyright, and/or literary property contracts is recommended. Experience proves that there is no substitute for knowledgeable counsel in contract negotiations.

Editorial cartooning

Editorial cartoonists are usually salaried staff artists on individual daily newspapers. Salaries range greatly with the circulation and status of the paper and the reputation and experience of the cartoonist. In some cases, however (i.e., Herblock, Mauldin, Oliphant, Auth), the work of editorial cartoonists is syndicated nationally, although they continue to remain on staff with their base papers. Usually their papers require that they do two locally oriented cartoons per week and the syndicates want at least three cartoons a week relating to national issues. As with comic strip or panel artists, the earnings that editorial cartoonists get from syndication depend on their contract and, based on that, the number and size of the newspapers using their work regularly. (See Syndication above).

Sometimes freelance cartoonists sell their work to major daily newspapers op-ed pages or to weeklies. Rates differ a good deal, but are generally established based on column width of the work used and whether the drawing is an original or reprint. Rates may be open to negotiation as well. In either case, it is best to check with individual papers regarding their interest in freelance contributions before sending work for consideration.

Books

In addition to collections of the published work of one or more cartoonists, there has been a recent trend toward publishing original cartoon works. Book contracts vary as much as syndication contracts, so it is a good idea to consult a qualified literary agent or lawyer. In fact, book publishers prefer to negotiate terms with a knowledgeable author's representative. Cartoonists should insist on an advance on royalties at contract signing. For a first-time cartoonist-author, the advance usually ranges from a minimum $3000 up to $10,000.

Licensing and merchandising

Another burgeoning aspect of cartooning is licensing and merchandising. When cartoon characters, such as *Snoopy, Kliban's Cats*, or *Superman** are licensed for a range of products from toys and apparel to designer sheets and stationery, the creator stands to earn considerable additional income *if* he or she retains all or a significant percentage of the subsidiary rights in the property.

It is generally assumed that only nationally known syndicate characters are sought by licensing agents or manufacturers. With the fast growth in this area, however, there are now possibilities for cartoonists to develop characters specifically for product use. Cartoonists interested in pursuing this potentially lucrative application of their work should seek counsel with an attorney specializing in this field so that adequate copyright protection is achieved *before* presenting work to licensers or manufacturers.

In May 1980 the first trade show in the character licensing and merchandising field was held in New York City. This show brought together creators, licensers, syndicates, and manufacturers and provided a place to explore business opportunities. Similar shows are already scheduled in the future on the East and West coasts and could become an important meeting ground for cartoonists seeking to expand in this field.

Pricing of magazine cartoons

The pricing of free-standing magazine cartoons is different from that of other forms of illustration because they are purchased as complete editorial elements-similar to freelance feature articles-at fixed rates. Generally, all black-and-white or color cartoons published at a particular unit size are paid for at the same rate. The exception is a handful of magazines (e. g., *The New Yorker*) that additionally compensate those cartoonist-contributors closely identified with their magazine. In these instances, an annual signature fee may be paid for first look at cartoons produced for magazines, as well as bonuses and, in a few cases, fringe benefits.

A number of factors affect prices for magazine cartoons. Among them are: finished art in black-and-white or color; unit size cartoon is published; national vs. regional distribution; circulation, impact, and influence of the magazine; importance of cartoons as a regular editorial element; the extent of rights being purchased; and the national reputation of the cartoonist. Since the list is composed of objective and subjective factors and the mix in each case is different, rates vary considerably among magazines. Consequently, this presentation is limited to a pricing range on captioned or uncaptioned magazine-type cartoons, not humorous illustrations, comic strips, or the other cartoon forms mentioned elsewhere in this section. Requests for additional information on cartooning may be addressed to the Cartoonists Guild *Graphic Artists Guild* 11 West 20th Street New York, New York 10011.

Basic terms of sale

1. Payment should always be made on acceptance of the work, not on publication.

2. First reproduction rights only should be sold, unless otherwise negotiated.

3. Under the new copyright law cartoonists retain copyright ownership of all work they create. Copyright can only be transferred in writing.

4. Cartoonists should never send the same original drawing to more then one U.S. publisher at a time. Multiple photocopy submissions are acceptable to many European and other overseas publishers.

5. Purchasers should make selection(s) promptly-within two to four weeks at the most-and return the unpurchased cartoons immediately to avoid tying them up.

6. All original art should be returned to the artist immediately after reproduction, regardless of rights purchased.

7. No work-for-hire provisions should be included in purchase agreements covering freelance cartoons.

8. Terms of sale should be specified in a contract or on the bill. For example, if work is to be reprinted in a textbook, the following should be included:

"For one-time, non-exclusive, English language, North American print rights only, in one hardcover edition, to be published by _____, entitled "_____." All additional requests for usage by your organization or any other publication, except as specified above, are to be referred to *(name of artist)* to determine the appropriate reprint fee."

Comparative fees for cartoon reprints

Consumer magazines

National, one column	$200 and up
National, two or more columns	250 and up
Other	100 and up

Trade magazines

Major	200 and up
Other	100 and up

Textbooks

North American one-time rights, English language	150 and up
World one-time rights, English language	200 and up
Foreign language rights	50 additional
All future editions or revisions	200 and up (in addition to fees for other rights)

Other trade hardcover and paperback books

One-time rights	100 and up

Cartoon anthologies

	Advance on royalties

Comparative fees for cartoons for national magazines*

Single panel	Black and White	Color
Quarter page or less	$150-350	$300-500
Full page	350-600	500-1200

Multipanel

Single-panel rate plus an additional rate per panel.

*These figures reflect the different rates now being paid for the purchase of first North American serial rights only by various general or special-interest magazines regularly using cartoons. For the reasons stated in the text of this section, listing average figures in each category would be unrealistic and misleading.

This section of the Guidelines is dedicated to

the memory of **Jan Giolito**.

Jan's commitment to the members of the Guild

and her contributions to Textile Design

have enriched our profession.

Textile Design

Textile designers are graphic artists who create illustrations, designs, or patterns to be used on surfaces, usually in repeat. Textile designers work in many areas including apparel, decorative, and home furnishings. Knowledge of the reproduction or printing methods, markets and trends is essential to textile designers.

Most freelance textile designers create individual designs which they sell to manufacturers, often stipulating a specific use or combination of uses. These artists are often commissioned to create a line of textile designs.

Factors for determining an appropriate price for a textile design include: (1) rights transferred; (2) credit on the selvage of the printed piece; (3) complexity of the design; (4) research; and (5) return of the original to the artist. In addition to the comparative fees and trade practices listed below, textile designers should be aware of the following conditions:

Quantity orders The Guild discourages reduced fees for large orders. Each textile design is individual in nature, and industry fee scales are already low.

Royalties The usual advance against royalties is often close to the fees listed in the table. Working without an advance against royalties is strongly discouraged by the Guild. There is no guarantee of income with such an arrangement, and it therefore amounts to speculation.

Commission The standard commission for an agent or representative who sells a textile designer's work is between 33 1/3 and 40 percent.

Trade Practices

The *freelancers perspective:* The following trade practices are relevant to freelance textile designers (see the textile design business and legal forms in the contracts section of this book).

Holding work: Individual judgement is necessary in this area. Previous work experience with a client who wishes to hold work helps establish reliability. The Guild discourages consenting to an extended holding time; shorter holding times help protect against damage, loss, or unauthorized reproduction of work. A maximum of five days is preferred by most artists; some limit holding to one day. As always, a written holding form should be used.

Billing for a sale: An invoice form is written at the time of sale. Payment to a textile designer should be prompt and negotiated at the time of sale. Because the major portion of the work represents labor, all invoices are payable in fifteen days (although thirty days is standard industry practice).

Appropriate speculation: The creation of work initiated by a textile designer for presentation and sale is standard practice in the industry. However, it is also standard practice to obtain a written guarantee of payment for creating *any* new work specifically requested by clients. The Guild opposes creating new work without such a guarantee accompanying the request.

Kill fees: When artwork commissioned by a client is not purchased, the artist should charge a cancellation fee which is based on the amount of labor invested in the work. Ownership of all copyright and artwork is retained by the artist. If a job is cancelled and is based on work belonging to a client (such as a repeat or coloring), a labor fee will be charged and the work will be destroyed.

Client responsibilities: Additional payment is due to an artist when: (1) artwork changes are requested by the client, but were not part of the original agreement; (2) extra expenses arise from the assignment including, but not limited to, photostats, mailings, shipping charges, and shipping insurance; (3) ordered corners are not developed into purchased sketches (a cancellation fee will be charged and ownership of all copyright and artwork is retained by the designer); and (4) sales taxes must be included on all artwork except when original work is returned to the designer or a resale certificate, signed by an officer of the company, is provided to the designer.

Royalties: Payments based on a percentage of the income earned by a design are becoming more common between clients and textile designers, but must be negotiated to include advance payment at the time of sale. Percentage rates range from 2 to 10 percent and depend largely on wholesale costs, sales volume of fabric house, and how much involvement the textile designer has in the project.

Limitations: The Guild strongly recommends limiting, in writing, the rights sold to the client's specific needs; the textile

Be sure to read any agreement carefully and try to restrict selling rights to specific markets. This can be done by crossing out inappropriate sections (see related material in the section on Business and Legal Practices). A word of caution, be sure to check any agreement for the words "work-for-hire," under this contract, you may be signing away "authorship" and all rights forever. See Professional Issues for more information on work for hire.

Artist/agent contracts: The Guild has developed a standard form for textile designer/agent contracts (pages 164 to 168). An agreement, even verbal, is legally binding, but it is an advantage to both parties to have the agreement in writing. Textile designers should have receipts for all work left with an agent.

Return of artwork: The Guild encourages textile designers to request the return of artwork. Textile designers are making these requests to obtain additional exposure (such as by display of designs as artwork).

Credit to artist: This is another practice that is becoming more prevalent in the industry. In particular, some designers receive credit on the selvage after they are known in the marketplace by designing a line or collection.

Artist agent responsibilities: In the textile design industry, the cost of shipping is usually billed to the client. In cases where the client is not billed, the agent pays-not the designer.

The Guild strongly recommends that a designer work for an agent strictly on a commission basis agreed upon by both parties in writing.

Knock-offs: A textile designer cannot ethically copy or "knock-off" a design by another artist. Although it is common practice, artists should be aware that it is illegal to infringe on anyone else's designs, and that infringement can lead to legal liability.

(Refer to page 125 for information on staff artists.)

Comparative fees for textile design
Prices shown are low/average/high

Apparel
Men, Women, Children

Corner	100-175-300
Design or Sketch	275-325-550
Repeat	200-300-800
Design in Repeat	475-600-1000
Coloring	60-100-200

Scarves (¹⁄₄ scarf)

Corner	175-300-600
Design or Sketch	300-500-900
Coloring	35-65-150

Hand-painted scarves

Corner	175-350-600
Design or Sketch	175-400
Lingerie (per garment hand-painted)	200-300
TV Costume (per garment hand-painted)	1000 or commission

Home Decorative
Wallpaper, Drapery, Upholstery, Bedspreads

Corner	125-300-500
Design or Sketch	375-600-1000
Repeat	375-500-850
Design in Repeat	750-950-1200
Coloring	100-150-250

Domestics**
Sheets

Corner	250-375-600
Design or Sketch	375-550-850
Repeat	450-650-1000
Design in repeat	750-900-1200
Coloring	100-150-250

Pillow case

Corner	150-250-350
Design or Sketch	300-500-600
Repeat	300-500-750
Design in repeat	650-900
Coloring	100-150-250

Hand towel

Design or Sketch	150-300
Coloring	100-150-250

Bath towel

Design or Sketch	300-700
Coloring	100-150-250

Face cloth

Design or Sketch	200-500
Coloring	100-150-250

Specialty/domestics
Tablecloth (¹/₄ tablecloth)

Corner	425-800
Design or Sketch	350-650
Repeat	650-1200 (tracing repeat)
Coloring	100-150-250

Tea towel

Design or Sketch	350-750
Coloring	100-150-250

Place mat

Design or Sketch	300-600
Coloring	100-150-250

Shower curtain

Design or Sketch	450-1200
Coloring	100-150-250

Rug design

Design or Sketch	300-600-900 or advance against royalty
Design in repeat	400-750-1200
Coloring	100-150-250

Specialty/home decorative
Kitchen accessories

Design or Sketch	150-400
Coloring	65-100-150

China/giftware/barware

Design or Sketch	200-300-700 or 200 with 3-5% royalty

Giftwrap/greeting cards

Design or Sketch	240-750-800
Repeat	250-500

Comparative fees for textile design (continued)

Woven design

Sample weaving	$35-60 per piece, 20-35 per hour
Analyses (pick-out)	30-45 per hour
Jacquard sketch	$600-1000
Coloring	$45-55 per piece
Several colors for one design	$750-1500
Prints developed for Jacquard	$500-750 per design
Developing a 'colorline' for solids	$1000
Developing a group of wovens ('styling a line')	$2000-10,000 per line
Consultation fee	$30-75 per hour

Special

Commissioned work and special orders	$20-30 per hour
Rug design consultation fee	$35-100 per hour
Consultation fees (plus expenses)	$35-100 per hour
Royalty arrangements	2-5-10% of wholesale price

Styling (freelance)	*Hourly and Per Diem*	*Per Week*
Apparel	$50-200 per hour, 200-1000 per day	$600-2500
Home decorative	$50-200 per hour, 200-1000 per day	$600-2500

Mill work *(excluding expenses)*		
Apparel	150-300 per day	750-1200
Home decorative	150-300 per day	750-1200

Notes:
These are average ranges. The higher fee can be much higher depending on the complexity of design and reputation of the designer.
Labor charges only apply to tracing layouts and corners, in which case all artwork remains property of the designer and no reproduction rights are transferred.
Art for home furnishings will be higher due to size and complexity of work.
Certain garment and home furnishings products are "engineered" to fit. In those cases, the prices for a design in repeat are applicable.

*Prices are based on items that are part of a total domestic package. If they are sold individually, prices increase accordingly.

Needleart design

Needleart designers are graphic artists who create designs and/or objects in a wide range of needleart media such as knitting, crochet, needlepoint, embroidery, lace, sewing, patchwork, applique, quilting, soft sculpture, macrame, weaving, basketry, braiding, latch hook and punch needle. Needleart designers work in many commercial markets, including publishing, advertising, apparel, decorative and home furnishings, toys, and novelties.

Most needleart designers are commissioned to create one-of-a-kind items for editorial, educational, promotional, or advertising use or as prototypes for multiple reproduction. Many also design items for resale in stores and/or galleries. Designers also work as industry consultants to develop and/or expand new or existing educational programs, product lines, needleart techniques and skills.

Rights sold

The terms of sale for a design vary with the needs of the client and designer. They can range from a one-time use to a buyout of all reproduction rights. Fees for reproduction rights do not include purchase of the original artwork *unless specified on writing*. This manner of selling rights applies whether the original design is reproduced photographically, as in editorial or reproduced by a manufacturer, as in product design.

For editorial purposes, one-time use generally refers to first North American reproduction rights. Additional rights to be sold may refer to publication in other geographic areas, markets, and mediums; reuse rights or the right for use of promotional purposes. If rights for pulblishing are not used within one year of delivery, they revert back to the artist. And, any rights not specified in a written contract remain the property of the artist. In the case of prototypes for manufacturing, rights should be enumerated and a royalty agreement should be negotiated at the beginning of the project. This applies to books, kits, leaflets, toys and home furnishings.

Many factors are used in determining an appropriate price for the sale of a needleart design or concept. They include: (1) complexity of design or concept; (2) complexity and/or multiplicity of techniques used; (3) uniqueness of design or concept and/or techniques used; (4) research and development time; (5) designer reputation, range skill, and ability; (6) rights transferred; and (7) return of original art to designer.

In addition, the fee should reflect reimbursement for out of pocket expenses including materials and supplies, messengers, toll telephone calls, transportation and travel, shipping and insurance. It is customary to increase the fee for rush delivery deadlines. The designer should be compensated for sketches and swatches done to the specifications of a client that do not result in a commission, and designs rejected by a client remain the property of the designer. Changes requested by a client once a project has been undertaken should be compensated for at the designer's hourly rate. Complexity of instructions (e.g., grading of patterns, conversions to knitting machines, etc.) will also affect pricing. If the designer is called in for consultations on a project beyond the initial project conference, a fee for consultation should be charged (please refer to pricing chart for fees).

Contracts

Since the transfer of rights is based on contractual agreement, it is imperative that the terms be clear to both client and designer. The written contract may be a document. In either case, the written document is legally binding. It is recommended that designers decide which form is most appropriate for the situation. They should not, however, begin a project before a contract or letter of agreement has been negotiated and signed.

Any contract should specify the conditions of sale in addition to enumerating rights that are transferred upon receipt of full payment. When a design is sold for publication, the contract should include the form of credit to be given. Name credit on the page where the design appears is expected. For limited reproduction rights, credit is in the form of a copyright notice in the designer's name and should appear adjacent to the work.

Specifications regarding the return of the original artwork are included when reproduction rights are being sold. Artwork should be returned in an undamaged condition within an agreed upon period from the date of delivery or the date of publication. The client should be billed for full market value if the work is lost, damaged or not returned.

The delivery date of any assignment is predicated on the receipt of all materials to be supplied by the client, by an agreed upon date.

Payment and delivery schedules are included in the contractual agreement. *Payment in full within thirty days of delivery* is standard, not upon publication (which may be delayed). If the major portion of the project represents labor and payment is preferred within fifteen days, it should be negotiated at the beginning of the assignment and included in the contract. A percentage increase (1 1/2 to 2 percent) on the fee for payment received after thirty days can be put in the contract and specified on the invoice at the time of delivery.

Other conditions that may be included in the contract are: conditional clauses to account for non-publication of the project and changes requested after delivery, etc.

Comparative fees

The comparative fees in the accompanying tables are arranged according to the category of the purchased. *Consumer product/magazine editorial* refers to work that will be photographed and reproduced in conjunction with specific editorial content of a magazine. *Advertising art* refers to any agency producing commercial advertising for printed publications, television media, etc.. The fees listed are for work specifically commissioned for an advertising program. Designers may offer existing work to an agency for a rental fee of 10 to 15 percent of the market value of that work. Clients are responsible for returning the work in its original condition. If damaged or lost, the client is liable for the full market value of the artwork. *Prototyped for manufacturers* refers to any market entity that produces any product entity in multiples (e.g., kits, books, leaflets, toys, novelties, clothing, home furnishings) or work related to packaged consumer goods.

As used in the tables, *average* refers to a design of normal intricacy in any one of the needleart media. *Complex* refers to a design of greater intricacy or scale. Extremely simple designs requiring less than average development and execution and extremely complex designs should be priced accordingly.

For information on the Needleart Designer's Confirmation Form please refer to the contracts section of this book.

The pricing ranges listed below do not constitute specific prices for particular jobs. They are guidelines that should be considered along with other factors specific to the commissioned work under consideration. Please refer to related material in other sections of this book.

Comparative fees for needleart design creating a textile structure or completely covering a textile surface

Garments	Consumer Products/ Magazine Editorial	Advertising Art	Prototype for Manufacturer
Half-body, average	$300-600	$600-1200	$400-600
Half-body, complex	600-1250	1200-3000	500-1000
Whole-body, average	600-800	1000-1500	500-800
Whole-body, complex	800-1500	1500-3000	800-1000
Accessories, average	150-350	400-600	350-500
Accessories, complex	350-1000	600-1000	500-1000
Soft sculpture			
Three dimensional	300-800	500-2000	
Props	300-800	500-2000	
Puppets	300-1000	500-2000	

Comparative fees for needleart design creating a textile structure or completely covering a textile surface (continued)

Environmental furnishing	Consumer Products/ Magazine Editorial	Advertising Art
Accessories, average	$150-250	$300-500
Accessories, complex	300-400	500-1000
Tableware, average	200-800	500-1000
Tableware, complex	800-2000	1000-2500
Window/wall treatment, average	200-800	500-1000
Window/wall treatment, complex	800-2000	1000-2500
Blankets or afghans, average	450-650	800-1500
Blankets or afghans, complex	650-1500	1500-300
Quilts, average	500-1000	1000-3500
Quilts, complex	1000-3500	1500-3000
Bedspreads, average	300-500	600-1000
Bedspreads, complex	500-2000	1000-3000
Banners, average	300-500	500-1000
Banners, complex	500-2000	1000-3000
Floor coverings, average	400-800	500-1000
Floor coverings, complex	800-2500	1000-3000

Logos and insignias

	Consumer Products/ Magazine Editorial	Advertising Art
Literal translation	300-500	1000-2000
Creative interpretation	500-1000	1500-3000

Toys and novelties

	Consumer Products/ Magazine Editorial	Advertising Art
Average	300-500	500-800
Complex	500-1500	800-2000

Comparative miscellaneous needleart fees	Per Hour	Per Day
Consulting	$25-50	$150-300
Instruction writing	25-40	125-300
Technical drawing	25-50	
Pattern drafting	30-55	

DESIGN
PRICES
AND TRADE CUSTOMS

General graphic design

Graphic designers are graphic artists who create communication tools incorporating the spectrum of graphic elements such as typography, illustration, photography, production and printing, to achieve the appropriate visual impact and message.

Graphic designers generally work within a studio that they may own and through which they may employ other graphic designers, illustrators, mechanical artists or photographers on a salaried or freelance basis. Almost all graphic designers buy *and* sell art.

Many graphic designers handle a range of projects and refer to themselves as general graphic designers. Specialized areas of design are described on the following pages. Trade customs and practices for these areas have been noted. Otherwise, the standards noted under general design apply.

As professional consultants, graphic designers can determine the feasibility of a project by incorporating their knowledge of the technical resources available. Often clients choose to develop projects and *then* bring in a designer. This can be inefficient since many decisions may be made that a designer should have been consulted on. The result can be unnecessary delays, additional costs and inadequate design solutions. The sooner designers are called in to consult on a project, the easier it is for them to help steer the project to the best graphic solution.

A client may choose to select a graphic designer with whom a long-term relationship can be established. This arrangement is appropriate when there is a string of projects which need a continuity of design. With such an ongoing relationship, a designer can be consulted during the early stages of a project for help in planning the visual thrust as well as the time and cost schedules.

Generally, estimates of the cost of each anticipated expense are made before starting work on a major project, and clients are presented with a proposal that reflects many of the following factors: (1) printing requirements (supervision, handling of printing); (2) reasearch; (3) complexity of style required by the project; (4) art and/or copy that will be developed by the designer; (5) typography, production, retouching that will be commissioned by the designer and; (6) intended use of the printed piece. (For more information, please refer to the Contracts section of this book.)

It is customary for project descriptions and cost proposals to be submitted to clients free of charge; however, any fees and expenses incurred on a client's behalf and with the client's consent are billable.

After the proposal is accepted by a client, the project direction is decided upon. The designer then develops the direction and makes decisions on size, length, color, visuals (e.g., illustration or photography), paper, printing methods and the specific "look" of the piece or package. At this stage, a presentation of a tight or loose comprehensive (comp) is shown to the client; the comp indicates what can be expected of the finished piece. Alterations or additions are made at this point since it is relatively easy and inexpensive to change a comp. It is only after the approval of the comprehensives that the designer proceeds to incur major expenses. It is important to note that changes that come after this stage can be expensive to the client and make the completion of the project difficult.

In many situations, graphic designers are entitled to credit and copyright, depending on the contractual arrangement. When other creative professionals are involved in a project through a designer, they may also deserve the same acknowledgement and rights on the piece or package of pieces.

Since graphic designers work with so vast an array of graphic resources, it is important that all conditions and expectations be spelled out before the work begins. The following points should be considered:

Payment: For larger projects, the standard system of payment is one-third upon approval of design comprehensives, and one-third within thirty days of delivery of mechanicals or printed pieces.

Markups: The standard markup to cover handling of billable expenses is from 15 to 25 percent of each expense.

Consultation fees: When a graphic designer is called in by a client to give advice on a project or design decision, a consultation fee is charged according an hourly rate. Such a fee is usually from $40 to $100 per hour.

(See the Graphic Designer's Estimate Confirmation/Invoice Form.)

The price ranges listed in this section do not constitute specific prices for particular jobs. They are guidelines that should be considered along with other factors specific to the commissioned work under consideration.

Corporate graphic design

Corporate graphic designers specialize in design for annual reports, corporate communications and identity programs, signage, newsletters and annual reports.

These designers often work in a studio that may include a principal of the studio, a production manager, a copywriter, and possibly an account executive. The nature of projects that corporate design studios are commissioned to handle often involve long term research and development. Many corporate design studios work on a retainer basis, acting as design consultants in peripheral areas besides their main projects. Consequently, corporate designers often are brought in at the early stages of a project and may be integrally involved in directing the project through fruition.

Of particular concern to corporate design studios is the somewhat complicated issue of copyright. Quite often, studios contract with freelance illustrators, designers and photographers on a limited-use basis for specific projects. In some instances, individual artists own copyright on the work they create, not the client. It is not uncommon, therefore, for copyrights to be held by different individuals within a project. Rather than having each contracted artist negotiate with the client, the studio often negotiates on their behalf within the scope of the art budget that the client has agreed to.

Since many clients commissioning corporate design groups don't buy art on a regular basis, it is often the responsibility of the studio to educate them on the intent, content and ethics of the copyright law. Studios frequently prepare documents explaining subcontractor relationships, billing procedures and contract terms.

In addition to copyright concerns, the studio's terms and conditions are clearly outlined in writing and generally are reviewed prior to the first commission. These standard customs are contained in the contract, letter of agreement or confirmation of engagement form (see Standard Contracts section).

Project Proposals

Most corporate design studios work in "phases."

Phase 1, programming: consists of all necessary research to determine a time schedule and clearly-defined program. A great deal of time is spent in this phase with the client defining the needs and problems that are to be solved. A rough budget is often prepared, showing a range of fees plus flexible expenses. A portion (normally 1/3) of the total budget is paid before the project begins.

Phase 2, schematic design: After a meeting between designer and client in phase 1, visual solutions are pursued that solve stated problems. Much of phase 2 is idea development, which results in a presentation showing *only* those ideas that the design team feels are viable, appropriate and meet the proscribed criteria.

Phase 3, design development: At this stage, the design team refines the accepted design. A final presentation is offered explaining the applications, tighter budget and time schedules. This phase is optional if the conditions are agreed upon prior to phase 3.

Phase 4, design production: Decisions are final at this point. Illustrations, photography, typography, copy and mechanicals and all other pre-print production elements are locked into place. Any changes made by the client after this point become billable as "client alterations."

Phase 5, production: Depending on the end product(s) a studio has been commissioned to produce, this phase may be a matter of going on press and/or supervising the manufacturing of products. Supervision is the key to this phase since all depends on the precision and quality achieved in this final phase. After the end product is approved, the project is considered billable. The studio normally retains control of design alterations, corrections and printing.

Billing

Billing expenses and fees may be handled in a number of ways. The studio arranges to bill on an hourly or project basis during the first phase. Expenses are always billed with handling charges or markups included. Sales tax and freight are never included in estimates and are normally billed at the end of the project along with client alterations, which are billed at a predetermined studio or principal's hourly rate.

The printing or manufacturing part of the project may be billed by the studio or directly to the client. This depends on the practice of the studio principals.

Regardless of who the invoice is sent to, the printer and all other professionals working with the design studio regard them-cally bound to the studio's direction while working on the project. This, of course, becomes a practical matter since designers are orchestrating many elements and must control them all to insure consistency.

The pricing ranges listed below do not constitute specific prices for particular jobs. They are guidelines that should be considered along with other factors specific to the commissioned work under consideration. Please refer to related material in other sections of this book.

Comparative fees for letterhead design*

	One or Two Colors
Corporate extensive use	$1500-2500
Corporate limited use	1250-1750
Nonprofit organization	1250-1750
Personal	750-1500

*Based on presentation of three versions of letterhead, card and envelope using an existing logo or simple typography; production charges are *not* included.

Comparative fees for newsletter design*

	Simple		Complex	
	4 pages	12 pages	4 pages	12 pages
Corporate, extensive use	$1500-3000	$2000-3500	$2000-3500	$3000-4000
Corporate, limited use	1250-2000	1500-3000	1500-2500	2000-3500
Consumer, extensive use	1500-3000	2000-3500	2000-3500	3000-4000
Consumer, limited use	1250-2000	1500-3000	1500-2500	1500-3000
Nonprofit organization/Institution	1000-1500	1500-2000	1250-1750	1500-2500

*Based on original concept and design including rought tissue layouts, three comprehensive layouts indicating masthead page, single page and spread format, and client consultation; production charges are *not* included.

Production charges*

Principal's hourly rate	$50-100
Studio staff hourly rate	25-50

Overtime rate is twice the above.

*Based on an hourly fee billable for unanticipated client consultations; selection, handling and supervision.

Comparative page rates for corporate annual reports*

	Text		Financial	
Corporate extensive use	*Two Color*	*Full Color*	*Two Color*	*Full Color*
Simple design	$275-500	$375-750	$225-400	$325-600
Complex design	325-750	450-900	325-600	375-750
Corporate limited use				
Simple design	$225-400	$275-650	$175-350	$275-450
Complex design	275-500	325-750	275-500	325-650
Nonprofit organization/Institution				
Simple design	$200-350	$250-500	$200-350	$250-400
Complex design	250-500	300-600	250-400	275-500

*Based on a 24-page annual report, broken down to 4 pages of financial and 20 pages of text; including client consultation, concept and design, research and presentation, rough tissue layouts and finished comprehensive dummy; production charges are *not* included.

Comparative fees for logo design*

	Research and Presentation	Development of Logo: Stationery Application	Development of Corporate Identity†
Corporate extensive use	$5000-10,000	$2500-5000	$5000-15,000 +
Corporate limited use	2500-500	1500-3500	2500-5000
Nonprofit organization/Institution	1000-2500	1000-2000	1500-3500

*Based on the presentation of three comprehensive layouts, rough tissue layouts, research, concept and design plus client consultation throughout the project; production charges are *not* included.

*Prices for standard programs are significantly higher for Fortune 500 companies.

†Corporate identity includes standardization of identity and manual.

Collateral advertising design

Graphic designers who specialize in collateral material handle the design of catalogs, packaging, brochures, press kits and direct mail packages.

While advertising agencies generally handle main campaigns for products and/or services, often clients will commission or retain a design studio to handle their collateral material. Studio designers understand the print capabilities since they specialize in that area and in general, are required to work on tighter deadlines with less design latitude and with more controls than other design areas.

Since collateral advertising is targeted to elicit a specific response, graphic designers must have a sophisticated awareness of advertising, marketing, and sales.

Clients or advertising agencies are apt to supply designers with existing art or photography, so it is important to know the rights that are transferred. If additional rights must be purchased, they should be negotiated *before* the design or production stage. It is normal for an agency to purchase rights for many uses of art or photography to avoid renegotiating each use.

It is also standard for designers to sell uses to the client, for first time print runs or extended uses if that is appropriate.

Comparative fees for promotional and self-mailer brochure design*

	Two Color		Four Color	
Major company	*8¹/₂x11*	*11x17*	*8¹/₂x11*	*11x17*
One to two folds	$500-1000	$750-1250	$750-1250	$1000-1500
	18x24	*20x28*	*18x24*	*20x28*
Multiple folds†	1000-2500	1500-3000	1500-3000	2000-5000
Smaller company	*8¹/₂x11*	*11x17*	*8¹/₂x11*	*11x17*
One to two folds	$350-750	$450-1000	$500-1000	$650-1250
	18x24	*20x28*	*18x24*	*20x28*
Multiple folds	$750-1500	$1000-2000	$1000-2000	$1500-3000

*Based on concept and design, rough tissue layouts, shooting format and final comprehensive layout; production charges *not* included.

†Prices for brochures with complex folds and/or die cuts should be estimated higher to account for complexity and usage, as well as size.

*Note: In the industry, publishing is considered separate from corporate; however unless the publishing company is a Fortune 500 firm, prices are the same as those for smaller companies.

Comparative fees for direct mail package design*

	Simple		Complex	
	Two Color	Full Color	Two Color	Full Color
Major company	$2000-3500	$3000-4500	$2500-4500	$3500-5500
Smaller company	1750-3000	2250-3500	2000-3500	2500-4000
Nonprofit organization/Institution	$1000-1750	1250-2000	1250-2000	1500-2500

*Based on design of a basic package including envelope, letter and brochure, reply card and return envelope; client consultation; rough tissue layouts showing format; comprehensive layout; production charges *not* included.

Production charges*

Principal's hourly rate	$50-100
Studio staff hourly rate	25-50

Overtime rate is twice the above.

*Based on an hourly fee billable for unanticipated client consultations; selection, handling and supervision of photography, illustration or printing; corrections.

Comparative fees for press kit design*

	Simple		Complex	
	Two Color	Full Color	Two Color	Full Color
Major company	$2500-3500	$3500-4500	$3000-4500	$4000-5500
Smaller company	2000-3000	2500-4000	2500-4000	3000-4500
Nonprofit organization/Institution	$1500-2500	2000-3000	2000-3000	2500-4000

*Based on design of a basic kit including press kit cover or folder, insert sheets showing, for example, advertising ideas, promotional and display material and additional data; client consultation plus concept and design, rough tissue layouts and a comprehensive layout; production charges *not* included.

Comparative page rates for product and service catalog design*

Major company	8-16 Page Rate	24 Page Rate	48 Page Rate
Color	$250-350	$200-325	$200-325
Black and white			
Color	200-300	200-275	200-250
Smaller company			
Color	$200-300	$175-300	$175-300
Black and white	200-250	175-250	150-225
Nonprofit organization/Institution			
Color	$125-200	$125-200	$125-175
Black and white	100-175	100-175	100-150

*Based on concept and design, rough tissue layouts showing format of spread, single page and cover design and final comprehensive layout. Price should be adjusted depending on the number of products required to be shown; production charges *not* included.

Advertising and promotion design

Graphic designers who specialize in advertising and promotion design handle the design and placement of magazine and newspaper advertising, poster, billboards, press kits, letterhead, and promotion campaigns. More and more studios are taking on advertising for clients who don't make advertising their main thrust for generating sales. In many areas studios must have agency status in order to place ads with magazines and newspapers.

Advertising designers must have a sophisticated knowledge of marketing, sales and advertising print production. Since they hire other graphic artists on a freelance basis and purchase art and photography on behalf of their clients, they must have a good working knowledge of advertising illustration and photography, including trade customs that govern both.

Expenses are often high for illustration and photography because of additional overhead factors (studio time, equipment and staff) and unusual time demands.

The investment clients make in advertising is often sizeable. Because of the value of advertising relative to the sales it produces, the risks must be calculated. This puts limits on the creative input that designers might have, sometimes to the *detriment* of the client. The designer's role is to work as part of a team comprised of a copywriter, possibly an account executive and/or client representative, such as a public relations person. The proposal given to the client should present a strategy as well as a design solution.

The price ranges listed below do not constitute specific prices for particular jobs. They are guidelines that should be considered along with other factors specific to the commissioned work under consideration. Please refer to related material in other sections of this book.

Comparative fees for magazine advertising design*

	Full	*Half*	*Less than Half Page*	*Spread*	*Cover*
National consumer	$2200-5500	$1650-3300	$1100-1650	$3850-6600	$2750-6050
Regional consumer	1650-2750	1100-1925	825-1375	2750-3850	2200-3300
Trade publication	1100-2200	825-1650	650-1100	1650-3300	1925-2750
Specialized audience	825-1925	660-1375	550-825	1650-2750	1925-2200
In-house magazine	700-1375	550-1100	450-750	1375-2200	1100-1925

*Based on concept and design of a maximum of three rough tissue layouts plus final comprehensive layout using the elements of photography or illustration, headline, subhead, body copy and company logo or sign off; production and art charges *not* included.

Comparative fees for newspaper advertising design*

	Full Page	Half Page	Less Than Half Page
National advertising campaign	$1500-3000	$1000-2000	$750-1500
Regional advertising campaign	1000-2500	750-1750	500-1250
Weekly newspaper	750-1500	500-1000	500-850

*Based on concept and design of a maximum of three rough tissue layouts; one final comprehensive layout using the elements of photography or illustration, headline, subhead, body copy and company logo or sign off; production and art charges *not* included.

Comparative fees for advertising and promotional campaign design*

	Simple	Complex
Corporate, extensive use	$2000-4000	$3000-5000
Corporate, limited use	1500-3000	2500-4000

*Based on concept and design including rough tissue layouts, comprehensive layout through to finished presentation; production charges *not* included.

Comparative fees for shopping bag designs*

	Simple		Complex	
	Two Color	Full Color	Two Color	Full Color
Corporate, extensive use	$735-1430	$825-2000	$935-1650	$1100-2200
Corporate, limited use	550-825	735-1100	825-1375	935-1650
Motion picture, extensive use	735-1650	825-2200	1375-1825	1650-2750
Motion picture, limited use	550-1100	735-1825	1100-1650	1325-2200
Theater	735-935	825-1100	1100-1650	1375-2200
Nonprofit organization/Institution	440-825	550-935	825-1210	935-1375

*Based on concept and design including rough tissue layouts and comprehensive layouts; production charges are *not* included.

Comparative fees for television advertising design*

National advertising campaign	$5500-11,000
Regional advertising campaign	3300-8250
Local area advertising campaign	2200-5500

*Based on client consultation; concept and design including storyboards.

Comparative fees for billboard design*

Major company	$1250-2500
Smaller company	1000-2000
Nonprofit organization/ Institution	750-1500

*Based on concept and design including rough tissue layouts and comprehensive layouts; client consultation; production charges are *not* included.

Comparative fees for public transportation advertising design*

Major company	$750-1500
Smaller company	500-1250
Nonprofit organization/ Institution	500-1000

*Based on concept and design including rough tissue layouts and comprehensive layouts; client consultation; production charges are *not* included.

Comparative fees for record album design*

	Front Only	Front and Back
Major label	$2750-3850	$3300-5500
Other	1650-2750	2200-3300

*Based on concept and design including rough tissue layouts, one finished comprehensive layout, supervision of photography or illustration; production charges *not* included.

Production, consultation, and supervision charges*

Principal's hourly rate	$50-100
Studio staff hourly rate†	25-50

*Based on an hourly fee billable for unanticipated client consultations; selection, handling and supervision of photography, illustration or printing; corrections.

†Overtime rate is twice the above.

Comparative fees for package design*

	Depending on number of concepts and complexity of design
National usage	$4500-8500
Local usage	2500-4500

*Fees are exclusive of all outside costs such as photography, illustration, typography, etc.

Display and novelty design

General graphic designers, needleartists, and illustrators often handle display and novelty design, although there are some artists who specialize in this field. Display and novelty design includes such items as posters, greeting cards, gift or boutique-type items, holiday decorations, eyeglass covers and the like.

Since manufacturing materials, resources and requirements for production of these items often limit the type of display and design, research into those factors can be an important part of an assignment of this type. The resourcefulness of artists in combining these limits with creative design is often the key to a successfully marketed display or novelty item.

The pricing ranges listed below do not constitute specific prices for particular jobs. They are guidelines that should be considered along with other factors specific to the commissioned work under consideration. Please refer to related material in other sections of this book.

Comparative fees for point-of-purchase display material design*

	Simple		Complex	
Counter cards	*Two Color*	*Full Color*	*Two Color*	*Full Color*
Consumer, extensive use	$550-1925	$825-2200	$825-2200	$1100-2750
Consumer, limited use	450-1375	550-1650	550-1650	825-2200
Posters				
Consumer, extensive use	825-1650	1100-2200	1100-2750	1650-3300
Consumer, limited use	660-1375	825-1650	935-1925	1375-2200
Banners				
Consumer, extensive use	725-1375	825-1650	825-1650	1100-2000
Consumer, limited use	550-1100	725-1375	550-1300	825-1650
Motion picture, extensive use	550-1375	825-1650	825-1650	1100-2000
Motion picture, limited use	500-1150	660-1375	660-1375	825-1650
Shopping bags				
Consumer, extensive use	550-1375	825-1650	825-1485	1100-2750
Consumer, limited use	440-1100	550-1375	660-1300	825-1650

*Based on design and concept including rough tissue layouts and a final comprehensive layout; production charges *not* included.

Comparative fees for design of exhibit display material*

	Simple		Complex	
Posters	Two Color	Full Color	Two Color	Full Color
Corporate, extensive use	$1375-2200	$1650-2750	$1375-2750	$1650-3300
Corporate, limited use	825-1650	1100-2200	1100-2200	1375-2750
Motion picture, extensive use	1375-2750	1650-3300	1375-3300	1650-3750
Motion picture, limited use	1375-2200	1650-2750	1100-2750	1650-3300
Theater	825-1650	1100-2200	1100-2200	1650-2750
Nonprofit organization/Institution	550-1100	825-1100	825-1650	1100-2200
Banners				
Corporate, extensive use	550-1375	825-1650	825-1650	1100-1980
Corporate, limited use	495-825	550-825	550-935	825-1100
Theater	495-1100	660-1375	825-1375	1100-1650
Nonprofit organization/Institution	495-1100	660-1375	925-1650	1100-2200
Billboards				
Corporate, extensive use	825-2200	1100-2750	1100-2750	1650-3300
Corporate, limited use	550-1430	825-1650	825-1650	1100-1980
Motion picture, extensive use	825-2200	1100-2750	1100-2750	1650-3300
Motion picture, limited use	550-1650	825-2200	825-2200	1100-2750
Theater	550-1650	825-2200	825-2200	1100-2750
Nonprofit organization/Institution	550-1375	1100-1650	825-1650	1100-2200

*Based on design and concept including rough tissue layouts and a final comprehensive layout; production charges *not* included.

Publication design

Publication designers create the formats and "look" of magazines or tabloids. These publications have an editiorial point of view and often contain advertising.

While most publication design is done on staff with in a parent company, there are freelance publication designers. For staff design information, please refer to the Salaried Artists chapter in this section.

A publication designer may, on a freelance basis, design the format for a magazine or tabloid, and be retained as a consultant for periodic oversight of the publication. In this case, the role filled by the publications designer is called art director. And, this art director may work with one or more associate art directors, assistant art directors, and/or designers and mechanical artists.

At the planning stages for each issue of the publication, the key editorial staff (most often the editor-in-chief, section editors and key writers for the issue) meet with the art director and appropriate staff to hold a story and cover conference. During this session, the strategy for several issues is mapped out, with a major focus on the current issue. A direction is established and concepts may be determined at this time. From this point on, the art director commissions art for the issues within the yearly budget constraints. However, editors of a publication have approval over dummies and story boards, since they are accepted as the authority for the publication. In all instances the publisher has final approval over the package.

Freelance artists who are commissioned to work on publications are often expected to sell on an all rights or work-for-hire basis. These types of contracts limit the pool of talent available to publications, since work for hire and all rights are not acceptable terms for many artists.

There are independent studios that produce magazines and/or tabloids on a periodic basis, but they are not the norm in this field.

Frequently, freelance or independent designers are commissioned to redesign an existing magazine and continue on as consultants, either on retainer or fee based on an estimated number of hours per issue.

The price ranges listed below do not constitute specific prices for particular jobs. They are guidelines that should be considered along with other factors specific to the commissioned work under consideration. Please refer to related material in other sections of this book.

Comparative fees for editorial magazine design*

Existing format	Masthead and Cover	Spread	Single Page
Extensive circulation, black and white	$ 825-1650	$375-550	$275-450
Extensive circulation, color	1650-2200	725-950	375-550
Limited circulation, black and white	650-1325	325-500	225-375
Limited circulation, color	1325-1650	550-825	325-500
Trade publication, black and white	650-1325	325-500	225-375
Trade publication, color	1325-1650	550-850	325-500
Special interest, black and white	550-1100	275-450	225-375
Special interest, color	825-1650	450-600	275-450
Corporate in-house, black and white	550-1100	275-450	225-375

Comparative fees for editorial magazine design (continued)*

Corporate in-house, color	825-1350	450-600	275-450
Nonprofit organization/Institution, black and white	500-1100	275-450	225-375
Nonprofit organization/Institution color	825-1650	450-600	275-450

New format	Masthead and Cover	Spread	Single Page
Extensive circulation, black and white	$1100-2200	$550-825	$375-550
Extensive circulation, color	1975-2750	825-1100	550-825
Limited circulation, black and white	825-1650	450-725	325-500
Limited circulation, color	1500-2200	650-950	450-700
Trade publication, black and white	825-1650	450-700	325-500
Trade publication, color	1550-2200	650-950	450-700
Special interest, black and white	675-1325	375-675	275-450
Special interest, color	1100-1925	550-825	375-675
Corporate in-house, black and white	675-1325	375-675	275-450
Corporate in-house, color	1100-1650	550-825	375-675
Nonprofit organization/Institution, black and white	675-1325	375-675	275-450
Nonprofit organization/Institution, color	1100-1825	550-825	375-675

*Based on concept and design including rough tissue layouts and comprehensive layouts; client consultation; production charges are *not* included.

Production, consultation, and supervision charges*

Principal's hourly rate	$50-100
Studio staff hourly rate	25-50

Overtime rate is twice the above.

*Based on an hourly fee billable for unanticipated client consultations; selection, handling and supervision of photography, illustration or printing; corrections.

Book jacket design

Book jacket designers are graphic artists who create the look of the jacket or cover of a book, or series of books using the graphic elements of typogaphy, illustration, photography, and/or designed letterforms.

After terms and fees are agreed upon by the publishing house's art director and the designer, one comprehensive is prepared for presentation. If additional comprehensives are required, it is customary for an additional fee to be paid. Once the comprehensive is approved, the designer proceeds to execute or commission illustration, lettering, or other graphic elements used in the finished art.

Generally, the comprehensive is as close as possible in appearance to the finished piece. Such tight comprehensives often entail expenses for typesetting, photostats, or color keys to achieve a finished look. All out-of-pocket expenses in the sketch and finished stages are billable to the client.

Because of the nature of publishing, there is a high rate of rejection on comprehensive presentations. This is accepted as a risk by designer and publisher. It should be noted, however, that the rejection fee is always considered separate from the expenses; the rejection fee reflects the amount of work completed at the time of termination of the project and any expenses are additional.

Copyright and credit for the designer should be agreed upon before work begins. If other creative elements (e. g., illustration or lettering) appear on the cover, they should be credited as well. If the publisher is preparing the flaps of the jacket or the back cover where the copyright will appear, all credit should be noted on the mechanical but outside of the reproduction area. When the rest of the jacket or cover is set in type, the credit will naturally be added; otherwise, it is easily overlooked. In any event, when confirming a job and on the invoice, book jacket designers should specify that artwork is prepared only for the named edition and title.

Designers usually sell one-time reproduction rights. The designer should receive additional payment for use of the art by other domestic or foreign publishers and book clubs, by film or television, or other sources of communication.

Production costs such as (but not necessarily limited to) photographic processing, type, mechanically reproduced lettering, and photostats should be billed by the designer over and above the design fee, or such costs can be directly assumed by the client.

It is suggested that a 15 to 25 percent handling fee be applied to expenses incurred (type, photostats, etc.) by the designer for a jacket design, when the publisher does not pick up these costs directly.

Additional rights for use of the finished art by the original client are usually limited to advertising and promotion of the original book in the edition initially contemplated. If any other rights are covered, a statement of those rights should appear on the designer's bill. Any bill should also state that all other rights are reserved to the designer and that original art should be returned to the designer.

Comparative fees for book jacket design concepts*

	Hardcover and Trade Paperback	Mass Market Bestseller
One concept for front jacket or cover with supplied mechanical for front and spine	$450-800	$600-1200
Additional concepts (per sketch)	200-400	200-400
One concept followed by voluntary termination	50% of original fee (minimum)	50% of original fee (minimum)

Note: These prices do not include expenses for comps.

*Some distinction should be made as to the difference of fees of 2-color and 3-color graphic designs, full-color spot design, and full-color bleed art. For juvenile book jackets, see Juvenile Book section.

Book design

Book designers are graphic artists who develop the style and visual flow of a book by using the graphic elements of typography, illustration, and photography. The functions of book designers range from highly creative to purely mechanical.

Before dealing with the creative aspects of a job, it is necessary to analyze the project in order to prepare a design brief that includes the information outlined below.

The design brief

The *design brief* includes: (1) a copy of the manuscript, and/or a selection of representative copy for sample pages, and a summary of all typographic problems, copy areas, code marks, etc.; (2) the compositor's name, method of composition, and a listing of typefaces; and (3) a description of the proposed physical characteristics of the book (e.g., trim size, page length, number of columns, number of colors, if more than one). The publisher should also indicate whether any particular visual style is expected.

The design brief may be prepared either by the publisher or by the freelance book designer. Pricing in the book design categories is based on preparation of the design brief by the publisher. When the designer's assignment includes this responsibility, it should be reflected by an increase in the design fee.

The following prices are based on preparation of as many layouts as the designer feels are necessary to show major design elements. When the client wishes to see highly detailed layouts showing elements which could just as easily be communicated to the compositor by typemarking of the sample manuscript pages, an increase of the fee is in order. Any additional considerations (such as a book in two or more colors) should also be reflected in an increase in the fee.

After the fee is agreed upon by the publisher and the book designer, layouts are prepared for chapter openings, title page and double-page spreads of the text that include all typographic elements, and treatment of illustrations or photographs. These typical examples of pages clearly show the design to the publisher and are used as a guide in production. Designers usually provide a "composition order" for a typesetter that spells out all type specifications in detail based on the layouts. They may also mark up all or part of the manuscript.

Most publishers use in-house or compositor's production facilities to take the book from sketches to page makeup. Designers should check galleys and page proofs to make sure the compositor has followed all design specifications. With complicated layouts, the publisher may request that the book designer dummy the book. *Dummying* is actually taking copies of galleys and stats of art or photographs which have been sized and placing them in position on dummy sheets. The dummy then may be used by the production staff or designer to prepare mechanicals for the printer.

Occasionally, a writer and book designer may team up to create a package for a publisher. Such a package includes camera-ready mechanicals or pasteups, relieving the publisher of these production responsibilities. This way of working is generally used when the idea of the book originated with the writer or designer.

Book design categories

The table below provides typical fees for simple, average, and complex book design format categories. The categories are defined as follows:

Trade books

Simple: A straightforward book such as a novel or short book of poetry. Design includes a layout showing a title page, a chapter opening, and a double spread of text, and spreads for front matter. These simple books are generally done in-house, but may be given to a freelance designer if the publisher is small and does not have an in-house design department.

Average: Non-fiction trade books, cookbooks, poetry or drama, anthologies, or illustrated books that are designed on a grid system. Design may include frontmatter (half-title, ad card, title, copyright, dedication, acknowledgments, preface, contents, list of illustrations, introduction), part opening, chapter opening, text comprising from three to six levels of heads, tabular matter, extracts, footnotes, and simple backmatter such as bibliographies and indexes. The design, exclusive of the frontmatter, may be set into sample pages by the publisher, to be ok'd before typesetting of the complete manuscript begins.

Complex: These are books such as workbooks, catalogs, and elaborate art or picture books, requiring special treatment of each page; two-color basic texts, cookbooks, or other books of greater complexity than in the previous category.

Textbooks

Simple: Mostly straight text with up to 3 levels of heads, simple tables and/or art.

Average: Up to 6 levels of heads, tables, extract, footnotes, and use of illustrations, diagrams and/or photographs in a grid system.

Complex: Foreign language texts, 2, 3 or 4-color texts, complicated workbooks, catalogues or illustrated books that require special treatment of each page.

The basic design fee

A basic fee includes an initial consultation with a publisher to discuss the project, analysis of manuscript or representative sample pages, cast off, preparation of tissue layouts and composition order, manuscript mark-up, and presentation of completed design. When sample pages are to be set, the basic fee includes specing of the sample manuscript and a review of samples after they have been set.

If a publisher requests minor changes in the design, revisions will be included in the basic design fee. If major changes are requested, the design fee may have to be renegotiated, or changes billed at the designer's hourly rate.

There are some unusual projects or books for small presses that may not fit easily into the categories below. In these cases, designers should use their hourly rates as the basis for a fee. If the design is to be used for a series of books, a re-use fee should be negotiated.

Dummying fee

The dummying fee covers checking of galleys and page proofs, cast off of galleys for the dummy; preparation of master mechanical boards to be pre-printed by the publisher, if necessary; the preparation of dummies, including sizing of art or photos; incorporation of changes into master galleys; and presentations of the completed dummys to the publisher. The dummying fee also includes the preparation of art or photo inserts.

Mechanical fee

A mechanical fee covers the preparation of mechanicals, finished art for ornaments, maps, etc., that a designer has agreed to provide, and the final corrections made by the publisher.

Extra charges

Supervision of an art program, including hiring of and coordination with illustrators or photographers; extra conference time and trips to the publisher; time spent handling stats or type, or other production work are billed at the hourly design rate.

Comparative fees for design of cover and interior text of juvenile books

	Type Layout after Illustrated Dummy	Format and Type Design	Format and Type Design Plus Art Illustration Direction
Trade Book	$750-950	$1000-1500	$1500-2500
Textbook	650-900	850	1250-1500

Comparative fees for book design*

Textbook	Simple Format	Average Format	Complex Format
Usual design	$500-600	$700-850	$850-1200
Highly stylized	575-750	800-1000	1100-1350
Unique design†	650-900	850-1100	1200-1750
Each additional book in series	25%	33%	50%
Trade book			
Usual design	550-650	650-750	750-1000
Highly stylized	700-850	850-1000	1500-3000
Unique design†	900-1000	1500-2000	2500-5000
Each additional book in series	25%	33%	50%

*See the text above for elaboration on the meaning of the range of formats.

†Prices in this category can exceed indicated ranges, depending on the complexity.

Letterforms

Hand letterers are graphic artists who use the characters of the alphabet and numbers to create graphic forms or original alphabets. Hand lettering includes calligraphy, built-up letterforms, designed letterforms, and alphabets.

Hand letterers work in a way similar to illustrators. Upon agreement of the terms and fee for the project, a letterer prepares sketches of possible solutions to a specific problem. Upon acceptance of the comprehensive or sketches, finished art is prepared for reproduction.

Hand lettering is used in all areas of the communications industry: advertising, corporate identity and promotion, publishing, and institutional.

Many hand letterers are also graphic designers or illustrators. In fact, it is rare to find a graphic artist who does hand lettering only, except in the area of calligraphy.

The dramatic development of photo and film lettering in recent years has, of course, made it necessary to restructure the pricing concepts for the creative professional letterers and alphabet designers. Among the many factors affecting the prices of lettering are the following: (1) The amount of design work involved; (2) the size of the original art; (3) medium to be used (pen, brush, ink paint); (4) styled lettering (typeface modification); (5) surface upon which it is to be executed (paper, color print, box, bottle, can); (6) distortion (perspective, condensing); and (7) number of comprehensives required.

The prices below reflect the average hand letterer's fee. All expenses are additional. The prices to a client may be higher if the lettering is being commissioned through a designer or art director because the end price must accommodate their additional participation.

Alphabet design

Alphabet design is a rather complex situation to make a determination about price arrangements. Most corporations have contracts that take complete possession of the design and continue to pay royalties for the sale to other corporations for extensive uses. It is up to the designer to communicate with the alphabet buyer (corporation) to negotiate changes in the contract. An advance against royalties of at least $500 is usually paid by the corporations for accepted alphabet designs.

Comparative fees for letterforms

Publication titling (one comprehensive, one finish)	Simple*	Average*	Complicated*
Major magazine	$550	$750	$1000-1200
Specific audience or minor publication	350	550	800
Publication masthead design logotype (three comprehensives, one finish; unlimited rights)			
Major magazine	4000	6500	8000
Specific audience	1800	2800	5000
Small publication (newsletter, in-house organ)	300	500	1000
Logotypes (three comprehensives, one finish; unlimited rights)			
Corporate	3000	5000-6000	7500-8500
Individual	750	1000-1200	1700-2000

Comparative fees for letterforms (continued)

	Average*	Complicated*
Hardcover book jacket lettering *(one comprehensive, one finish; one-time rights limited to specific editions involved)*		
Mass market	550-750	750-1100
Trade market	450	650
Paperback cover lettering *(One comprehensive, one finish; one-time rights limited to the specific edition involved)*		
Mass market	600	750-800
Trade market	450	700

Rough lettering: $30-45 per hour, $150-300 per sketch

Comprehensive lettering: $30-45 per hour

Finish lettering: $50-75 per hour

Calligraphy on certificates or envelopes: $2 per work or line, depending on the height and weight of the words and the quality required.

Reworking or altering letterforms *(in house):* $30-45 per hour.

Advertising *(including packaging, television and film):* See advertising illustration section for comparable prices for any built up, designed or calligraphic letterforms.

*These classifications indicate both numbers of words and the complexity of typeface.

Comparative fees for alphabet design*

	Simple	Complicated
Corporate	$6000-7500	$10,000 +
Type house†	–	–
Magazine or publication	5000-7000	8500 +

*Includes upper and lowercase and numerals in one weight (approximately seventy characters); unlimited rights, but not for resale.

†$100 advance is paid on delivery and royalty arrangement is negotiated based on unit sales. The advance should be negotiated based on the number of characters, the weights, slants, small capitals, numerals, and upper and lowercases required. No outright sales is suggested for a purchase price less than $5000.

Retouching

Retouchers are graphic artists who alter, enhance, or add to a photograph by using bleaches, dyes, brush, or airbrush techniques. The resulting photograph usually appears remained untouched. This "invisible art" requires a highly skilled hand and eye in order to be successful. Therefore, the retoucher most often specializes in one area of retouching and concentrates on the skills and technical knowlwedge of that area.

When pricing a retouching project, many factors come into play:

Surface: Most color work of high quality is done on transparencies, chromes or dye transfers because of the subtleties that can be achieved on these surfaces. A retoucher uses dyes and bleaches when working on a chrome. C prints are often used for presentation purposes, but when extreme detail is required, often lack the dependability of chromes and dye transfers for the printer to use as a reproduction art. Brush, pencil, dyes, bleaching, etching, and airbrush techniques are used in retouching on all surfaces. In black-and-white retouching, photographic prints of high quality are most commonly used as a surface to be retouched.

Complexity: Retouching can run the gamut of change in the photo, from simply adding a few highlights to actually creating photorealistic, hand-wrought backgrounds, shapes, or figures, or stripping two or more photos together to create a montage.

Expenses: Typography, photography, props, and other out-of-pocket expenses are considered to be additional, billable expenses.

Overtime: Retouching, by its nature, should not be a last-minute project. It's important, therefore, to know how the retoucher charges for extraordinary time requirements. Normal timing for any average-size project is three days. Overtime rates for less than three days turnover are figured at: Two days: 50 percent more; one day: 100 percent more (rush job status). If the job requires evening, weekend or holiday time, there is often a 100 percent overtime charge.

Rights: Unlike the other graphic artists, retouchers always work on an existing piece of art and are usually not entitled to copyright or reuse fees. The fee that they charge initially represents the total income from that project, unlike artists who are working on the basis of selling future rights.

Studio: A retouching studio has full equipment and staff to provide multiple talents, flexibility in handling larger projects, and accessibility. Studio rates are higher than freelance rates.

Freelance: Freelance retouchers handle each project themselves and generally work out of their own studios. They rarely work on the client's premisis. Since free-lancers often have less overhead, rates may reflect it.

Comparative fees for retouching

Advertising	*Average to extensive*
National, color	$1500-3000 +
National, black and white	600-1500 +
Trade, color	900-2000
Trade, black and white	500-1200
Editorial	
National, color	800-2000
National, black and white	500-1200
Trade, color	900-1500 +
Pharmaceutical	
Color	1000-2000 +
Black and white	500-1500
Photo-comping (on 8x10)	200-250 Per element

Notes:
Retouching fees vary from studio to studio depending on quality, technical know-how and other factors, etc. Time is a major factor in pricing. Two-day service is priced at +50% of normal fee. One-day service is priced at +60%-100% of normal fee. Overtime for holidays and weekends is +150%-200% of normal fee.

Comparative hourly rates for retouching

	Studio	Free-lance
Color, chromes or dye transfers	$125-200	$50-100
Color, C prints (comp retouching)	80-125	50-80
Black and white prints	75-125	40-60

Note:

The above prices are based on average job, working conditions, talent, and client as the guide. Deviations from average may reflect in higher or lower prices and/or rates.

Production

Production artists are graphic artists who execute the finished mechanical or pasteup for a graphic designer or art director to their layout specifications. Production artists, in short, make the project camera ready for the printer. The subtle decisions and interpretations that production artists must make on the board determine the final product. The details are critical.

Advanced production artists are adept at keyline ruling, overlays, and all other complicated production techniques.

Some of the considerations production artists use in determining the cost of producing a mechanical or pasteup are: (1) conditions of the job and tightness of the layout; (2) extent of responsibility in gathering materials for the job; (3) location of job (on site or in own studio): (4) complexity of style; and (5) deadline (amount of overtime involved).

Most production artists base their prices on their hourly rates. Occasionally, prices are worked out on a per-page rate.

Comparative hourly rates for preparing camera-ready art

Pasteups

Corporate	$17-20
Publishing	12-18
Advertising	20-25

Mechanicals

Corporate	20-30
Publishing	15-20
Advertising	23-28

SALARIED
PRICES
AND TRADE CUSTOMS

Salaried Artists

For more detailed descriptions of positions mentioned in the pricing sections of this chapter, please refer to the appropriate freelance sections, which describe the role of each discipline. The positions included here are those that do not appear in those freelance sections.

A salaried graphic artist is usually employed solely by one company. Unless contractual arrangements are made to the contrary, all art created on company time is considered work-for-hire. In the more creative jobs, often it is considered unethical to moonlight for a competitor. Generally, the scope of employee limits the income of the salaried graphic artist to the artist's employing company.

Many of the disciplines listed below are not exclusive of each other. For instance, an art director may also produce illustrations, designs, or letterforms. In fact, very few salaried graphic artists specialize so rigidly as to only have talents in one given area. The needs of the position must, therefore, dictate the talents required. Using the primary role to be filled, the salaries outlined below should give an idea of the ranges that can be expected by professional artists being interviewed for staff positions.

These salary ranges are based on a standard 35-hour week with a benefits package including health insurance, vacation pay, holiday and sick pay. Bonuses, stock options, and retirement plans are negotiable,. The jobs described are creative positions and do not include purely executive or supervisory functions.

Generally, larger companies hire full-time art staff (i.e., companies that produce a significant amount of graphic art in-house such as catalogs, textile designs, advertising, packaging, or corporate graphics). Freelance talent is often used to supplement an art staff. At times, independent agencies or studios are on retainer when there is no art staff or the company chooses to subcontract large areas of concern (e.g., advertising, corporate identity programs, or annual and quarterly reports).

Employment conditions

When applying for a full-time salaried position, artists should consider conditions of employment along with salary and type of work. Among the conditions generally accepted as standard for full-time workers are:

Staff policy: Many employers have written staff policies that outline the way in which a company relates to its employees. In fact, New York state companies are required by law to notify employees "in writing or by publicly posting" policy on sick leave, vacation, personal leave, holidays and hours. Other items that may be included in staff policies are: maternity/paternity leave, employee grievance procedures, criteria for salary increases and promotions, cause for firing, etc. A staff policy can often give potential employees an impression of an employer's attitude towards his/her staff, so it is useful to know what is included in a staff policy before deciding to accept a job.

Job benefits: Most companies offer some benefits packages to their employees that may include health, disability, life and dental insurance plans. In larger companies and corporations, there are occasionally profit-sharing and stock option plans, day care facilities or child-care subsidies, although these benefits are rare for most lower to middle management positions.

Job descriptions: Just as a contract serves as a clear understanding between a client and a freelance artist, a written job description can give artists a clear indication of what is expected of them during the term of employment. The Guild recommends that written job description for all artists seeking a salaried position, since it helps both employer and employee to avoid expectations and assumptions that are not shared by the other party. A written job description is also useful in the event that a job changes significantly during the term of employment. When substantial changes are made in a job, have the description re-written and discuss title changes and salary adjustments.

Job review: A regular job review (semi-annual or annual) is a helpful practice for both employer and employee. A review allows employees to get valuable feedback on how they are performing, and to bring up questions about job expectations. The employer has, at review times, the opportunity to discuss changes in job descriptions and performance critiques. Formal job reviews also provide opportunities for both employer and employee to suggest ways to improve the "product" or the role being considered . When handled well, job reviews can head off problems that might arise and help maintain good and productive relationships between

employer and employee. It is recommended that the results of the job review be kept on file and that employees have access to their reviews.

While many of the above conditions of employment are not mandatory, they are recommended to help insure that both employer and employee develop and maintain good relations during the term of employment.

Broadcast designers

The demands of the one-eyed television medium that sits in 98 percent of the living rooms in the United States present a unique challenge to broadcast designers. The challenge demands knowledge and creativity in every aspect of design.

For on-air duties, broadcast designers are required to be illustrators, cartoonists, and type designers. It is necessary to know, prepare and sometimes shoot animations on both film and tape. Knowledge of stand and remote still photography is essential. For print media, broadcast designers devise everything from small-space program-listing ads to full-page newspaper ads as well as trade publication ads, booklets, brochures, invitations and similar material.

Broadcast designers double as corporate designers who coordinate everything from the on-air look, to the stationery, memo pads, and sales promotion materials. Broadcast designers even design news vehicle markings and occasionally design helicopter markings.

In addition to the preceding fields, scenic design is another area of responsibility. Here the understanding of construction techniques, materials, and paints is important, along with an awareness of staging, furnishing, lighting, spatial relationships, and camera angles.

It is necessary for art directors in this field to be proficient in managerial skills such as organization, budgeting, purchasing, directing a staff, and working with upper management.

Obviously, not all of these skills apply to every individual or situation, and each design staff is built around personal strengths; nevertheless, a broad spectrum of design possibilities does exist. The broadcast designer is called upon to meet these requirements and others.

This section on the broadcast designer was written by Gil Cowley, art director at WCBS -TV; Chairman of the advisory board and former president of the Broadcast Designer's Association.

Textile designers

The following tr
vant to the salaried tex

1. *Physical wor*
designers should surv
space and evaluate su
ventilation, cleanlines
and other conditions i
work.

2. *Freelance:* (.
freelance work is a common
industry. Freelance work is permi
the converter requires the textile designe.
sign a form stating that the textile designer will not work for other companies while employed by the converter. In-company freelance work should be competitively priced according to current market guidelines. It is to the converter's advantage to have textile designers at hand to complete work quickly and in the way wished. Textile designers should therefore not be penalized for helping the converter.

3. *Mill work:* Long-standing, unfair practices have existed concerning mill work by staff employees. Extended travel time, 24-hour shifts with sleep deprivation, working weekends and weekdays, and enduring poor physical conditions at mills are common practices that are rarely given appropriate compensation. These extra duties are expected for the usual in-studio salary and benefits. Trends are changing, however, by providing compensation such as days off, overtime pay, and by increasing personnel to limit shift hours. These goals require that textile designers firmly negotiate from their own point of view.

4. *Work Practices:* According to the New York State Labor Board at least one-half hour for lunch in a 9 a.m. to 5 p.m. workday must be provided. Contact the Board for other information on rest periods and working conditions. It is important for every textile designer to know his or her rights as an employee. The Guild discourages working extra hours consistently without overtime pay.

5. *Salary reviews:* Most converters evaluate work quality and salary advancement on an annual basis. Each staff artist should be acquainted with the policies of the company. Most converters are stringent about the limited amounts and numbers of raises given. Each textile designer should know what to expect and negotiate or act accordingly.

6. *Artists on per diem:* Per diem rates are usually not beneficial to textile designers

e lower than prevailing
s. In addition, textile designers
e medical or life insurance and
nefits. However, hiring a per diem
signer for even one day requires the
y to pay taxes, social security, and
ployment insurance to the government
hat textile designer. Also, according to
vernment regulation, consistent per diems
can make a worker automatically eligible for
benefits. With respect to wages for per diem
work, the Guild strongly recommends that
textile designers review the ability level
required and the work assigned. The work
day should be priced accordingly.

7. Knock-offs: Ethically, textile designers should not be forced to knock-off or copy
designs for an employer unless that converter
is willing to sign a release that the converter
line accepts full responsibility in the event of
any potential infringement. Knocking off
designs is a common practice, but textile
designers must be aware that it is improper
to infringe on anyone else's designs and that
any infringement can lead to serious legal
liabilities.

8. Changing jobs: Textile staff artists
change jobs frequently in order to improve
salaries, achieve promotions or better working conditions. The Guild advises giving
present employers a standard two-week
notice when leaving a job. Anything less can
jeopardize severance or vacation pay due.

Note: Some companies request test
coloring samples as part of the interview
process. The Guild recommends against this
process unless the test colorings are paid for
or remain the property of the artist.

9. Converters: Staff art converters in
the textile field may include:

Stylist: Creative & managerial heads
of departments, sometimes referred to as
style directors or art buyers.

Assistant stylists: Managerial and creative assistants to stylists; may or may not
work at drawing board; may or may not
buy art.

Studio head: Directly in charge of non-
management studio personnel; answers to
stylist; usually works at drawing board.

Designer: Executes original art work.

Colorist: Executes color combinations,
usually painted but occasionally "chipped."

Repeat artist: Executes precise continuous repeat patterns, imitating original artist's
"hand."

Mill worker: Can be any of the above
employees trained to shade fabric at the mills.

10. Studios: Staff at studios may
include:

Studio director: Creative and managerial head, in some cases the studio owner.

Rep: Sells original artwork or seeks
clients who need colorings, repeats, etc. A
few also solicit mill work.

Artists: Usually work at the studio;
may execute original artwork, colorings,
repeats.

Earnings gap still a problem: The textile design field has historically been composed of many more women designers than
men. While this fact is well known in the
industry, the corollary that men and women
are not paid equally for the same job is less
well publicized. According to 1983 U.S. Census Bureau statistics, "women working year
round at full-time jobs still earn only about
62% of what men make." The commissioner
of labor statistics cites clothing and textile
industries as areas where "most women continue to work in the country's lowest paying
industries."

The 1983 Graphic Artists Guild survey
found that the situation for textile designers is
at least in keeping with the general Census
Bureau statistics. For example, the majority
of members surveyed report that their annual
gross salaries are $20,000 and under. Only
1% of the respondents report gross incomes
of $40,000 or more. Since the survey includes
freelance as well as salaried designers, the
net figures for income are significantly lower.

In one case, a man with 11 years of
design experience was being paid $4,000
more per year in a salaried position than a
woman with 17 years of experience in a comparable job.

The issue of equal pay for equal work
has received a great deal of attention from
women's groups and labor organizations. The
Guild believes that equal pay standards should
be promoted and supported. It encourages
members with information on problems in this
area to contact the Guild.

Comparative salaries of advertising agency staff*

	Small Agency	Large Agency
Senior art director	$40,000-50,000	$65,000+
Art director	16,000-30,000	35,000-50,000
Junior art director	–	20,000-35,000
Assistant art director	10,000-12,000	10,000-14,000
Creative director	80,000-125,000	125,000+
Associate creative director or supervisor	75,000-80,000	80,000-125,000
Comp illustrator	–	20,000-35,000
Promotion art director (Direct mail and collateral)	27,000-38,000	35,000-50,000

*A small agency has between $5 and 10 million in annual billings; a large agency has more than $75 million.

Note:
In many instances relative size of agency has little or no bearing on salaries paid.

Comparative salaries of corporate art department staff*

	Medium	Large or Fortune 500
Consultant art director	$–	$125,000-160,000
Senior art director	40,000-50,000	75,000-125,000
Graphic designer	25,000-37,000	35,000-45,000
Production artist	–	18,500-32,000

*A medium corporation has less than $300 million in annual sales revenues; a large corporation has $300 million or more.

Comparative salaries of book publishing art department staff

	Small Publisher	Large Publisher
Art director	$25,000-35,000	$70,000-90,000
Production artist/production supervisor	25,000-30,000	35,000-50,000

Comparative salaries of graphic design office or studio staff*

	Small Studio	Large Studio
Design director	$–	$45,000-60,000
Senior graphic designer	35,000-45,000	45,000-50,000
Junior graphic designer	18,000-27,000	20,000-30,000
Entry level graphic designer	–	16,000-22,000
Junior packaging designer	–	18,000-25,000
Senior packaging designer	–	25,000-35,000
Packaging design director	–	35,000-45,000
Senior production supervisor	–	100,000-125,000
Senior production artist	–	20,000-35,000
Entry level production artist	–	16,000-22,000

*A small design studio has less than $250,000 in annual sales revenue; a large design studio has $750,000 or more.

Notes:
All salaries are exclusive of additional job incentives such as bonuses, retirement packages, stock options and annual leave, etc. In many cases there is no difference in relative salaries at small and large design studios especially for production artists and entry level positions.

Comparative salaries of broadcast station art department staff

	Smallest Markets, 51-100*	Largest Markets, 1-10*
Art director of design manager	$35,000-40,000	$55,000-70,000
Graphic designer	20,000-30,000	40,000-55,000

*Market sizes are ranked according to population in the broadcast area. The most populous market (i.e., New York metropolitan area) is ranked number 1.

Comparative salaries of animation staff artists*

	Hourly	Weekly		Hourly	Weekly
Director	$24.00	$840.00	Preplanner/checker (animation)	11.25	393.75
Story, story sketch	17.25	603.75			
Layout	17.25	603.75	Apprentice preplanner, first 3 months	9.00	315.00
Assistant layout	11.25	393.75	Apprentice preplanner, second 3 months	10.05	351.75
Apprentice layout (8 months)	9.45	330.75			
Animator I†	18.00	630.00	Junior checker (ink and paint only)	8.85	309.75
Animator II	12.75	446.25	Junior checker apprentice, first 3 months	6.45	225.75
Assistant animator	11.25	393.75			
Apprentice assistant animator, first 6 months	9.00	315.00	Junion checker apprentice, second 3 months	7.50	262.50
Apprentice assistant animator, second 6 months	10.05	351.75	Inker	8.85	309.75
			Apprentice inker, first 3 months	6.45	225.75
Inbetweener	9.75	341.25			
Apprentice inbetweener, first 3 months	7.50	262.50	Apprentice inker, second 3 months	7.50	262.50
			Graphic film artist I	13.50	472.50
Apprentice inbetweener, second 3 months	8.55	299.25	Graphic film artist II	12.33	431.55
Production coordinator	12.39	433.65	Apprentice graphic film artist, 0-6 months	5.25	183.75
Background	14.79	517.65			
Assistant background	11.25	393.75	Apprentice graphic film artist, 7-9 months	6.30	220.50
Apprentice background, first 3 months	7.55	278.25	Apprentice graphic film artist, 10-12 months	$7.35	$257.25
Apprentice background, second 3 months	9.45	330.75	General apprentice, 0-6 months	5.25	183.75
Apprentice background, third 3 months	$10.83	$379.05			

(Continued on next page)

Comparative salaries of animation staff artists (continued)*

	Hourly	*Weekly*
General apprentice, 7-9 months	6.30	220.50
General apprentice, 10-12 months	7.35	257.25

Benefits: medical plan, annuity, 10 day sick time, 13 paid holidays, 2 week vacation (under 5 years), 3 weeks vacation (5-10 years), 4 weeks vacation (over 10 years).

*The above salaries are based on union rates and supplied by the Animators Union, Local 841, IATSE.

Comparative salaries of textile studio or converter art department staff

	Weekly	*Yearly*
Beginning artist (colorist, designer)	$275-350	$14,300-18,200
Colorist, junior designer, sample weaver	300-600	15,600-31,200
Repeat artist	300-600	15,600-31,200
Senior designer (with & without millwork)	500-900	26,000-46,800
Studio head	450-700	23,400-36,400
Assistant stylist	500-800	26,000-41,600
Stylist*	600-2500	31,200-130,000
Student trainee		Minimum wage

Note: In most cases woven design personnel are not paid as much as print design personnel.

*In many cases, stylists get perks and bonuses based on success of line.

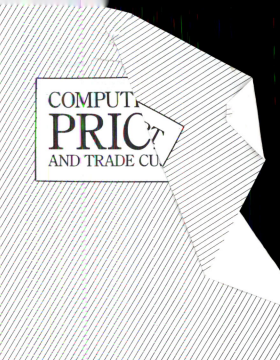

...ter generated art

Art produced by computer is like any other area of the graphic arts where pricing and business practices are concerned. In pricing computer-generated art, start with the final applications for the work: that is, the price will depend, in part, on whether the art will be used as illustration, text design, in broadcast, etc. And, like pricing for other forms of artwork, consideration must be made for the ways in which the art will be used. The applications covered here are primarily for work done on a personal computer or for videotex broadcasting. Work created on larger and more powerful paint and animation systems are best priced by referring to the other pricing sections of this book that apply to the final product and then applying the formula that appears in the chart below.

A computer is not a "self-functioning" tool. Like pencils, airbrushes and other graphics tools, computers do not generate work of and by themselves. *Any conmputer-generated art is the result of the artist's talent, skill, experience and knowledge of software.*

Computer-generated artwork, referred to as computer graphics, presents a new level of options for artists and clients. It can speed up the design process, give some new special effects, textures and patterns that are impossible to create with other tools, and can be faster and more cost-effective for certain types of work.

Among the many varieties of work done on computer are: TV station logos, weather and news graphics, videotext, color-retouching, automatic pate make-up and design, high resolution presentation graphics for audio-visual multi-media shows, computer simulated models for scientific applications and much more.

Factors to be considered when pricing computer graphics include:

Time: a job done on computer may be more efficient or may take longer than art produced with traditional media. Unlike traditional approaches, using computers allows for revisions to be made directly on the finished work, in fact, a rough comp can be turned immediately into a finished work on computer. Time can be saved in alterations, multiple uses and for additions or revisions of color.

Extra expenses: post production costs for video, slide houses that shoot slides from computer disks, film development, delivery services, film, possible rental of support equipment, etc., will add expenses to the cost of the art.

The work done on personal computer and videotex is in digital format, that is, it remains in the form produced by the computer. Whereas other uses of computer-generated works require conversion into more commonly-known applications such as 35 mm film, slides and videotape, etc.

Broadcasting is an area where computer-generated work has been most commonly used. Computer technology is used to create and augment titles and commercials through both illustration and animation. However, even though the original work is created on computer, the final product is displayed on 35 mm film or videotape. The technology to produce computer-generated art directly on hardcopy is not of high enough print quality for standard printing techniques at this time. Similarly, business graphics and presentations are created on computer and then photographed onto film. Therefore, any use of computer-generated art for print illustration must employ the "raster lines" of the monitor as part of the aesthetic of the style and requires conversion of the computer image into some form of "hardcopy" that is photographable.

Applications

Hardcopy includes all applications for standard print illustration. Follow illustration pricing sections for any work that will be used in conventional print or media applications.

Broadcast and audio-visual refers to presentation and business graphics (Geni-graphics, Dicomed, Artonics, etc.) such as charts and graphs, broadcast graphics and commercials. Refer to pricing sections for broadcast and audio-visual art.

Software and electronic publishing includes title page illustration, interior illustration, structured or formated pages, game title pages and interior screens.

Artists working in this area will be creating illustrations or designs on specific operation systems (i.e., Apple, Atari, IBM). The most realistic way to work with these systems is to use a system that includes an electronic digital drawing board, rather than trying to write complex and time-consuming programs. Art created for software will follow very standard print models: Title and chapter screens for games and programs, illustrations, and formated pages (pages laid out for text with borders, windows, etc.).

In all probability, publishing will use electronic downloading digital information via telephone services before 1985. Because of this, artists should establish royalty payment structures for art used in software and electronic down loaded publishing.

Videotex is a broadcast industry that uses vertical band intervals to transmit digital information. Services in this area include advertising, public bulletin boards, games and information services. Videotex should also require royalty arrangements since it is billed by per-frame use. Whatever its final form, the concept is one of interactive digital-based information and entertainment services through which artists will illustrate game screens, title screens and advertisement screens.

Consideration should be given to the potential use of the work when pricing. Royalties should be established for the work if it is to be used for continued resale.

Copyright: Work for use in digital format-software, electronic publishing , and videotex is copyrightable. In fact, it can be copyrighted as text (printed source code), as graphic art (hardcopy printout, photo, etc.) and as an audio visual work. In most instances, registering a work as an audio-visual is the choice of the artist.

The contract for computer-generated art appearing in this book is applicable to software, electronic publishing and videotex. Because of the newness of the field, the contract is a starting point, which can be amended as the technology and industry practices change.

Computer graphics for video

Computer graphics for the video industry fall into three categories: industrial, broadcast—non-advertising, and broadcast—advertising (Bosch, Quantel Systems, etc.). When computer graphics are used in video for either animation or other special effects, they are usually part of a larger work and are frequently combined with live footage and traditional techniques. This can make pricing a little more complicated than when art is being commissioned as the whole project.

Computer graphics for commercial videos normally are not done by individuals, but by various sized animation/video companies. These companies range from small studios, which do animation and art on computer only, to large studios that provide full video services as well as full film services, handling total production for a project. Even the larger companies frequently contract freelance artists on special jobs and/or rent special equipment from other facilities.

Because of equipment costs, it is unusual for individual artists to be able to provide all of these services for a client. Even large companies do not always own all of the video equipment necessary for a particular job.

Industrials: Industrials are usually 3/4" videos used for non-broadcast purposes such as training films, video newsletters or brochures, sales videos, video catalogues and how-to's for the home VCR market. These videos are also referred to as non-theatrical releases.

Generally computer graphics account for only a percentage of the total video/film, with images such as growth charts, location maps and logos (sometimes including animation) the most likely applications.

The choice of visual concepts for industrial use affects the final price of a job. In some cases, more than one computer graphics system may have to be used to produce the desired effect. The job may, therefore, end up being produced in more than one location on more than one piece of equipment. Pricing should reflect this factor as well as post-production costs for special techniques.

Pre-production consultation is vital in determining the price and for describing to the client the best and most efficient processes for arriving at the final product.

Broadcast/non-advertising: This category is usually 1" video and includes title sequences, educational films and maps and charts (such as weather maps).

Many of the same factors in determining prices for industrials apply to this section as well. Maps and charts are generally priced at the same rate as title sequences.

Broadcast/advertising: These jobs are usually done by medium to large-sized animation studios who have large permanent staff and who occasionally hire freelance artists for special projects. Fees for this type of work are not determined by usage, but by time, complexity and type of equipment needed-including the use of outside equipment.

Videotex/interactive computer graphics: Videotex or interactive computer graphics, refers to the electronic delivery of information. This form of communication has been under development since 1976 and is still in its infant stages.

This technique uses an electronic signal that delivers information to a monitor in an area between TV field transmissions. These frequencies are visualized as 21 lines of black between frames that have beeen used by TV technicians for testing.

Electronic information services are developed through the coordinated efforts of graphic designers, writers, technicians, engineers and marketing personnel. Their combined creative ideas result in electronic pages or screens.

The public views this electronic information through a personal computer or television with a modem and telephone hook-up, a public information kiosk, cable delivery or as an independent interactive software program disk.

The input of graphics and type is achieved by designers through the use of computer graphics software. The frames that are created are stored in specific file formats, ASCII (American Standard Code of Information Interchange), and NAPLPS (North American Presentation Level Protocol Syntax). ASCII is presented to the viewer as text only frames, while NAPLPS is viewed as a 16-color graphic and text presentation.

Teletex: Teletex is a non-interactive electronic service also delivered through the vertical blank interval of a TV broadcast signal. While it is similar to Videotex, Teletex is display only. Videotex and Teletex can be used for the following applications.

Business-to-Business Services: These services are generally used by large corporations to interconnect their offices and offer new and direct modes of communication for anything from memos to training manuals.

Business-to-Consumer Services: The goal of these services is to educate consumers with up-to-date information that allows them to make an intelligent assessment of the product or service being advertised. The most readily available forms for this service are in-home personal computers with telephone and modem hook-up and public access available at a public kiosk.

Public Access Services: These services collect and distribute information electronically. They appear wherever people congregate: at public events, transportation centers, hotels, etc..

Entertainment Services: Recently advertisers have begun to develop a form of "entertainment advertising," through which a viewer can learn about a product or service while enjoying the entertainment value of an interactive service. The interactive nature of videotex makes it suitable for games, entertainment and education.

CD-ROM: Compact Disks-Read Only Memory is a non-interactive peripheral device attached to a personal computer. The CD-ROM has a storage capacity of about 250,000 still pictures of high resolution quality. At present, these disks are expensive and are only being implemented for professional use in such areas as hospitals, libraries and corporate offices. CD-ROM's will most likely be available to individual consumers in late 1986.

Comparative fees for software imagery for educational use

Title screen	$350-700
Full screen (multiples of 6 to 10)	250-400
Animation/windows (Depending on size of characters, size of windows and multiples)	50-200

Comparative fees for computer generated business graphics

Title	$30-60
Tabular (Depending on columns and rows)	40-200
Illustration or logo (Depending on system)	150-1000 +
Formatted screen	hourly rate* for first screen, base rate thereafter

*Hourly rate is $150-1000 + (see pricing formula chart)

Note: Artist hourly rate is $15-35

Comparative rates for computer graphics for video

Industrials	Staff	Freelance
Computer graphics operator	$8-20/hr.	
Storyboard (pencil roughs)	8-20/hr.	$5-10/frame
Storyboard (color finishes)		$20/frame
Operator consultant	$8-20/hr.	$20-50/hr.
Full service: includes pre-production* consultation, equipment rental, operators and post-production editing		$1000/day
Editing (including staff and equipment)		$150/hr.
Computer graphics (including staff and equipment)		$150/hr.

Broadcast/non-advertising		
Title sequences (6 seconds) (includes animation, rental, post-production editing, operator/consultant and storyboard)		$5000-6000 ($1000 + /per second)
Educational spots (40 seconds) (depending on complexity includes video tape, materials and operator fee, rental expenses)		$2000-5000
Maps and charts		$1000/per second

Broadcast/advertising		
Animation directors fees		$2000-2500/week (add 20% for post-production)
Paintbox with operator/artist		$175/hr.
Paintbox only, no artist		$135/hr.
Paintbox and Harry with operator/artist		$500/hr.
Editing		$300/hr.
Editing plus ADO		$575-600/hr.
Editing plus mirage		$700/hr.

* $1/4$ to $1/3$ total video price.

Pricing formula for computer graphics in normal print media

Creative fee
(see appropriate
specialty) Machine rental/
payback fee Added efficiency
Added effect Total computer
design fee

Computer Graphics Glossary

ASCII: American Standard Code for Information Interchange. This code gives specific numbers to alphabetic characters and is one of the few ways in which different computers can exchange information.

Binary: A numbering system based on 2's rather than 10's, which uses only the digits 0 and 1.

Bit: Binary digit—a single piece of binary data.

Buffer: Temporary data-storage device, often used to store a single image.

Byte: A sequence of binary digits operated on as a unit, e.g., an 8-bit or 16-bit byte.

CAD/CAM: Computer Aided Design/Computer Aided Manufacture—used to design and test parts, machinery, generate schematics, calculate manufacturing specifications, etc.

Chip: A miniature electrical circuit etched from silicon.

Color map/palette: Synonym for the range of colors from which an artist/operator chooses the particular colors used in an individual image.

CPU: Central Processing Unit—hardware which performs the main calculations of the computer.

Cursor: A position indicator on a computer screen indicating where data will be entered.

Data: A general term for the basic elements of information, alphanumeric or graphic, which can be processed by a computer.

Digital: A way of representing information (words, pictures, music, etc.) in discrete numerical values.

Documentation File: A stored collection of data treated as a unit.

Hardcopy: Any non-electronic version of what is viewed on the computer screen, e.g. black-and-white or color print-outs, slides or photographic prints.

Hard disk/floppy disk: A means for storing both computer programs and the data created with those programs (i.e., drawings, animations, novels, etc.). Both are record-like disks coated with magnetic material. Hard disks are faster, have a greater capacity, and generally stay with the computer system, while floppy disks can be easily transported. The implication is that an artist's work is less vulnerable to copyright infringement if saved on a floppy disk over which the artist maintains control.

Hardware: The physical components of a computer system.

Jaggies: The saw-toothed, stair-stepped quality of a line produced by most computer programs.

Image-processing: Manipulation of an image (usually video scanned), i.e., enhancement, colorizing, or distortions.

Input: Information or data entered into a computer's memory; the act of doing so; devices enabling the data to be entered.

Menu: A list of functions of a particular program from which the operator chooses the specific action desired. In graphic programs, it is usually displayed on the screen or on the graphics tablet.

Output: Computer results, devices which accept and display these results.

Pixel: Picture element, the individual dots on the display device, arranged in a grid, that comprise the image.

RAM/ROM: Random Access Memory/Read Only Memory—types of internal computer memory. RAM can hold changing data such as programs and the data created with the programs, and is erased when the power is shut off. ROM cannot be changed by the user, and holds various instructions used by the computer to do its work.

Raster System: A graphics system which draws shapes pixel-by-pixel.

Resolution: The absolute number of pixels across and down on a display device. This determines the fineness of detail available, much as grain in a photograph.

RGB: Red-green-blue. The primary colors of light and, therefore, of video screens. Also describes a type of high quality monitor where the signal for each color is handled as a separate electronic signal.

Software: Programs for the operation of the computer.

Teletext: A generic term describing the broadcast of text and graphics in an ordinarily unused part of the television signal. Television sets must be equipped with a decoding device in order to display the information.

Terminal: An input/output device that may look like a microcomputer, but does not do the computations. Many terminals may be connected to a single large computer.

Time-sharing: Renting time on a computer that is at a different location other than the terminal from which the work is being done, usually accomplished through telephone lines or a special data communication network.

Vector System: A graphics system that draws shapes in line segments rather than pixel-by-pixel. Many high-resolution drawing or presentation programs operate on vector systems.

Standard Contracts

The Guild has created a number of standard contracts for use by its members and other professionals. The Guild's contracts conform to the Code of Fair Practice and provide a basis for fair dealing between the parties. The purpose of these standard forms is to aid both creators and art buyers in reaching a thorough understanding of their rights and obligations.

A contract is a binding agreement between two or more parties. Normally each party gains certain benefits and must fulfill certain obligations. To be valid a contract must include the important terms of an assignment such as the fee and the job description. Other terms, such as a time when payment must be made, will be presumed to be reasonable (such as within thirty days of submitting an invoice or completing the assignment), if the parties have not actually specifed them in writing. Although it is wise to have written contracts, oral contracts are also binding in many cases and can be the basis of a legal suit. Thus contracts can take many forms: oral, purchase orders, confirmation forms, letters, an exchange of letters, or formal documents.

Both parties need not sign a contract to make it binding, although it is wise to do so. For example, if a buyer receives a confirmation form from an artist and does not object to the terms of the form, the artist is justified in starting work with the uncontested form as a binding contract. Even if purchase orders or invoices are not complete enough to be called contracts, they can be used as evidence of the terms of the unwritten contract on which the artist relied to start work.

A common way of entering into a contract is to have one party send a letter to the other party. If the party receiving the letter agrees with the terms set forth in the letter, he or she signs at the bottom of the letter beneath the words "Agreed to" and returns a signed copy of the letter to the party who sent it. While informal, such a letter of agreement is binding. Both artist and art buyer may feel more comfortable in some situations if the letter-of-agreement format is used. In the event that one party is signing a contract on behalf of a corporation, that person should give the corporate name, their own name, and their title that authorizes them to sign for the corporation, such as "XYZ Corp. By Alice Buyer, Art Director."

In creating a contract, there must be an offer and an acceptance. If one party makes an offer and the other party makes a counteroffer, the original offer is automatically terminated. For a contract to be binding, each party must give somthing of value to the other party. This giving of value is called consideration. The most common form of consideration is a promise to do something or refrain from doing something. So a promise to work or a promise to pay could be consideration, although doing the work or making the payment would also be consideration. For a contract to be enforceable, its purpose must be both legal and not against public policy, as might occur if, for example, a contract provided that the public be misinformed as to some aspect of a product.

One common problem that arises in contracts is the battle of the forms. Each party sends its own forms to the other, but the terms are never the same. The question then arises: whose form will govern if a dispute arises? If work is begun on the basis of one form, that form should take precedence over forms sent after completion of the work (such as invoices or a check with a condition on its back). However, the best way to resolve this problem is to deal with it directly. As soon as either party realizes that agreement has not been reached, the other should be notified. The points of disagreement should then be discussed and worked out to the satisfaction of both parties. Only in this way can the ambiguities that cause contractual problems be avoided.

Each of the Guild's contracts is a model that can be used directly or that can be modified to suit individual needs and circumstances.

Purchase orders and holding forms

Purchase orders often are used by clients at the beginning of an assignment. If the purchase order is merely an assignement description, artists will want to use a confirmation form, or order-acknowlgement form, detailing rights, payments, and other terms. An estimate is normally given before a purchase order is issued.

Holding forms are used by artists when they leave work for consideration by a client. These forms detail the work that is being left by the artist, the date and time the client received the work, and the projected response date. An invoice is normally presented to a client with the finished work.

Most of the forms have been discussed in detail in various parts of the text (the Textile Designer-Agent Agreement is accompanied by its own introduction). All contracts and forms in this book are based on the U.S. Copyright Law, which provides for the sale of individual reproduction rights by artists based on the needs expressed by their clients. Each right of usage is clearly specified, as are all terms for usage.

Usage limitations take the following format:

Title or product: Limits specific uses to advertising, promotion, editorial, corporate, or other uses, so that, for example, artwork purchased for editorial art may not be used in advertising without further agreement or consideration.

Medium of use: Specifies the form in which the art will reach the public, such as trade magazine, brochure, annual report, album cover, etc.

Edition: Limits usage to a given edition, such as a hardcover, quality paperback, or other edition.

Geographic area: Limits the territory in which the art can be distributed.

Time period: Limits the length of time during which the art can be used.

All of these concepts can be refined to fit the exact needs of artist and client. Clients establish the usage needed, and artists set appropriate fees based on the usage required. If further uses are necessary after the a contract is negotiated, an appropriate reuse fee can be established in most cases.

Writing a proposal

Graphic designers often provide clients with full service design projects from concept to production through final delivery. In the process of providing this service, they often coordinate their own art direction and design services with copywriters, illustrators, photographers, retouchers and printers, and bill the client for the entire package.

Standard contracts such as the ones appearing in this book, do not provide the detail and explanatory material required by this kind of complex, multi-phased project. In such cases, a proposal is a more effective vehicle since it can provide a greater scope and a more comprehensive bidding structure. And when signed by both client and artist, a proposal is as legally binding as a standard contract.

Although proposals often require significant research and development time, including contacts with suppliers and indications of initial design ideas, they are provided free of charge. The information supplied is only for the design directions already discussed, specified and agreed upon by client and artist at their initial meeting. Since clients often compare a number of proposals before choosing an artist for the job, a proposal should be clear and thorough enough to be reviewed without the artist present.

At their initial meeting, it is important for both client and artist to discuss *specific* directions about what is being bid on. Being specific serves two purposes: it will ensure that the proposal will cover the same project and items as other proposals submitted, and both parties will be able to avoid surprises in the scope and estimates of the project after the proposal is accepted.

When preparing a proposal for a new client, it helps to include collateral material such as resumes of those involved in the project, promotion pieces, reprints of published work, samples of similar projects, etc. Always make at least two copies of the proposal for both client and artist to retain as original signed copies if the commission is accepted. Once signed, the proposal becomes the legal contract for the commission.

What to include

A proposal should begin with a clear and concise description of the project, concept, time frame, size of the project, photography, copywriting, etc. All proposals should also include a disclaimer that prices and fees quoted are based on rough verbal specifications of the items listed. If the items change, fees will change accordingly.

Proposals, like the projects they reflect, are divided into parts. These parts include: *(l)* a description of design and production, *(2)* a description of fees, *(3)* a payment schedule for the phases of work involved, and *(4)* rights, usages and terms.

Defining and describing the phases for a project helps facilitate the billing process and insures that the work will not proceed to the next phase until payment is received according to agreed upon schedules. These check points also give clients very clear and tangible input at appropriate times as the project develops.

Parts and phases of a proposal

Part 1: Design and production: Phase l, design: describe the design phase of the project fully, including what form the design presentation will take, how many versions will be presented, the client approval process and the time schedule for this phase.

Phase 2, mechanical preparation: after approval of phase l, phase 2 will begin. Explain the production process including photography, copywriting, illustration, typesetting, proofreading and who will supervise, exact print/production time estimates, client approval schedules and time required.

Phase 3, final production: after client approval of previous phases, final production can begin. After release for final production, designate the supervision of this phase and the time required.

Part 2: Fees: Again, outline the project in briefer form than Part 1 and the fees required for design, copywriting, photography, illustration, etc. Clients sometimes request estimates for a variety of solutions to a design project. This is common practice and gives the client a choice of directions.

It is important at this stage to explain what these fees *do* include (i.e. design, mechanical, production, type specification, preliminary proofreading, etc.) and, more important, what they *do not* include (i.e., out-of-pocket expenses, author's alterations, overtime charges, photographic art direction, long distance travel, etc.). These non-fee expenses, including mark-ups, should be stated and estimates of charges should be included if possible.

When supplying production prices such as printing, be sure to state that these estimates are based on rough verbal specifications and are budget estimates only. More exact quotations can be furnished at such time as a comp or mechanicals are viewed by the printer.

Part 3, Payments: Next, outline a payment schedule: *Phase 1* —40 percent of design fees due on receipt of invoice and inception of project. *Phase 2*—30 percent of design fees and out-of-pocket expenses to-date, due on completion of phase and receipt of invoice. *Phase 3*—30 percent of design fees and balance of out-of-pocket expenses due on final delivery of completed project and receipt of invoice.

Part 4, Rights, usage and credit: Discuss usage, ownership of rights and artwork, credit lines, approvals and interest charged for late payments and any other terms deemed necessary. For clarification on these items, refer to the standard contracts in this book.

Signature lines for both client and artist, and date that the agreement is signed should follow. A signed original and copy should be retained by both parties.

All-Purpose Purchase Order

TO	COMMISSIONED BY
	DATE
	PURCHASE ORDER NUMBER

ASSIGNMENT DESCRIPTION

(remove all italics before using this form)

(indicate any preliminary presentations required by the buyer)

DELIVERY DATE	FEE

BUYER SHALL REIMBURSE ARTIST FOR THE FOLLOWING EXPENSES

RIGHTS TRANSFERRED. BUYER PURCHASES THE FOLLOWING EXCLUSIVE RIGHTS OF USAGE

TITLE OR PRODUCT	*(name)*
CATEGORY OF USE	*(advertising, corporate, promotional, editorial, etc.)*
MEDIUM OF USE	*(consumer or trade magazine, annual report, TV, book, etc.)*
EDITION (IF BOOK)	*(hardcover, mass market paperback, quality paperback, etc.)*
GEOGRAPHIC AREA	*(if applicable)*
TIME PERIOD	*(if applicable)*

ARTIST RESERVES ANY USAGE RIGHTS NOT EXPRESSLY TRANSFERRED. ANY USAGE BEYOND THAT GRANTED TO BUYER HEREIN SHALL REQUIRE THE PAYMENT OF A MUTUALLY AGREED UPON ADDITIONAL FEE. SUBJECT TO ALL TERMS ON REVERSE SIDE OF FORM.

Terms:

1. Time for Payment. All invoices shall be paid within thirty (30) days of receipt.

2. Changes. Buyer shall make additional payments for changes requested in original assignment. However, no additional payment shall be made for changes required to conform to the original assignment description. The Buyer shall offer the Artist first opportunity to make any changes.

3. Expenses. Buyer shall reimburse Artist for all expenses arising from this assignment, including the payment of any sales taxes due on this assignment. Buyer's approval shall be obtained for any increases in fees or expenses that exceed the original estimate by 10% or more.

4. Cancellation. In the event of cancellation of this assignment, ownership of all copyrights and the original artwork shall be retained by the Artist, and a cancellation fee for work completed, based on the contract price and expenses already incurred, shall be paid by the Buyer.

5. Ownership of Artwork. The Artist retains ownership of all original artwork, whether preliminary or final, and the Buyer shall return such artwork within thirty (30) days of use.

6. Credit Lines. The Buyer shall give Artist and any other creators a credit line with any editorial usage. If similar credit lines are to be given with other types of usage, it must be so indicated here:

_____

_____

_____

_____

☐ If this box is checked, the credit line shall be in the form:

©_____198____

7. Releases. Buyer shall indemnify Artist against all claims and expenses, including reasonable attorney's fees, due to uses for which no release was requested in writing or for uses which exceed authority granted by a release.

8. Modifications. Modification of the Agreement must be written, except that the invoice may include, and Buyer shall pay, fees or expenses that were orally authorized in order to progress promptly with the work.

9. Arbitration. Any disputes in excess of $_____ (maximum limit for small claims court) arising out of this Agreement shall be submitted to binding arbitration before the Joint Ethics Committee or a mutually agreed upon arbitrator pursuant to the rules of the American Arbitration Association. The Arbitrator's award shall be final, and judgment may be entered upon it in any court having jurisdiction thereof. The Buyer shall pay all arbitration and court costs, reasonable attorney's fees, and legal interest on any award or judgment in favor of the Artist.

_____
CONSENTED AND AGREED TO

_____
DATE

_____
ARTIST'S SIGNATURE

_____
COMPANY NAME

_____
AUTHORIZED SIGNATURE

_____
NAME AND TITLE

MEMBER

Artist-Agent Agreement

Agreement, this_____day of
_____, 19_____, between

_____
(hereinafter referred to as the
"Artist"), residing at

_____ ,

and_____ ,
(hereinafter referred to as the
"Agent" residing at

_____ .

Whereas, the Artist is an established artist of proven talents; and

Whereas, the Artist wishes to have an agent represent him or her in marketing certain rights enumerated herein; and

Whereas, the Agent is capable of marketing the artwork produced by the Artist; and

Whereas, the Agent wishes to represent the Artist;

Now, therefore, in consideration of the foregoing premises and the mutual covenants hereinafter set forth and other valuable consideration, the parties hereto agree as follows:

1. Agency. The Artist appoints the Agent to act as his or her exclusive representative: (A) in the following geographical area:

_____

_____

(B) for the markets listed here (specify publishing, advertising,etc.):

_____

_____

The Agent agrees to use his or her best efforts in submitting the Artist's work for the purpose of securing assignment for the Artist. The Agent shall negotiate the terms of any assignment that is offered, but the Artist shall have the right to reject any assignment if he or she finds the terms thereof unacceptable.

2. Promotion. The Artist shall provide the Agent with such samples of work as are from time to time necessary for the purpose of securing assignments. These samples shall remain the property of the Artist and be returned on Termination of this Agreement. The Agent shall take reasonable efforts to protect the work from loss or damage, but shall be liable for such loss or damage only if caused by the Agent's negligence. Promotional expenses, including but not limited to promotional mailings and paid advertising, shall be paid _____% by the Agent and _____% by the Artist. The Agent shall bear the expenses of shipping, insurance, and similar marketing expenses.

3. Term. This Agreement shall take effect on the_____day of _____, 19_____, and remain in full force and effect for a term of one year, unless terminated as provided in Paragraph 9.

4. Commissions. The Agent shall be entitled to the following commissions: (A) On assignments incurred by the Agent during the term of this Agreement, twenty-five (25%) percent of the billing. (B) On house accounts, ten (10%) percent of the billing. For purposes of this Agreement, *house accounts* are defined as accounts obtained by the Artist at any time or obtained by another agent representing the Artist prior to the commencement of this Agreement and are listed in Schedule A attached to this Agreement.

It is understood by both parties that no commissions shall be paid on assignments rejected by the Artist or for which the Artist fails to receive payment, regardless of the reason payment is not made. Further, no commissions shall be payable in either (A) or (B) above for any part of the billing that is due to expenses incurred by the Artist in performing the assignment, whether or not such expenses are reimbursed by the client. In the event that a flat fee is paid by the client, it shall be reduced by the amount of expenses incurred by the Artist in performing the assignment, and the Agent's commission shall be payable only on the fee as reduced for expenses.

5. Billing. The ☐Artist ☐Agent shall be responsible for all billings.

6., Payments The Party responsible for billing shall make all payments due within ten (10) days of receipt of any fees covered by this Agreement. Late payments shall be accompanied by interest calculated at the rate of_____% per month thereafter.

7. Accountings. The party responsible for billing shall send copies of invoices to the other party when rendered. If requested, that party shall also provide the other party with semi-annual accountings showing all assignments for the period, the clients' names, the fees paid, expenses incurred by the Artist, the dates of payment, the amounts on which the Agent's commissions are to be calculated, and the sums due less those amounts already paid.

8. Inspection of the books and records. The party responsible for the billing shall keep the books and records with repect to commissions due at his or her place of business and permit the other party to inspect these books and records during normal business hours on the giving of reasonable notice.

9. Termination. This Agreement may be terminated by either party by giving thirty (30) days written notice to the other party. If the Artist receives assignments after the termination date from clients originally obtained by the Agent during the term of this Agreement, the commission specified in Paragraph 4(A) shall be payable to the Agent under the following circumstances. If the Agent has represented the Artist for six months or less, the Agent shall receive a commission on such assignments received by the Artist within ninety (90) days of the date of termination. This period shall increase by thirty (30) days for each additional six months that the Agent has represented the Artist, but in no event shall such period exceed one hundred eighty (180) days.

10.Assignment. This Agreement shall not be assigned by either of the parties hereto. It shall be binding on and inure to the benefit of the successors, administrators, executors, or heirs of the Agent and Artist.

11. Arbitration. Any disputes arising under this Agreement shall be settled by arbitration under the rules of the American Arbitration

Association in the City of

_____

Any award rendered by the arbitrator may be entered in any court having jurisdiction thereof.

12. Notices. All notices shall be given to the parties at their respective addresses set forth above.

13. Independent Contractor Status. Both parties agree that the Agent is acting as an independent contractor. This Agreement is not an employment agreement, nor does it constitute a joint venture or partnership between the Artist and Agent.

14. Amendments and merger. All amendments to this Agreement must be written. This Agreement incorporates the entire understanding of the parties.

15. Governing Law. This Agreement shall be governed by the laws of the State of

_____

In witness whereof, the parties have signed this Agreement as of the date set forth above.

SCHEDULE A: HOUSE ACCOUNTS	
DATE	*(remove all italics before using this form)*
1.	*(name and address of client)*
2.	
3.	
4.	
5.	
6.	
7.	
8.	
9.	

_____
ARTIST

_____
AGENT

MEMBER

Needleart Designer's Confirmation/Invoice Form

PRIMARY CLIENT	DATE
	COMMISSIONED BY
	TITLE

CONTRIBUTING CLIENT	COMMISSIONED BY
	TITLE

DELIVERY DATE	
THIS DELIVERY DATE IS PREDICATED UPON RECEIPT OF ALL MATERIALS TO BE SUPPLIED BY CLIENT(S)	
MATERIALS SUPPLIED BY	
PUBLICATION DATE	

ASSIGNMENT DESCRIPTION

(remove all italics before using this form)

(Describe each item in terms of

technique, design, size, material, coloration, complexity

and instructions required for duplication)

FEES	PRIMARY CLIENT	CONTRIBUTING CLIENT
FIRST NORTH AMERICAN REPRODUCTION RIGHTS	*(list figures in column)*	*(list figures in column)*
OTHER REPRODUCTION RIGHTS		
	(remove all italics before using this form)	
OTHER USES OR RIGHTS	*(list figures in column)*	*(list figures in column)*
CLIENT RETENTION OF COMPLETED PROJECTS	*(list figures in column)*	*(list figures in column)*
MATERIALS AND SUPPLIES	*(list figures in column)*	*(list figures in column)*
ADDITIONAL EXPENSES	*(list figures in column)*	*(list figures in column)*
	(toll telephones, transportation and travel, shipping and insurance)	
SUBTOTAL		
SALES TAX		
TOTAL		

ARTIST RESERVES ANY USAGE RIGHTS NOT EXPRESSLY TRANSFERRED. ANY USAGE BEYOND THAT GRANTED TO BUYER HEREIN REQUIRES THE PAYMENT OF A MUTUALLY AGREED UPON ADDITIONAL FEE. SUBJECT TO ALL TERMS ON SECOND SHEET OF FORM.

Terms:

1. Publication rights. The negotiated fee (unless specified otherwise below) is for first North American reproduction rights only for photographs of each project and instructions for their execution. All other rights, including copyright, are retained by the Artist. If publication does not take place within one year of delivery of the design, all rights granted hereunder revert to the Artist.
Other rights:

_____

_____

2. Name credit. On any contribution for magazine or book use, the Artist shall receive name credit in print. If name credit is to be given with other types of use, it must be specified here:

_____

_____

3. Return of projects and borrowing privileges. The negotiated fee assumes that the project(s) remains the property of the Artist and is to be returned to the Artist within_____months following photography. If the Client desires to retain the project(s), an additional fee of_____dollars will be charged.

The Client has the right to borrow a project on a short-term basis, for dislay promotion purposes only, for a period of _____months from the project's date of publication, and for a fee of_____dollars each time. The Artist shall receive name credit as the designer on all promotional displays of the project. All transportation costs for the pickup and return of the project to the Artist will be borne by the borrower.

The Artist shall be reimbursed by the Client for the replacement value of the artwork if the Client loses, damages, or fails to return a project. This reimbursement payment is in addition to the nego-

tiated project fee(s) and will be _____dollars.

4. Materials purchase. Should the Artist be required to purchase materials for a project, unless specified otherwise, the Artist will submit these bills to the Client for reimbursement. These charges are subject to the same payment terms as the negotiated fee.

5. Proof of publication. When a project is published, the Artist shall receive_____tearsheets and/or _____ copies of the magazine as proof of publication.

6. Project cancellation. Work cancelled by the Client while in progress shall be compensated for on the basis of work completed at the time of cancellation and assumes that the Artist retains the project, whatever its stage of completion. Upon cancellation, all rights, publication and other, revert to the Artist. If the negotiated fee is to be paid by both Client and "Secondary Source," the Client is obligated to pay the Artist's total cancellation fee.

7. Project revisions. Any changes in a project that require additional work on the part of the Artist, and are not the result of an error by the Artist, require supplementary confirmation in writing and additional compensation to the Artist, to be specified at the time.

Any changes in a project, due to an error on the part of Artist, require no additional compensation to the Artist.

8. Projects used for publication covers. Should the photograph of a project be used as a publication cover, an additional fee of _____dollars will be charged. This fee will be billed at the time of the cover decision and is subject to the same payment terms as the original fee.

9. Right to timely publication. Since

most design projects are subject to trends within the marketplace, the Artist is guaranteed the right of timely publication. If a project is not photographed within six months of its delivery, it is assumed that the project is cancelled, and that all rights to the project revert to the Artist, with no cost or penalty to the Artist. Further, should the design not be published within one year of its date of delivery, it is assumed that the project is cancelled and all rights to the design revert to the Artist, with no cost or penalty to the Artist.

10. Multiple billing. If the Artist's Client is a publication, but the Artist's fee is to be paid by both the publication and a contributing manufacturer, it is the responsibility of the publication, unless the Artist chooses to assume this responsibility, to negotiate the Artist's fee with the manufacturer and arrange for prompt payment of this fee in accordance with the Artist's payment terms for the publication.
☐ If this box is checked, the Artist shall receive copyright notice adjacent to the work in the form:

© _____ 198____.

11. Unauthorized use. Client will indemnify Artist against all claims and expenses, including reasonable attorney's fees, due to uses for which no release was requested in writing or for uses which exceed authority granted by a release.

12. Modifications. Modification of the Agreement must be written,except that the invoice may include, and Client shall be obligated to pay, fees or expenses that were orally authorized in order to progress promptly with the work.

13. Arbitration. Any disputes in excess of $_____(maximum small claims court limit) arising out of this Agreement shall be submitted to binding arbitration before the Joint Ethics Committee or a mutually agreed upon arbitrator pursuant to the rules of the American Arbitration Associaton. The Arbitrator's award shall be final and judgment may be entered upon it in any court having jurisdiction thereof. The Client shall pay all arbitration and court costs, reasonable attorney's fees, and legal interest on any award or judgment in favor of the Artist.

14. The above terms incorporate Article 2 of the Uniform Commercial Code. If not objected to within ten (10) days, these terms shall be deemed accepted.

15. The Client and Artist agree to comply with all the provisions of the Joint Code of Ethics, a copy of which may be obtained from the Joint Ethics Committee, P.O. Box 179, Grand Central Station, New York, New York 10017.

CONSENTED AND AGREED TO

DATE

ARTIST'S SIGNATURE

COMPANY NAME

AUTHORIZED SIGNATURE

NAME AND TITLE

MEMBER

Illustrator's Confirmation of Engagement

TO	DATE
	AUTHORIZED ART BUYER
	ILLUSTRATOR'S JOB NUMBER
	CLIENT'S JOB NUMBER

ASSIGNMENT DESCRIPTION

DELIVERY SCHEDULE

FEE (PAYMENT SCHEDULE)

ADDITIONAL ESTIMATED EXPENSES

CANCELLATION FEE (PERCENTAGE OF FEE)

BEFORE SKETCHES

AFTER SKETCHES

AFTER FINISH

RIGHTS TRANSFERRED (ALL OTHER RIGHTS RESERVED BY THE ILLUSTRATOR)	
FOR USE IN MAGAZINES AND NEWSPAPERS, FIRST NORTH AMERICAN REPRODUCTION RIGHTS UNLESS SPECIFIED OTHERWISE HERE	
	(remove all italics before using this form)
FOR ALL OTHER USES, THE CLIENT ACQUIRES ONLY THE FOLLOWING RIGHTS	
TITLE OR PRODUCT	*(name)*
CATEGORY OF USE	*(advertising, corporate, promotional, editorial, etc.)*
MEDIUM OF USE	*(consumer or trade magazine, annual report, TV, book, etc.)*
GEOGRAPHIC AREA	*(if applicable)*
TIME PERIOD	*(if applicable)*
NUMBER OF USES	*(if applicable)*
OTHER	*(if applicable)*
ORIGINAL ARTWORK, INCLUDING SKETCHES AND ANY OTHER PRELIMINARY MATERIAL, REMAINS THE PROPERTY OF THE ILLUSTRATOR UNLESS PURCHASED BY A PAYMENT OF A SEPARATE FEE.	

Terms:

1. Time for Payment. Payment is due within thirty (30) days of receipt of invoice. A 1½% monthly service charge will be billed for late payment. Any advances or partial payments shall be indicated under Payment Schedule on front.

2. Default in Payment. The Client shall assume responsibility for all collection and legal fees necessitated by default in payment.

3. Grant of Rights. The grant of reproduction rights is conditioned on receipt of payment.

4. Expenses. The Client shall reimburse the Illustrator for all expenses arising from the assignment.

5. Sales Tax. The client shall be responsible for the payment of sales tax, if any such tax is due.

6. Cancellation. In the event of cancellation or breach by the Client, the Illustrator shall retain ownership of all rights of copyright and the original artwork, including sketches and any other preliminary materials.

7. Revisions. Revisions not due to the fault of the Illustrator shall be billed separately.

8. Credit Lines. On any contribution for magazine or book use, the Illustrator shall receive name credit in print. If name credit is to be given with other types of use, it must be specified here:

_____

_____

☐ If this box is checked by the Illustrator, the Illustrator shall receive copyright notice adjacent to the work in the form:
©_____198_____

9. Return of Artwork. Client assumes responsibility for the return of the artwork in undamaged condition within thirty (30) days of first reproduction.

10. Unauthorized Use. Client will indemnify Illustrator against all claims and expenses, including reasonable attorney's fees, arising from uses for which no release was requested in writing or for uses which exceed the authority granted by a release.

11. Arbitration. Any disputes in excess of $_____ (maximum limit for small claims court) arising out of this Agreement shall be submitted to binding arbitration before the Joint Ethics Committee as a mutually agreed upon arbitrator pursuant to the rules of the American Arbitration Association. The Arbitrator's award shall be final, and judgment may be entered upon it in any court having jursidiction thereof. The client shall pay all arbitration and court costs, reasonable attorney's fees and legal interest on any award or judgment in favor of the Illustrator

12. Acceptance of Terms. If the terms of this confirmation are not objected to within ten (10) days of receipt, the terms shall be deemed accepted.

_____

CONSENTED AND AGREED TO

_____

DATE

_____

ILLUSTRATOR'S SIGNATURE

_____

COMPANY NAME

_____

AUTHORIZED SIGNATURE

_____

NAME AND TITLE

MEMBER

Illustrator's Invoice

FRONT: ILLUSTRATOR'S LETTERHEAD

TO	DATE
	AUTHORIZED ART BUYER
	ILLUSTRATOR'S JOB NUMBER
	CLIENT'S JOB NUMBER

ASSIGNMENT DESCRIPTION	
	FEE

ITEMIZED EXPENSES (OTHER BILLABLE ITEMS)	
CLIENT'S ALTERATIONS	
SALE OF ORIGINAL ART	
MISCELLANEOUS	
	TOTAL
	SALES TAX
	PAYMENTS ON ACCOUNT
	BALANCE DUE

ORIGINAL ARTWORK, INCLUDING SKETCHES AND ANY OTHER PRELIMINARY MATERIALS, REMAIN THE PROPERTY OF THE ILLUSTRATOR UNLESS PURCHASED BY PAYMENT OF A SEPARATE FEE SUBJECT TO TERMS APPEARING ON REVERSE SIDE.

RIGHTS TRANSFERRED (ALL OTHER RIGHTS RESERVED BY THE ILLUSTRATOR)	
FOR USE IN MAGAZINES AND NEWSPAPERS, FIRST NORTH AMERICAN REPRODUCTION RIGHTS UNLESS SPECIFIED OTHERWISE HERE	
(remove all italics before using this form)	
FOR ALL OTHER USES, THE CLIENT ACQUIRES ONLY THE FOLLOWING RIGHTS	
TITLE OR PRODUCT	*(name)*
CATEGORY OF USE	*(advertising, corporate, promotional, editorial, etc.)*
MEDIUM OF USE	*(consumer or trade magazine, annual report, TV, book, etc.)*
GEOGRAPHIC AREA	*(if applicable)*
TIME PERIOD	*(if applicable)*
NUMBER OF USES	*(if applicable)*
OTHER	*(if applicable)*
ORIGINAL ARTWORK, INCLUDING SKETCHES AND ANY OTHER PRELIMINARY MATERIAL, REMAINS THE PROPERTY OF THE ILLUSTRATOR UNLESS PURCHASED BY A PAYMENT OF A SEPARATE FEE.	

Terms:

1. Time for Payment. Payment is due within thirty (30) days of receipt of invoice. A 1½ % monthly service charge will be billed for late payment.

2. Default in Payment. The client shall assume responsibility for all collection and legal fees necessitated by default in payment.

3. Grant of Rights. The grant of reproduction rights is conditioned on receipt of payment.

4. Credit Lines. On any contribution for magazine or book use, the Illustrator shall receive name credit in print. If name credit is to be given with other types of use, it must be specified here:

_____

☐ If this box is checked by the Illustrator, the Illustrator shall receive copyright notice adjacent to the work in the form
©_____ 198_____

5. Additional Limitations. If Illustrator and Client have agreed to additional limitations as to either the duration or geographical extent of the permitted use, specify here:

_____

6. Return of Artwork. Client assumes responsibility for the return of the artwork in undamaged condition within thirty (30) days of first reproduction.

7. Unauthorized Use. Client will indemnify Illustrator against all claims and expenses, including reasonable attorney's fees, arising from uses for which no release was requested in writing or for uses which exceed the authority granted by a release.

8. Arbitration. Any disputes in excess of $_____ (maximum limit for small claims court) arising out of this Agreement shall be submitted to binding arbitration before the Joint Ethics Committee or a mutually agreed upon arbitrator pursuant to the rules of the American Arbitration Association. The Arbitrator's award shall be final, and judgment upon it may be entered upon it in any court having jurisdiction thereof. The client shall pay all arbitration and court costs, reasonable attorney's fees, and legal interest on any award or judgment in favor of the Illustrator.

9. Acceptance of Terms. If the terms of this invoice are not objected to within ten (10) days of receipt, the terms shall be deemed accepted.

MEMBER

Magazine Purchase Order for Illustrators

This letter is to serve as our contract for you to create certain illustrations for us under the terms described herein.

1. Job Description. We, the Magazine, retain you, the Illustrator, to create_____Illustrations(s) described as follows (indicate if sketches are required):

_____

_____

_____

to be delivered to the Magazine by

_____ 19__, for publication in our magazine

titled _____ .

2. Grant of Rights. Illustrator hereby agrees to transfer to the Magazine first North American magazine rights in the illustrations. All rights not expressly transferred to the Magazine hereunder are reserved to the Illustrator.

3. Price. The Magazine agrees to pay Illustrator the following purchase price: $_____ in full consideration for Illustrator's grant of rights to Magazine.

4. Changes. The Illustrator shall be given the first option to make any changes in the work that the Magazine may deem necessary. However, no additional compensation shall be paid unless such changes are necessitated by error on the Magazine's part, in which case a new contract between us shall be entered into on mutually agreeable terms to cover changes to be done by the Illustrator.

5. Cancellation. If, prior to the Illustrator's completion of finishes, the Magazine cancels the assignment either because the illustrations are unsatisfactory to the Magazine or for any other reason, the Magazine agrees to pay the Illustrator a cancellation fee of 50% of the purchase price. If, after the Illustrator's completion of finishes, the Magazine cancels the assignment, the Magazine agrees to pay 50% of the purchase price if cancellation is due to the illustrations not being reasonably satisfactory and 100% of the purchase price if cancellation is due to any other cause. In the event of cancellation, the Illustrator shall retain ownership of all artwork and rights of copyright, but the Illustrator agrees to show the Magazine the artwork if the Magazine so requests so that the Magazine may make its own evaluation as to degree of completion of the artwork.

6. Copyright Notice and Authorship Credit. Copyright notice shall appear in the Illustrator's name with the contribution. The illustrator shall have the right to receive authorship credit for the illustration and to have such credit removed if the Illustrator so desires due to changes made by the Magazine that are unsatisfactory to the Illustrator.

7. Payments. Payment shall be made within thirty (30) days of the billing date.

8. Ownership of Artwork. The Illustrator shall retain ownership of all original artwork and the Magazine shall return such artwork within thirty (30) days of publication.

To constitute this a binding agreement between us, please sign both copies of this letter beneath the words "Consented and Agreed to" and return one copy to the Magazine for its files.

CONSENTED AND AGREED TO
_____

DATE
_____

ARTIST'S SIGNATURE
_____

MAGAZINE
_____

AUTHORIZED SIGNATURE
_____

NAME AND TITLE

MEMBER

Textile Designer's Holding Form

TO	DATE

NUMBER OF DESIGNS HELD	
DESIGN I.D. NUMBER	SKETCH PRICE
DESIGN I.D. NUMBER	SKETCH PRICE
DESIGN I.D. NUMBER	SKETCH PRICE
DESIGN I.D. NUMBER	SKETCH PRICE
DESIGN I.D. NUMBER	SKETCH PRICE
DESIGN I.D. NUMBER	SKETCH PRICE
DESIGN I.D. NUMBER	SKETCH PRICE

Terms:

The submitted designs are original and protected under the copyright laws of the United States, Title 17 United States Code. These designs are submitted to you in confidence and on the following terms:

1. Ownership and Copyrights. You agree not to copy, photograph, or modify directly or indirectly any of the materials held by you, nor will permit any third party to do any of the foregoing. All artwork, photographs, and photostats developed from these designs, including the copyrights therein, remain my property and must be returned to me unless the designs are purchased by you.

2. Responsibility for Artwork. You agree to assume responsibility for loss, theft, or any damage to the designs while they are being held by you. It is agreed that the fair market value of each design is the price specified above.

3. Holding of Artwork. You agree to hold these designs for a period not to exceed _____ working days from the above date. Any holding of artwork beyond that period shall constitute a binding sale at the price specified above. You further agree not to allow any third party to hold designs unless specifically approved by me.

4. Arbitration. All disputes in excess of $_____ (maximum limit for small claims court) arising out of this agreement shall be submitted to binding arbitration before the Joint Ethics Committee or a mutually agreed upon arbitrator pursuant to the rules of the American Arbitration Association. The Arbitrator's award shall be final, and judgment may be entered upon it in any court having jursidiction thereof. The party holding the designs shall pay all arbitration and court costs, reasonable attorney's fees, and legal interest on any award or judgment in favor of the Textile Designer.

5. The above terms incorporate Article 2 of the Uniform Commercial Code.

CONSENTED AND AGREED TO

_____
DATE

_____
DESIGNER'S SIGNATURE

_____
COMPANY NAME

_____
AUTHORIZED SIGNATURE

_____
NAME AND TITLE

MEMBER
TEXTILE DESIGNERS
GUILD

A DISCIPLINE OF
THE GRAPHIC ARTISTS
GUILD

Textile Designer's Confirmation Form

TO	DATE
	PATTERN NUMBER
	DUE DATE

ESTIMATED PRICES	
SKETCH	
REPEAT	
COLORINGS	
CORNERS	
TRACINGS	
OTHER	

DESCRIPTION OF ARTWORK		
REPEAT SIZE		
COLORS		
TYPE OF PRINTING		
½ DROP	☐ YES	☐ NO

SPECIAL COMMENTS

Terms:

1. Time for Payment. Because the major portion of the above work represents labor, all invoices are payable fifteen (15) days net. A 1½% monthly service charge is payable on all unpaid balances after this period. The grant of textile usage rights is conditioned on receipt of payment.

2. Estimated Prices. Prices shown above are minimum estimates only. Final prices shall be shown in invoice.

3. Payment for Changes. Client shall be responsible for making additional payments for changes requested by Client in original assignment.

4. Expenses. Client shall be responsible for payment of all extra expenses arising from assignment, including but not limited to photostats, mailings, messengers, shipping charges, and shipping insurance.

5. Sales Tax. Client shall assume responsibility for all sales taxes due on this assignment.

6. Cancellation Fees. Work cancelled by the client while in progress shall be compensated for on the basis of work completed at the time of cancellation and assumes that the Designer retains the project whatever its stage of completion. Upon cancellation, all rights, publication and other, revert to the Designer. Where Designer creates corners which are not developed into purchased sketches, a labor fee will be charged, and ownership of all copyrights and artwork is retained by the Designer.

7. Insuring Artwork. The client agrees when shipping artwork to provide insurance covering the fair market value of the artwork.

8. Arbitration. Any disputes in excess of $_____ (maximum limit for small claims court) arising out of this agreement shall be submitted to binding arbitration before the Joint Ethics Committee or a mutually agreed upon arbitrator pursuant to the rules of the American Arbitration Association. The Arbitrator's award shall be final, and judgment may be entered upon it in any court having jurisdiction thereof. The Client shall pay all arbitration and court costs, reasonable attorney's fees, and legal interest on any award or judgment in favor of the Designer.

9. The above terms incorporate Article 2 of the Uniform Commercial Code.

CONSENTED AND AGREED TO
_____

DATE
_____

DESIGNER'S SIGNATURE
_____

COMPANY NAME
_____

AUTHORIZED SIGNATURE
_____

NAME AND TITLE
_____

Textile Designer's Invoice

TO	DATE
	INVOICE NUMBER
	PURCHASE ORDER NUMBER
	STYLIST
	DESIGNER

PATTERN NUMBER	DESCRIPTION	PRICE
		SUBTOTAL

ITEMIZED EXPENSES	
	SUBTOTAL
	TOTAL
	SALES TAX
	TOTAL DUE

Terms:

1. Receipt of Artwork. Client acknowledges receipt of the artwork specified above.

2. Time for Payment. Because the major portion of the above work represents labor, all invoices are payable fifteen (15) days net. The grant of textile usage rights is conditioned on receipt of payment. A 1½% monthly service charge is payable on unpaid balance after expiration of period for payment.

3. Adjustments to Invoice. Client agrees to request any adjustments of accounts, terms, or other invoice data within ten (10) days of receipt of the invoice. These terms incorporate Article 2 of the Uniform Commercial Code.

4. Arbitration. All disputes in excess of $_____ (maximum limit for small claims court) arising out of this agreement shall be submitted to binding arbitration before the Joint Ethics Committee or a mutually agreed upon arbitrator pursuant to the rules of the American Arbitration Association. The Arbitrator's award shall be final, and judgment may be entered upon it in any court having jursidiction thereof. The Client shall pay all arbitration and court costs, reasonable attorney's fees, and legal interest on any award or judgment in favor of the Designer.

_____
CONSENTED AND AGREED TO

_____
DATE

_____
DESIGNER'S SIGNATURE

_____
COMPANY NAME

_____
AUTHORIZED SIGNATURE

_____
NAME AND TITLE

Introduction: Textile Designer-Agent Agreement

The Textile Designer-Agent Agreement has been drafted by the Steering Committee of the Textile Designers Guild in consultation with the Graphic Artists Guild's General Counsel. It seeks to clarify Designer-Agent Relationships by providing a written understanding to which both parties can refer. Its terms are not immutable and can be modified to meet the special needs of either Designer or Agent. The Agreement has been drafted with a minimum of legal jargon, but this in no way changes its legal validity.

The Agreement balances the needs of both Designer and Agent. The agency in Paragraph 1 is limited to a particular market. In that market the Agent has exclusive rights to act as an agent, but the Designer remains free to sell in that market also (except to accounts secured by the Agent). Because both Agent and Designer will be selling in the same market, the Designer may want to provide the agent with a list of clients previously obtained by the Designer and keep this list up to date.

If the Agent desires greater exclusivity—such as covering more markets—the Designer may want to require that the Agent exercise best efforts (although it is difficult to prove best efforts have not been exercised) and perhaps promise a mimimum level of sales. If the level is not met, the Agreement would terminate.

Paragraph 2 seeks to protect the Designer against loss or damage to his or her artwork, in part by requiring the Agent to execute with the client contracts that protect the designs.

Paragraph 3 sets forth the duration of the Agreement. A short term is usually wise, since a Designer and Agent who are working well together can simply extend the term by mutual agreement in order to continue their relationship. Also, as time goes on, the Designer may be in a better position to negotiate with the Agent. The term of the Agreement has less importance, however, when either party can terminate the agency relationship on thirty days notice as Paragraph 10 provides.

The minimum base prices in Paragraph 4 ensure the Designer of a minimum remuneration. Flexibility in pricing requires that the Designer and Agent consult one another in those cases in which a particular sale justifies a price higher than the base price. The Designer can suggest that the Agent follow the Graphic Artists Guild's *Pricing and Ethical Guidelines* to establish the minimum base price.

The Agent's rate of commission in Paragraph 5 is left blank so the parties can establish an acceptable rate. If the Designer is not paid for doing an assignment, the Agent will have no right to receive a commission. Nor are commissions payable on the amount of expenses incurred by the Designer for work done on assignment (as opposed to work done on speculation). Discounts given by the Agent on volume sales of the work of many designers shall be paid out of the Agent's commission.

Optional provisions

Additional provisions could be used to govern certain aspects of the Designer-Agent relationship. Such provisions might include:

The scope of the agency set forth in Paragraph 1 is limited to the following geographic area:

_____

Despite any provisions of Paragraph 1 to the contrary, this agency shall be nonexclusive and the Designer shall have the right to use other Agents without any obligation to pay commissions under this Agreement.

The Agent agrees to represent no more than _____ designers.

The Agent agrees not to represent conflicting hands, such hands being designers who work in a similar style to that of the Designer.

The Agent agrees to have no designers as salaried employees.

The Agent agrees not to sell designs from his or her own collection of designs while representing the Designer.

The Agent agrees to employ _____ full time and _____ part time sales people.

The Agent agrees that the Designer's name shall appear on all artwork by the Designer that is included in the Agent's portfolio.

The Agent agrees to seek royalties for the Designer in the following situations:

_____

The Agent agrees to hold all funds due to the Designer as trust funds in an account separate from funds of the Agent prior to making payment to the Designer pursuant to Paragraph 8 hereof.

Additional provisions

Or the additional provisions might be requirements for terms that the Agent must obtain from the client, such as:

The Agent agrees to enter into a written contract with each client that shall include the following provision:

Credit line for designer: The designer shall have the right to receive authorship credit ; for his or her design and to have such credit removed in the event changes made by the client are unsatisfactory to the designer. Such authorship credit shall appear as follows on the selvage of the fabric:

_____

☐ If this box is checked, such authorship credit shall also accompany any advertising for the fabric:

_____

Copyright notice for designer: Copyright notice shall appear in the Designer's name on the selvage of the fabric, the form of notice being as follows:

© _____ 19_____ .

The placement and affixation of the notice shall comply with the regulations issued by the Register of Copyrights. The grant of right in this design is expressly conditioned on copyright notice appearing in the Designer's name.

☐ If this box is checked, such copyright notice shall also accompany any advertising for the fabric.

Paragraph 6 covers the Agent's obligations when commissioned work is obtained for the Designer. Of particular importance are the terms of the order form secured by the Agent from the client. The Agent is required to use the order form developed by the Textile Designers Guild or a form incorporating similar terms.

Holding of designs by clients can present a problem which Paragraph 7 seeks to resolve by establishing a maximum holding time of five working days. Again, the Agent is required to use the holding form developed by the Textile Designers Guild or a form with similar terms.

In Paragraph 8 the Agent assumes responsibility for billing and pursuing payments which are not made promptly. The reason for keeping any single billing under the maximum allowed for suit in small claims court is to make it easier to collect if a lawsuit is necessary. The Agent is required to use the invoice form of the Textile Designers Guild or a form with similar provisions.

Paragraph 9 allows the Designer to inspect the Agent's books to ensure that proper payments are being made.

Termination is permitted on giving thirty days written notice to the other party. Paragraph 10 distinguishes between sales made or assignment obtained prior to termination (on which the Agent must be paid a commission, even if the work is executed and payment received after the termination date) and those after termination (on which no commission is payable). Within thirty days of notice of termination, all designs must be returned to the Designer.

Paragraph 11 provides that the Agreement coannot be assigned by either party since the relationship between Designer and Agent is a personal one.

In Paragraph 12, arbitration is provided for disputes in excess of the maximum limit for suits in small claims court. For amounts within the small claims court limit, it is probably easier to simply sue rather than seek arbitration.

The manner of giving notice to the parties is described in Paragraph 13.

Paragraph 14 affirms that both Designer and Agent are independent contractors, which avoids certain tax and liability issues that might arise from the other legal relationships mentioned.

This Agreement is the entire understanding of the parties and can only be amended in writing. In stating this, Paragraph 15 points out a general rule that a written contract should always be amended in writing that is signed by both parties.

Paragraph 16 leaves room for the parties to add in any optional provisions that they consider necessary. Some of the optional provisions that might be agreed to appear under Optional Provisions below.

Finally, Paragraph 17 sets forth the state whose law will govern the Agreement. This is usually the law of the state in which both parties reside or, if one party is out of state, in which the bulk of the business will be transacted.

Textile Designer-Agent Agreement

Agreement, this_____day of
_____, 19_____, between
_____
(hereinafter referred to as the
"Designer"), residing at:
_____
_____ ,
and_____
(hereinafter referred to as the
"Agent"), residing at:

_____
_____ .

Whereas, the Designer is a professional textile designer; and
Whereas, the Designer wishes to have an Agent represent him or her in marketing certain rights enumerated herein; and
Whereas, the Agent is capable of marketing the artwork produced by the Designer, and
Whereas, the Agent wishes to represent the Designer;
Now, therefore, in consideration of the foregoing premises and the mutual covenants hereinafter set forth and other valuable consideration, the parties hereto agree as follows:

1. Agency. The Designer appoints the Agent to act as his or her representative for:
☐Sale of textile designs in apparel market,
☐Sale of textile designs in home furnishing market,
☐Securing of service work in apparel market. Service work is defined to include repeats and colorings on designs originated by the Designer or other designers,
☐Securing of service work in home furnishing market
☐Other_____
_____
_____

The Agent agrees to use his or her best efforts in submitting the Designer's artwork for the purpose of making sales or securing assignments for the Designer. For the purposes of this Agreement, the term *artwork* shall be defined to include designs, repeats, colorings, and any other product of the Designer's effort. The Agent shall negotiate the terms of any assignment that is offered, but the Designer shall have the right to reject any assignment if he or she finds the terms unacceptable. Nothing

contained herein shall prevent the Designer from making sales or securing work for his or her own account without liability for commissions except for accounts which have been secured for the Designer by the Agent. This limitation extends only for the period of time that the Agent represents the Designer. Further, the Designer agrees, when selling his or her artwork or taking orders, not to accept a price which is under the price structure of his or her Agent.
After a period of _____ months, the Designer may remove his or her unsold artwork from the Agent's portfolio to do with as the Designer wishes.

2. Artwork and Risk of Loss, Theft or Damage. All artwork submitted to the Agent for sale or for the purpose of securing work shall remain the property of the Designer. The Agent shall issue a receipt to the Designer for all artwork which the Designer submits to the Agent. If artwork is lost, stolen, or damaged while in the Agent's possession due to the Agent's failure to exercise reasonable care, the Agent will be held liable for the value of the artwork. Proof of any loss, theft, or damage must be furnished by the Agent to the Designer upon request. When selling artwork, taking an order, or allowing a client to hold artwork for consideration, the Agent agrees to use invoice, order, or holding forms which provide that the client is responsible for loss, theft, or damage to artwork while being held by the client, and to require the client's signature on such forms. The Agent agrees to enforce these provisions, including taking legal action as necessary. If the Agent undertakes legal action, any recovery shall first be used to reimburse the amount of attorney's fees and other expenses incurred and the balance of the recovery shall be divided between Agent and Designer in the respective percentages set forth in Paragraph 5. If the Agent chooses not to require the client to be responsible as described herein, then the Agent agrees to assume these responsibilities. If the Agent receives in-

surance proceeds due to loss, theft, or damage of artwork while in the Agent's or a client's possession, the Designer shall receive no less than that portion of the proceeds that have been paid for the Designer's artwork.

3. Term. This Agreement shall take effect on the_____day of _____19_____, and remain in full force and effect for a term of one year, unless terminated as provided in Paragraph 10.

4. Prices. At this time the minimum base prices charged to clients by the Agent are as follows:
Sketch (apparel market):
_____
Repeat (apparel market):
_____
Colorings (apparel market):
_____
Sketch (home furnishing market):
_____
Repeat (home furnishing market):
_____
Colorings (home furnishing market):
_____
Other:
_____

The Agent agrees that these prices are minimum prices only and shall be increased whenever possible as the work become larger or more complicated than is usual. Higher prices shall also be charged for rush jobs, whenever possible. The Agent also agrees to try to raise the base price to keep pace with the rate of inflation. The Agent shall obtain the Designer's written consent prior to entering into any contracts for payment by royalty.
No discounts shall be offered to clients by the Agent without first consulting the Designer.
When leaving a design with the Agent for possible sale, the Designer shall agree with the Agent as to the price to be charged if the design should bring more than the Agent's base price.

5. Agent's Commissions. The rate of commission for all artwork shall be_____. It is mutually agreed by both parties that no commissions shall be paid on assignments rejected by the Designer or for which the Designer does not receive payment, regardless of the reasons payment is not made.

On commissioned originals and service work, expenses incurred in the execution of a job, such as photostats, shipping, etc. shall be billed to the client in addition to the fee. No Agent's commission shall be paid on these amounts. In the event that a flat fee is paid by the client, it shall be reduced by the amount of expenses incurred by the Designer in performing the assignment, and the Agent's commission shall be payable only on the fee as reduced for expenses. It is mutually agreed that if the Agent offers a client a discount on a large group of designs including work of other designers, then that discount will come out of the Agent's commission since the Agent is the party who benefits from this volume.

6. Commissioned Work. Commissioned work refers to all artwork done on a nonspeculative basis. The Agent shall provide the Designer with a copy of the completed order form which the client has signed. The order form shall set forth the responsibilities of the client in ordering and purchasing artwork. To this the Agent shall add the date by which the artwork must be completed and any additional instructions which the Agent feels are necessary to complete the job to the client's satisfaction. The Agent will sign these instructions. Any changes in the original instructions must be in writing, signed by the Agent, and contain a revised completion date.

It is mutually agreed that all commissioned work generated by the Designer's work shall be offered first to the Designer. The Designer has the right to refuse such work.

The Agent agrees to use the order confirmation form of the Textile Designers Guild, or a form that protects the interests of the Designer in the same manner as that form. The order form shall provide that the Designer will be paid for all changes of original instructions arising out of no fault of the Designer. The order form shall also provide that if a job is can-

celed through no fault of the Designer, a labor fee shall be paid by the client based on the amount of work already done and the artwork will remain the property of the Designer. In a case in which the job being cancelled is based on artwork which belongs to the client such as a repeat or coloring, a labor fee will be charged as outlined above and the artwork will be destroyed. If the artwork is already completed in a satisfactory manner at the time the job is canceled, the client must pay the full fee.

7. Holding Policy. In the event that a client wishes to hold the Designer's work for consideration, the Agent shall establish a maximum holding time with the client. This holding time shall not exceed five (5) working days. Any other arrangements must first be discussed with the Designer.

The Agent agrees to use the holding form of the Textile Designers Guild, or a form that protects the interests of the Designer in the same manner as that form. All holding forms shall be available for the Designer to see at any time.

8. Billings and Payments. The Agent shall be responsible for all billings. The Agent agrees to use the invoice form of the Textile Designers Guild, or a form that protects the interests of the Designer in the same manner as that form. The Agent agrees to provide the Designer with a copy of all bills to clients pertaining to the work of the Designer. The Designer will provide the Agent with a bill for his or her work for the particular job. The Designer's bill shall be paid by the Agent within one week after the delivery of artwork or, if the Agent finds it necessary, within ten (10) working days after receipt of payment from the client. The terms of all bills issued by the Agent shall require payment within thirty (30) calendar days or less. If the client does not pay within that time, the Agent must immediately pursue payment and, upon request, inform the Designer that this has

been done. The Agent agrees to take all necesary steps to collect payment, including taking legal action if necessary. If either the Agent or Designer undertakes legal action, any recovery shall first be used to reimburse the amount of attorney's fees and other expenses incurred and the balance of the recovery shall be divided between Agent and Designer in the respective percentages set forth in Paragraph 5. The Agent agrees, whenever possible, to bill in such a way that no single bill exceeds the maximum that can be sued in small claims court.

Under no circumstances shall the Agent withold payment to the Designer after the Agent has been paid. Late payments by the Agent to the Designer shall be accompanied by interest calculated at the rate of 1½ percent monthly.

9. Inspection of Books. The Designer shall have the right to inspect the Agent's books and records with respect to proceeds due to the Designer. The Agent shall keep the books and records at the Agent's place of business and the Designer may make such inspection during normal business hours on the giving of reasonable notice.

10. Termination. This Agreement may be terminated by either party by giving thirty (30) days written notice by registered mail to the other party. All artwork executed by the Designer not sold by the Agent must be returned to the Designer within these thirty (30) days. In the event of termination, the Agent shall receive commissions for all sales made or assignments obtained by the Agent prior to the termination date, regardless of when payment is received. No commissions shall be payable for sales made or assignments obtained by the Designer after the termination date.

11. Assignment. This Agreement shall not be assigned by either of the parties hereto. It shall be binding on and inure to the benefit of the successors, administrators, executors, or heirs of the Agent and Designer.

12. Arbitration. Any disputes in excess of $_____ (maximum limit for small claims court) arising out of this agreement shall be submitted to binding arbitration before the Joint Ethics Committee or a mutually agreed upon artibrator pursuant to the rules of the American Arbitration Association. The Arbitrator's award shall be final, and judgement may be entered upon it in any court having jurisdiction thereof. The Agent shall pay all arbitration and court costs, reasonable attorney's fees, and legal interest on any award or judgment in favor of the Designer.

13. Notices. All notices shall be given to the parties at their respective addresses set forth above.

14. Independent Contractor Status. Both parties agree that the Agent is acting as an independent contractor. This Agreement is not an employment agreement, nor does it constitute a joint venture or partnership between the Designer and Agent.

15. Amendments and Merger. All amendments to this Agreement must be written. This Agreement incorporates the entire understanding of the parties.

16. Other Provisions

_____
_____
_____

17. Governing Law. This Agreement shall be governed by the laws of the State of

_____

In witness whereof, the parties have signed this Agreement as of the date set forth above.

_____
DESIGNER

_____
AGENT

Computer Illustration/Graphics Job Order Form

This job order form is a sample of a possible contract for computer-generated art. Since the field is so new, the artist should view this as a model and amend it to fit their situations and the needs of their client, based on a negotiated agreement.

DATE		
AUTHORIZED BUYER		
CLIENT		
FOR USE IN	ISSUE	DATE
DEFINITION/TYPE OF ASSIGNMENT		
ADDITIONAL USES	*(promotional, packaging, etc.)*	
NUMBER OF SCREENS OR IMAGES	*(single frame, multiple frame)*	
STILL FRAME		
*SECTOR LENGTH PER SCREEN: MAXIMUM	PREFERRED	MINIMUM

JOB DESCRIPTION/APPEAL   *(nature of market):*
COPY TO READ
*BE SURE COPY IS CORRECTLY SPELLED AND TITLED. ARTIST IS NOT RESPONSIBLE FOR ANY COPY OTHER THAN EXACTLY WHAT APPEARS ABOVE.

PRODUCTION SCHEDULE:
FIRST SHOWING
REVIEW
FINAL ACCEPTANCE
RIGHTS TRANSFERRED   *(one time use, etc.)*
TYPE OF USE   *(game program, advertising, etc.)*
MEDIUM OF USE   *(floppy, documentation, packaging, promotion, etc.)*
DISTRIBUTION/GEOGRAPHICAL AREA   *(method of distribution, electronically downloaded, floppy disk, store distribution)*
TIME/NUMBER OF PRINTINGS

COMPUTER FORM BACK

SYSTEM APPLICATIONS	*(for use on specific machine, or compiled into other operation languages.)*
PURCHASE PRICE/PAYMENT SCHEDULE	

Terms:

1. Time for Payment. All invoices are payable within thirty (30) days of receipt. A 1½% monthly service charge is payable on all overdue balances. The grant of any license or right of copyright is conditioned on receipt of full payment.

2. Estimates. If this form is used for an estimate or assignment confirmation, the fees and expenses shown are minimum estimates only. Final fees and expenses shall be shown when invoice is rendered. Client's approval shall be obtained for any increases in fees or expenses that exceed the original estimate by 10% or more.

3. Changes. Client shall be responsible for making additional payments for changes requested by Client in original assignment. However, no additional payment shall be made for changes required to conform to the original assignment description. The Client shall offer the Illustrator the first opportunity to make any changes.

4. Expenses. Client shall reimburse Illustrator for all expenses arising from this assignment, including the payment of any sales taxes due on this assignment, and shall advance $_____ to the Illustrator for payment of said expenses.

5. Cancellation. In the event of cancellation of this assignment, ownership of all copyrights and the original artwork is retained by the Illustrator and a cancellation fee for work completed, based on the contract price and expenses already incurred, shall be paid by the Client.

6. Ownership of Artwork. The Illustrator retains ownership of all original artwork, whether preliminary or final, and the Client shall return such artwork within thirty (30) days of use.

7. Credit Lines. The Illustrator shall be given credit in:
(a) floppy disk, (b) documentation, (c) packaging, (d) illustrator's mark on art.

8. Any electronic alteration of original art (color shift, mirroring, flopping, combination cut and paste, deletion) creating additional art, shall constitute additional use and will be billed accordingly.

9. Other operating systems conversions. Illustrator shall be given first option at compiling the work for operating systems beyond the original use.

10. Unauthorized use and program licenses. Client will indemnify illustrator against all claims and expenses arising from uses for which client does not have rights to or authority to use. The Client will be responsible for payment of any special licensing or royalty fees resulting from the use of graphics programs that require such payments.

11. Illustrators guarantee for program use. Illustrator guarantees to notify Client of any licensing and/or permissions required for art generating/driving programs to be used.

12. Arbitration. Any disputes in excess of $____ (maximum limit of small claims court) arising out of this agreement shall be submitted to binding arbitration before the Joint Ethics Committee or a

mutually agreed to arbitrator pursuant to the rules of the American Arbitration Association. The arbitrator's award shall be final and judgement upon it may be entered upon it in any court having jurisdication thereof. The Client shall pay all arbitration and court costs, attorney's fees and legal interest on any judgement or award in the favor of the Illustrator.

13. The Client must copy protect all final art which is the subject of this agreement against duplication or alteration.

14. The Client waives the right to challenge the validity of the Illustrator's ownership of the art, subject to this agreement because of any change or evolution of the law.

15. Acceptance of terms: If the terms of this agreement are not objected to within ten (10) days of receipt, the terms shall be deemed accepted.

Member

Graphic Designers Estimate/Confirmation/Invoice Form

FRONT: DESIGNER'S LETTERHEAD

☐ ESTIMATE	☐ ENGAGEMENT CONFIRMATION	☐ INVOICE
TO		DATE
		COMMISSIONED BY
		ASSIGNMENT NUMBER
		INVOICE NUMBER
		CLIENT'S PURCHASE ORDER NUMBER

ASSIGNMENT DESCRIPTION	DELIVERY DATE
	(PREDICATED ON RECEIPT OF ALL MATERIALS TO BE SUPPLIED BY CLIENT)
	MATERIALS SUPPLIED BY
	FEE

ITEMIZED EXPENSES. CLIENT SHALL REIMBURSE DESIGNER FOR ALL EXPENSES. IF THIS IS AN ESTIMATE OR ASSIGNMENT CONFIRMATION, ANY EXPENSE AMOUNTS ARE ESTIMATES ONLY. IF THIS IS AN INVOICE, EXPENSE AMOUNTS ARE FINAL.

ILLUSTRATION PHOTOGRAPHY	
MATERIALS AND SUPPLIES	
MECHANICALS	
MESSENGERS	
PHOTOGRAPHIC REPRODUCTION	
PRINTING	
TOLL TELEPHONES	
TRANSPORTATION AND TRAVEL	
MODELS AND PROPS	
SHIPPING AND INSURANCE	
TYPE	
STATS	
OTHER	EXPENSES SUBTOTAL
	TOTAL
	SALES TAX
	TOTAL DUE

ANY USAGE RIGHTS NOT EXCLUSIVELY TRANSFERRED ARE RESERVED TO DESIGNER. USAGE BEYOND THAT GRANTED TO CLIENT HEREIN SHALL REQUIRE PAYMENT OF A MUTUALLY AGREED UPON ADDITIONAL FEE SUBJECT TO ALL TERMS ON REVERSE.

RIGHTS TRANSFERRED. DESIGNER TRANSFERS TO THE CLIENT THE FOLLOWING EXCLUSIVE RIGHTS OF USAGE. *(remove all italics before using this form)*	
TITLE OR PRODUCT	*(name)*
CATEGORY OF USE	*(advertising, corporate, promotional, editorial, etc.)*
MEDIUM OF USE	*(consumer or trade magazine, annual report TV, book, etc.)*
EDITION (IF BOOK)	*(hardcover, mass market paperbook, quality paperback, etc.)*
GEOGRAPHIC AREA	*(if applicable)*
TIME PERIOD	*(if applicable)*
ANY USAGE RIGHTS NOT EXCLUSIVELY TRANSFERRED ARE RESERVED TO DESIGNER. USAGE BEYOND THAT GRANTED TO CLIENT HEREIN SHALL REQUIRE PAYMENT OF A MUTUALLY AGREED UPON ADDITIONAL FEE SUBJECT TO ALL TERMS ON REVERSE.	

Terms:

1. Time for Payment. All invoices are payable within thirty (30) days of receipt. A 1½% monthly service charge is payable on all overdue balances. The grant of any license or right of copyright is conditioned on receipt of full payment.

2. Estimates. If this form is used for an estimate or assignment confirmation, the fees and expenses shown are minimum estimates only. Final fees and expenses shall be shown when invoice is rendered. Client's approval shall be obtained for any increases in fees or expenses that exceed the original estimate by 10% or more.

3. Changes. Client shall be responsible for making additional payments for changes requested by Client in original assignment. However, no additional payment shall be made for changes required to conform to the original assignment description. The Client shall offer the Designer the first opportunity to make any changes.

4. Expenses. Client shall reimburse Designer for all expenses arising from this assignment, including the payment of any sales taxes due on this assignment, and shall advance $_____ to the Designer for payment of said expenses.

5. Cancellation. In the event of cancellation of this assignment, ownership of all copyrights and the original artwork is retained by the Designer and a cancellation fee for work completed, based on the contract price and expenses already incurred, shall be paid by the Client.

6. Ownership of Artwork. The Designer retains ownership of all original artwork, whether preliminary or final, and the Client shall return such artwork within thirty (30) days of use.

7. Credit Lines. The Designer and any other creators shall receive a credit line with any editorial usage. If similar credit lines are to be given with other types of usage, it must be so indicated here:

_____

_____

8. Releases. Client will indemnify Designer against all claims and expenses, including reasonable attorney's fees, due to uses for which no release was requested in writing or for uses which exceed authority granted by a release.

9. Modifications. Modification of the agreement must be written, except that the invoice may include, and Client shall be obligated to pay, fees or expenses that were orally authorized in order to progress promptly with work.

10. Arbitration. Any disputes in excess of $_____ (maximum limit of small claims court) arising out of this agreement shall be submitted to binding arbitration before the Joint Ethics Committee or a mutually agreed to arbitrator pursuant to the rules of the American Arbitration Association. The arbitrator's award shall be final and judgement upon it may be entered upon it in any court having jurisdiction thereof. The Client shall pay all arbitration and court costs, attorney's fees and legal interest on any judgement or award in the favor of the Designer.

11. Acceptance of terms: The above terms incorporate Article 2 of the Uniform Commercial Code. If not objected to within ten (10) days, these terms shall be deemed acceptable.

12. Code of Fair Practice. The Client and Designer agree to comply with the provisions of the Code of Fair Practice, a copy of which may be obtained from the Joint Ethics Committee, P.O. Box 179, Grand Central Station, New York, New York 10017.

CONSENTED AND AGREED TO

_____

DATE

_____

DESIGNER'S SIGNATURE

_____

COMPANY NAME

_____

AUTHORIZED SIGNATURE

_____

NAME AND TITLE

MEMBER

Business Management

As creators of unique products, graphic artists have the right to share in the economic proceeds that the uses of their products generate. Securing economic interests and rights is the responsibility of individual graphic artists.

In addition to producing quality artwork, artists must develop a competent business aptitude to market and protect their art successfully. This is *the* basic survival skill for independent practitioners.

The commissions offered to graphic artists must be accurately evaluated, often at a moment's notice. Artists must have the skills and knowledge to pinpoint critical provisions and to take steps to avoid loss of economic control or legal problems down the road.

Since, for most artists, skillful negotiation is the key to a fair and profitable commission or job, negotiation skills must be learned and continuously honed. This "fine art" of negotiation with a client can often make the difference in an artist's ability to reach his or her business goals.

If problems should develop during or after the job, artists must also be prepared to act. They, therefore, should be aware of the resources available if problems should occur.

As with any other business, record-keeping is important both for tracking how the business is doing and for providing accurate data should problems occur after a job has been completed. Records of jobs must be maintained, invoices sent and accurately stated, and outstanding fees tracked.

In short, the viability of the artist's professional life is dependent to a great degree on acquiring relevant business and legal knowledge. This chapter of the *Handbook* discusses the fundamental business management issues common to all graphic art professionals.

Negotiation

In the graphic arts industry a great deal depends on repeat business, and a professional and honorable reputation. In negotiations, a "winner-take-all" attitude can do more harm than good. Whenever possible, an atmosphere of mutual trust and collaboration should be established and encouraged by the parties involved. From that point, both sides can create an agreement that will satisfy their respective needs.

This cooperation is attained not merely by the exchange of concessions, but through the attitudes and professional manner of the persons negotiating. Since the terms of a final agreement may not be those stated by either party at the outset, the participants must use their creative energies to manufacture solutions that meet the needs of all concerned.

It is important for artists to remember that art buyers are not "the enemy." During the years the Guild has handled grievance procedures between artists and clients, a common source of complaints has been a failure on the part of both sides to communicate effectively prior to the commencement of work. Both sides must take responsibility for knowing their own needs, articulating them and taking the other party's needs into account. Even if only one of the negotiators is making a conscientious effort to understand and elicit both the other party's point of view as well as their own, chances of a misunderstanding and/or conflict are greatly reduced.

Many artists are reluctant to ask questions or raise objections to clients' demands for fear of appearing difficult to work with. The Guild's experience shows, however, that as long as the discussion is carried out in an appropriately professional manner, clients appreciate artists who can be specific in their dealings, since it prevents misunderstandings later.

Attitude

Relaxation is very important in negotiation. By preparing properly and making the situation as comfortable as possible, it is possible to relax. Focusing on breathing and concentrating on relaxing muscles in the head, neck and shoulders can be surprisingly useful in a stressful situation. Even though, at the moment, the deal at hand may seem like a "make it or break it" proposition, that is usually not the case. In fact, most careers in the graphic arts are built upon hundreds of projects, not one. It is important to create a mental distance from the desperation and anxiety that can come into play in the middle of a negotiation. It can also help with maneuverability and the ability to respond quickly so that the opportunity to get the right job at the right price won't slip away.

When faced with a negotiation, both sides begin by implying or stating a set of demands based on their needs. These demands should not be confused with underlying needs. It is these needs that a skilled negotiator attempts to discern.

When the problem stated is, "My company is looking for a first-class brochure that we can produce for under $10,000," there may be several underlying needs that are not articulated directly. The art buyer may be asking, "Do you want this project?"; "Are you excited about it?" and "Are you going to mess up and cost me my job?" In attempting to determine what kind of brochure is required, what degree of work is involved, and the amount of money the client will have to pay for it, a skilled negotiator is communicating other messages as well, i.e., "I'm just the right person for this job, I know what I'm doing, and I'm going to make you look good."

It is important to convey positive expectations about the job. Instead of "What is the deadline?", use a phrase like, "When would you want me to deliver the art?" From the outset, contact with a client can show a personal interest and attachment to the project that is contagious.

The answer to a stated problem will not always be obvious. It is critical to be able to relax and perceive the other person's position. By understanding that, there can be a positive response to the "sub-text" of what's being said, and the negotiation can proceed with harmony.

Know when to quit. Getting greedy when things start to go well, or pushing too far can lead the other party to abandon the whole deal out of spite. A show of generosity may pay off in future negotiations.

Preparation and research

Adequate preparation is a key ingredient to successful negotiation. Artists should attempt to know everything possible about a client prior to a meeting. Business libraries contain valuable information about the marketplace: directories for corporations and advertising agencies show amounts of billing, circulation, officers, media, etc.

In addition, publication directories list magazines with circulation, advertising rates, names of staff, etc.

Subscriptions for all appropriate major trade magazines should be maintained.

Active membership in arts organizations such as the Guild helps to give artists the extra "edge" they may need in a job situation. Magazine stands, mass transit posters, billboards, retail stores, supermarkets, bookstores all contain valuable information about clients that artists may use with a new client.

Agendas and contracts

When a negotiation begins, it is important to ask the right questions and formulate an *agenda* for meetings or phone calls that outlines the topics to be covered. Additionally, artists should establish a "position paper" that will help answer the most important question of all, "What do I want from this job?", and "What will I do *instead* if I turn it down or am not right for it?"

Whether a project is interesting purely for the money, because it is a valuable showcase or because it will help establish a working relationship with a new client, an agenda will affect what the artist will agree to in negotiations (consult checklist in this section for suggestions on an agenda and checklist).

Prior to starting work, agreements should be put in writing whenever possible. This protects the client as well as the artist by confirming terms before a misunderstanding can occur. The document can be as simple or complicated as the situation requires, from an informal "letter of agreement," to a complicated contract requiring the signatures of all parties. Formulating such letters and contracts or analyzing contracts offered by clients requires a thorough working knowledge of copyright law and its phraseology. By reviewing model contracts and supplementary sections of this book and other publications carefully, artists will be able to rephrase contractual terms on the spur of the moment.

The majority of art directors and creative services personnel who commission art have little or no expertise in the area of copyright and contracts. Like artists, most of them would prefer not to have to deal with the subject. They are attempting to conduct business in what are usually hectic, high-pressure surroundings. Having a clear understanding of how to suggest, phrase and put contract amendments into writing, can help solve any problems that might appear.

When clients use work-for-hire clauses in contracts or demand all rights to artwork, every effort should be made to determine what the client *really* needs. Often such terms in a contract were put in by a lawyer trying to cover all bases. But such terms are usually excessive and, if priced accordingly, make work too expensive to afford.

Keep thorough written records of a job's progress, including the initial checklist containing job description, deadlines, fees and expenses, notes on the person representing the client, records of follow-up meetings and phone calls, hours on the job, layouts, memos, sketches, contracts, invoices and business letters. This should form a "job packet" that is a "paper trail" in the event that a disagreement or misunderstanding gets in the way of completing a project and payment.

The meeting

As much as possible, create an environment for meeting that will allow as comfortable a situation as possible. If negotiating "on your own turf" is impossible, bring your own turf with you. Clothing should always be professional and neat, but make sure it is also *comfortable.* Any presentation or portfolio should show the very best work. An unusual and creative presentation that shows thought and is well designed goes a long way in establishing the expertise of an artist—and making a sale.

Negotiations should be avoided if the artist lacks sleep, is overtired, is taking medication, under the influence of alcohol, or has recently eaten a heavy meal. Very expensive errors can occur when artists are not as sharp as they should be. If the situation is uncomfortable or potentially disruptive, arrange to conduct the negotiation another time. There is a right and wrong time for negotiation. Recognize an opportunity and make use of it, but recognize also when there is *no* opportunity and wait for another day.

The golden rules during a meeting are: Stop, look and listen. Stop—quiet down, breathe, relax and get "centered." Refrain from lots of "small talk," unless what's being said has a purpose for the business at hand. A well-placed word here and there does more to establish professional credibility, however, giving out information not asked for can give clues about the artist's situation and weakness

inadvertently. Conducting presentations can also distract clients from carefully reviewing the work.

Look—a great deal can be learned by close attention to physical clues and the behavior of others. Office environments (wallpaper, furniture, desktops, artwork and photographs) can give clues about the personality of the client. Notice if a seat is offered, if the client consults a watch constantly, or is interrupting and not focused on the discussion. If understood, behavioral clues can give a substantial advantage of knowing how to deal with someone during a negotiation.

Listen—people appreciate someone who is alert, attentive and indicates that he or she understands what is being said. It is important to indicate that *understanding* even if the listener doesn't agree with the point made. Listen *actively,* with nods of agreement, encouraging the other party to express themselves. It is very useful to repeat what was heard, such as, "let me see if I understand correctly, you're saying that, etc...." This indicates a good listener who is eager to understand. Listening effectively helps to determine and address the other party's needs and expectations.

Power

Negotiation itself cannot turn every situation into a golden opportunity. There are some relationships where the balance of power is so out of alignment that one party must either yield to unfavorable conditions or give up the negotiation. However, it is possible to maximize assets and protect yourself from an agreement that may be detrimental.

Remembering that not every negotiation is destined to end in a *deal* is important. Two parties can "agree to disagree" most amicably and part ways hoping for another try at a later date. It is this ability to regard a negotiation with a level-headed objectivity, keeping it in perspective, that provides a skilled negotiator with the relaxation and attitude necessary to obtain the most favorable agreement.

Parties in a discussion should bear in mind what their course of action will be if the negotiation ends without agreement. "What other jobs do I have?" or "What else will I do with my professional time if I don't take this assignment?" are questions that artists should ask themselves, just as the client is asking, "What else can I do, or who else can I hire to make this project work?" These questions provide both parties with a realistic assessment of how much power they actually have in a negotiation. Power can be regarded as the ability to say *no*, assessing alternatives, therefore, clarifies a position.

Often parties will establish an arbitrary limit from which they will not bend, such as "I won't pay more than $25,000," or "I won't accept less than $3,000." Since the figures or conditions are often arbitrarily selected in the first place, it is important to be able to *ignore* such a limit if necessary. A bottom line can become a focal point that inhibits the imagination necessary to establish terms that meet both parties' needs.

When entering into negotiations, it's important to decide what to do if negotiations break off. It's much easier to say no when there is a favorable alternative to pursue. As the saying goes, a bank will lend money if you prove you don't need it. In the same way, it's much easier to get a job if you already have one. If an artist is not busy with other jobs, the best alternative is to create a mental "priority" list of important and valuable projects to pursue. This help alleviate the often, ill-founded notion that the deal must be made "at any cost."

Tactics

Tactics are used throughout every negotiation, whether intentional or not. By separating emotional responses from calm, detached observations of tactics, the effectiveness of the tactic is defused. It is important not to take things personally in any phase of negotiation. Performance and ability to maneuver are seriously hampered when egos take charge.

Consider a few examples: (1) Limited authority: a person claims to have no final say on the terms of a deal. This enables one negotiator to make rigid demands, leaving the other to offer concessions in order that some headway is made. One possible solution is to treat the project under discussion as a joint venture, recruiting the other person as your new found "partner." By emphasizing terms that create partnership and sharing a stake in decisions, that person is encouraged to "go to bat" with the higher ups to defend the artist's needs and goals. (2) Phony legitimacy: it is stated that a contract is a "standard contract" and cannot be changed . Contracts are working documents that serve to protect two or more parties in an agreement. Don't agree to sign standardized contracts if they don't protect you. Don't be reluctant to strike out unfavorable sections or terms. If necessary, the

defense "my attorney has instructed me not to sign contracts with these conditions," may be used to suggest alterations (see GAG sample contracts for guidelines). (3) Emotions: anger, threats, derisive laughter, tears or insults may be convincing and may, in fact be genuine, but should be regarded as tactical maneuvers. Listen carefully to the *point* of the message and separate it from the style of delivery. Never escalate an emotional situation. Any attempt to "roll up your sleeves and jump in" is very risky.

Phone

Telephones seem to be very easy for some to work with and much harder for others. Like personal contact, negotiating by phone has its good and bad parts. Phone calls have distinct advantages over in-person meetings. They provide ample opportunity to refer to written materials for reference and support. Often, when calling from the office or home, being surrounded by one's own environment can bolster confidence.

Skill in the use of the phone is very important to a good negotiator: some individuals go as far as to write "scripts" for particularly difficult situations, where performing under pressure can cause confusion. A simpler negotiation "agenda" or checklist can be used to outline all the points that need to be covered. This prevents the problem of forgetting important details and helps keep the conversation centered on the important matters at hand. Note taking during phone conversations is highly recommended. Artists often are attempting to understand the esthetic requirements of a project, all the details of a business arrangement, and build up a personal understanding of the individual on the phone. These are complicated details and should be written down. Such notes can also be valuable references should a misunderstanding occur during the project.

Use of the phone has disadvantages as well. It's easier to refuse someone over the phone. If a difficult demand has to be made, it might be preferable to arrange a meeting. It is also difficult to judge reactions to what is being said when it is impossible to see the other person's face. A person's attention to what is being said may not be focused, and this can make it more difficult to establish the rapport and "partnership" that is so important to any successful negotiation. Should a discussion become difficult, it is easy to put the caller on hold or get off the telephone and call back when it is more advantageous. This allows time for consultation of research materials, other phone calls for research, cooling off if emotions are in play, or just time to make a difficult decision.

Money

Money should be the last item in a discussion, for several reasons. It is the one area where the majority of disagreements can occur, and it is important in the earliest stages of a negotiation to focus on areas where there is accord. In this way the partnership stressed earlier is given time to bloom. Also, money should only be a reflection of all the factors that lead up to it.

The job description, deadline, expenses, usage and reproduction rights, difficulty of execution, etc., all tell the story of how much a job should cost. So negotiating money before this information has been clearly agreed to is premature and can be a costly error.

When discussing money, insofar as is possible, outline the expectations, then attempt to get the other side to make the first offer. The old game of "I say 10, you say 6, I say 9, you say 7, we agree on 8," is still played out but is not always necessary,. Depending on how it is stated, though, a first offer is rarely a final offer and should almost always be tested. Once again, one must weigh the risk of losing a possible working relationship by refusing to budge past a certain price. It always depends on the situation.

Don't feel obligated to respond right away if someone starts out a negotiation with, "I only have $500, but I think you'd be great for the job." One can acknowledge the figure and still bring it up *later* when there is a foundation of a working relationship on which to base requests for more money.

Often, artists are asked to bid on jobs. It is important to clarify the nature of the bid. Is the client looking for a sealed bid that will be used to compete against other artists? Is this bid an attempt to help structure a budget? Is it only a "ballpark" estimate? Do they wish to negotiate directly? Since a sealed bid encourages negotiation against yourself, it should be clarified whether the bid is final and binding. It is unfair to ask an artist to develop a competitive sealed bid and then use that figure as the starting point for future negotiations. In a "ballpark" estimate, the client will often hear only the low figure, so use care to offer a set of figures that brackets your price in the middle.

It is not only practical, it's actually good business to ask for a price slightly higher than what you would expect. Like it or not, people in business often like to feel that they've gotten you to bend somewhat, and in that sense it is an obligation to manufacture a few concessions without harming your own interests.

Hourly rate formula

Another way to figure pricing, as opposed to "the going rate" or supply and demand, is the *hourly rate formula*. This formula takes into consideration factors that make up overhead such as rent, utilities, salaries, benefits, promotion, outside professional services, equipment, transportation, office and art supplies, business taxes and entertainment. In order to come up with an hourly rate, divide the annual total for "overhead" figures by 1800, which is the number of hours worked in an average year. The resulting figure would be an hourly rate (based on a 35-hour week) that could be expected to cover all of your costs *including* your salary.

However, most artists, especially those who are self-employed, bill at some smaller number, for example dividing the yearly overhead figure by 900 hours. This may give a more practical rate since it allows for the fact that self-employed artists rarely work on a full-time basis for one or two clients.

When a project is being considered, it is important to figure a close estimate of hours of work. This estimate multiplied by the hourly rate will demonstrate whether the client's fee for the project will mean profit or loss or a "break-even" amount. At that point, the artist has the option of figuring out a solution to the project that will mean fewer hours of work to make the job more profitable, or rejecting the job because the fee is too small.

Many large jobs, such as corporate design projects, require that the hours involved be used as a gauge to see if the project is on budget.

Copyright registration

Although the copyright law automatically protects original artwork from the moment it is created, there are advantages in formally registering the art with the Copyright Office. Registration establishes a public record of the artist's copyright claim to the artwork. Then if someone infringes or copies the art to the artist's detriment, the

FORM VA
UNITED STATES COPYRIGHT OFFICE

REGISTRATION NUMBER

VA   VAU

EFFECTIVE DATE OF REGISTRATION

(Month)   (Day)   (Year)

DO NOT WRITE ABOVE THIS LINE. IF YOU NEED MORE SPACE, USE CONTINUATION SHEET (FORM VA/CON)

(1) Title

TITLE OF THIS WORK:
THE CITY BEAUTIFUL

NATURE OF THIS WORK: (See instructions)
GOUACHE PAINTING

Previous or Alternative Titles

PUBLICATION AS A CONTRIBUTION: (If this work was published as a contribution to a periodical, serial, or collection, give information about the collective work in which the contribution appeared.)

Title of Collective Work PRESERVATION ANNUAL   Vol   No   Date 1987   Pages

(2) Author(s)

IMPORTANT: Under the law, the "author" of a "work made for hire" is generally the employer, not the employee (see instructions). If any part of this work was "made for hire" check "Yes" in the space provided, give the employer (or other person for whom the work was prepared) as "Author" of that part, and leave the space for dates blank.

1
NAME OF AUTHOR:
LAWRENCE DAVIDSON
Was this author's contribution to the work a "work made for hire"?   Yes   No ✓

DATES OF BIRTH AND DEATH:
Born 1938   Died —
(Year)   (Year)

AUTHOR'S NATIONALITY OR DOMICILE:
Citizen of USA   or   Domiciled in
(Name of Country)   (Name of Country)

WAS THIS AUTHOR'S CONTRIBUTION TO THE WORK:
Anonymous?   Yes   No ✓
Pseudonymous?   Yes   No ✓
If the answer to either of these questions is "Yes," see detailed instructions attached

AUTHOR OF: (Briefly describe nature of this author's contribution)
ARTWORK

2
NAME OF AUTHOR:
Was this author's contribution to the work a "work made for hire"?   Yes   No

DATES OF BIRTH AND DEATH:
Born   Died
(Year)   (Year)

AUTHOR'S NATIONALITY OR DOMICILE:
Citizen of   or   Domiciled in
(Name of Country)   (Name of Country)

WAS THIS AUTHOR'S CONTRIBUTION TO THE WORK:
Anonymous?   Yes   No ✓
Pseudonymous?   Yes   No ✓
If the answer to either of these questions is "Yes," see detailed instructions attached

AUTHOR OF: (Briefly describe nature of this author's contribution)

3
NAME OF AUTHOR:
Was this author's contribution to the work a "work made for hire"?   Yes   No

DATES OF BIRTH AND DEATH:
Born   Died
(Year)   (Year)

AUTHOR'S NATIONALITY OR DOMICILE:
Citizen of   or   Domiciled in
(Name of Country)   (Name of Country)

WAS THIS AUTHOR'S CONTRIBUTION TO THE WORK:
Anonymous?   Yes   No
Pseudonymous?   Yes   No
If the answer to either of these questions is "Yes," see detailed instructions attached

AUTHOR OF: (Briefly describe nature of this author's contribution)

(3) Creation and Publication

YEAR IN WHICH CREATION OF THIS WORK WAS COMPLETED:
Year
(This information must be given in all cases.)

DATE AND NATION OF FIRST PUBLICATION:
Date
(Month)   (Day)   (Year)
Nation
(Name of Country)
(Complete this block ONLY if this work has been published.)

(4) Claimant(s)

NAME(S) AND ADDRESS(ES) OF COPYRIGHT CLAIMANT(S):
LAWRENCE DAVIDSON
1520 MOSS PARK ROAD
BOULDER   CO 80302

TRANSFER: (If the copyright claimant(s) named here in space 4 are different from the author(s) named in space 2, give a brief statement of how the claimant(s) obtained ownership of the copyright.)

- Complete all applicable spaces (numbers 5-9) on the reverse side of this page
- Follow detailed instructions attached   • Sign the form at line 8

DO NOT WRITE HERE
Page 1 of . . . . pages

---

artist possesses presumptive evidence of ownership, leaving the burden to prove differently on the other party. With registration, the artist also gains a broader range of legal remedies in the event of infringement.

The registration procedure is not at all complex or lengthy. Form VA is generally used by graphic artists to register pictorial, graphic or sculptural artwork. Along with the properly completed form, one or two copies of the entire artwork must be enclosed (depending on whether the art is unpublished or published) with a $10 fee. The accompanying example of a completed Form VA is for a published illustration appearing in a book.

At times other registration forms may be needed by graphic artists. If audiovisual work is created, including motion pictures, then Form PA is the appropriate registration form. When both art and text in a work are to be registered by the artist and the text predominates, then Form TX should be used. For computer software Form TX is used and for computer graphics, Form VA. All forms are accompanied by line-by-line instructions.

The protection of the copyright law may be lost easily if a proper *copyright notice* does not accompany a public distribution or

EXAMINED BY:	APPLICATION RECEIVED:	
CHECKED BY:		FOR COPYRIGHT OFFICE USE ONLY
CORRESPONDENCE ☐ Yes	DEPOSIT RECEIVED	
DEPOSIT ACCOUNT FUNDS USED: ☐	REMITTANCE NUMBER AND DATE	

DO NOT WRITE ABOVE THIS LINE. IF YOU NEED ADDITIONAL SPACE, USE CONTINUATION SHEET (FORM VA/CON)

PREVIOUS REGISTRATION:

- Has registration for this work, or for an earlier version of this work, already been made in the Copyright Office? Yes ..... No ....

- If your answer is "Yes," why is another registration being sought? (Check appropriate box)
  ☐ This is the first published edition of a work previously registered in unpublished form.
  ☐ This is the first application submitted by this author as copyright claimant.
  ☐ This is a changed version of the work, as shown by line 6 of the application.

- If your answer is "Yes," give: Previous Registration Number .... Year of Registration ....

5 Previous Registration

COMPILATION OR DERIVATIVE WORK: (See instructions)

PREEXISTING MATERIAL (Identify any preexisting work or works that this work is based on or incorporates.)

MATERIAL ADDED TO THIS WORK: (Give a brief, general statement of the material that has been added to this work and in which copyright is claimed.)

6 Compilation or Derivative Work

DEPOSIT ACCOUNT: (If the registration fee is to be charged to a Deposit Account established in the Copyright Office, give name and number of Account.)

Name ....

Account Number ....

CORRESPONDENCE: (Give name and address to which correspondence about this application should be sent.)

Name LAWRENCE DAVIDSON

Address 1520 MOSS PARK ROAD – (Apt.)

BOULDER CO 80302
(City) (State) (ZIP)

7 Fee and Correspondence

CERTIFICATION: ✱ I, the undersigned, hereby certify that I am the: (Check one)
☒ author ☐ other copyright claimant ☐ owner of exclusive right(s) ☐ authorized agent of
(Name of author or other copyright claimant, or owner of exclusive right(s))
of the work identified in this application and that the statements made by me in this application are correct to the best of my knowledge.

Handwritten signature (X) *Lawrence Davidson*

Typed or printed name LAWRENCE DAVIDSON Date 4/16/87

8 Certification (Application must be signed)

LAWRENCE DAVIDSON
(Name)
1520 MOSS PARK ROAD
(Number Street and Apartment Number)
BOULDER CO 80302
(City) (State) (ZIP code)

MAIL CERTIFICATE TO

(Certificate will be mailed in window envelope)

9 Address For Return of Certificate

✱ 17 U.S.C. § 506(e): FALSE REPRESENTATION – Any person who knowingly makes a false representation of a material fact in the application for copyright registration provided for by section 409, or in any written statement filed in connection with the application, shall be fined not more than $2,500.

☆ U.S. GOVERNMENT PRINTING OFFICE: 1978–261-022/4

Jan. 1978–300,000

publication of any art. Refer to page 31 for the elements that make up a copyright notice. Rather than having the art enter the public domain and thus losing esthetic and economic control over it, a notice should accompany *all* publications of the art. The form and placement of the notice should be covered by written agreements with the client. When use of the art has been temporarily granted to a client, the name in the notice should preferably be the artist's, but may be the client's for the duration of the usage.

A means for cutting costs on repeated registration fees for *unpublished* artwork is to register a group of artworks under a single title. For example, the artist may collect 75 drawings, put them into an orderly unit and then register them under a single identifying title. A similar inexpensive means of group registration is possible for *published* artwork having appeared in periodicals. Such contributions to periodicals must have been made within a one-year period and must include the individual artist's copyright notice. In this latter instance, Form GR/CP must be completed in addition to any of the other forms noted.

In submitting copies of the artwork along with the registration form, original art need not be submitted. The artist can submit tearsheets, photocopies or transparencies.

Whatever type of copies are submitted, they should show all copyrightable contents of the artwork.

A basic discussion of the copyright law is provided in other sections of this book. The Copyright Office is also a resource for artists. Information on the copyright law and registration procedures can be obtained at 202/287-8700 and forms can be requested at 202/287-9100. Additionally, literature about the various elements of registration are available for free. A list of these publications may be found in *Publications on Copyright* (Circular 2). The forms and literature may also be obtained by writing:

Copyright Office
Information & Publications Section
Library of Congress
Washington, D.C. 20559

Invasions and Infringements

Any illustration or design could involve problems of invasion of privacy and copyright infringement. For example, the "advertising or trade" use of a living person's name or likeness without permission is an invasion of privacy. In this field claims may be in the hundreds of thousands of dollars for an infringement. Since "advertising or trade" means virtually all uses outside of the factually correct editorial contents of magazines, newspapers, books, television programs, etc., uses include print and TV ads, company brochures, packaging, etc. Public and private figures are protected equally in this connection.

The test of "likeness" is whether an ordinary person would recognize the complainant as the person in the illustration in question. It needn't be a perfect likeness. The best protection in these cases is a signed release from the person whose likeness is used and any contract should provide for this if a problem is likely to arise.

In addition, if the artist copied another work (say a photograph) in making the illustration, then the photographer or copyright holder might sue for copyright infringement. The test of an infringement is whether an ordinary person would say that one work is copied from the other; the copying need not be exact.

Given the substantial amount of photography used in reference files for illustration as well as the frequent incorporation of photographs into designs, it is likely that everyone should be exercising extreme caution in this area. Of course, common themes and images (such as squares or triangles) are in the public domain and may be used freely.

Infringement requires the copying of a substantial portion of a work, so a mere similarity of style or concept will not be an infringement. The Guild is currently developing a form to prevent "knock-offs" in the textile design field.

Because of the privacy and infringement risks, many firms carry "advertisers' (or publishers') liability" insurance to cover claims pertaining to these subjects. That, however, is not the ultimate salvation. Claims and lawsuits mean increased insurance premiums or loss of coverage altogether. For that reason, caution in the use of artwork is always necessary.

Checks with conditions

It is not uncommon for artists to receive payment in the form of a check with several conditions stated on the back. Most commonly these will be conditions to the effect that endorsement of the check constitutes a transfer of all reproduction rights and/or ownership of the original art to the payer. Although legal opinion is divided on the matter, it is doubtful that endorsement of such a check would constitute a legal contract, especially if it conflicts with a previous contract. An artist has at least three options to consider when handling checks with conditions.

First, simply return the check and request a new check be issued without conditions. If the conditions on the check violate a prior contract, a refusal to issue a check without conditions will be a breach of contract.

Second, if an artist has signed a contract or sent an invoice that restricts the client's rights of use, the artist should strike out the conditions on the check and deposit it if the artwork has already been used. In making the deposit, the artist should probably not sign the back of the check, but instead use an endorsement stamp after striking out all the conditions. If the artwork has not been used, the artist should notify the client in writing that he or she is striking out the conditions on the check. If the artist does not hear from the client within two weeks, the check can be deposited safely.

Finally, if the artist has neither signed a contract with the client nor sent any prior invoice restrictions on the rights of use, that check should be returned in order to protect all rights. Along with the check the artist should include an appropriate invoice restricting the rights of use. Of course, the best procedure is to specify in writing which rights will be transferred, before beginning an assignment.

Records, billing and bill-tracking

Getting paid on time and in the full amount is the just entitlement of any artist. Proper planning and preparation at the right time—and in writing—can do much towards having this expectation met. These preparations may, at times, require an extra effort on the artist's part, but they will certainly *pay-off* in the long run.

At the start of each job, artists should have a complete understanding of the negotiated terms and obtain a final agreement in writing to help insure timely and proper payment of fees.

To encourage timely payment, artists may include additional terms providing penalties for accounts that are past due and the retention of rights until payment is made. Since job changes often alter the original terms, it becomes particularly important to confirm in writing any additional fees due to the artist as a result of such changes.

Model business forms prepared by the Guild incorporate a number of these measures and can aid members in securing their agreement and rights.

To facilitate accurate billing, artists should maintain proper records through job files, job ledgers, or similar means. Tracking invoices provides the means to remind buyers of outstanding obligations and to take such follow-up steps as are necessary to obtain payment.

When a buyer refuses to make payment, written agreements and invoices can serve as a basis to protect the artist's rights, either through negotiation, arbitration or a lawsuit.

Keeping records

All artists should have a system for recordkeeping. Such a system facilitates billing, bill tracking, fees collection, and provides

a basis for claiming and verifying tax deductions.

Job file: One common method of recordkeeping is the use of a folder or envelope for each job. As a new job is received a job file is prepared to retain all information and documents such as agreements, receipts, letters, invoices, and so on. The job file then provides a single and complete record.

Identifying information is usually placed on the cover. This may include the job number, the title of the project, the buyer's name and the delivery date. If the job is complex, the job file should be subdivided into sections to permit easy access to information.

Job ledger: A job ledger contains standard columns for information such as the *job description* (Job Number, Client, Description of Artwork, Delivery Date), *rights granted* (Usage Rights, Status of Original Artwork), *fees and expenses* (Fee, Reimbursable Expenses, Sales Tax, Advance, etc.), and *billing information* (Balance Due, Invoice Date, Payment Due Date, and Payment Received Date).

The artist could then, at a glance, determine the status of each aspect of the job. The ledger's format can vary from a form specifically created by the artist to a printed journal readily available in stationery stores.

Billing procedure

Most art assignments, whether written or verbal, are contractual arrangements. Essentially, the buyer promises to make a specific payment in return for the artist's grant of usage rights. Invoices serve as formal communications to the buyer of monies that have or will become due.

The manner and time of payment are normally established in the written agreement. If the parties have not specified a payment due date, the generally accepted practice is payment within 30 days of delivery of the art.

An invoice should be presented whenever a payment becomes due. In many instances, invoices should accompany delivery of the finished art. When a partial payment is due or costs are to be billed during the job, the invoice(s) should be delivered accordingly. If cancellation or rejection occurs, the buyer should be billed immediately according to the agreement or, if such a provision is absent, according to Guild policy discussed in the Professional Issues section of this book.

Verbal requests for payment are not substitutes for invoices but are additional means to use in the collection process. In many businesses an invoice is mandatory for the buyer or others to authorize and issue a check. A copy of the invoice should also be sent to the accounting department, if the business is large enough to have one, to facilitate prompt processing.

The wording of invoices should be accurate and complete to avoid payment delays. Copies of receipts for reimbursable costs are usually attached to document expenditures. At least one copy of the invoice should be retained by the artist.

Tracking outstanding payments

Once the invoice has been given to the buyer, artists will need to retrack or monitor the outstanding debt until it is paid. A tracking method should be established that ties into the artist's recordkeeping.

One simple method is to set up a separate folder marked as "Accounts Receivable." Copies of all invoices forwarded to buyers, in an order based upon payment due dates, the artist's job numbers, or the billing dates, should be kept in this folder.

To track fees, these invoices should be reviewed periodically. When payments are received, the invoice is pulled and placed into the individual job file.

When using a job ledger, artists can determine at a glance which payments remain outstanding by referring to the "Payment Due Date" column. When payment is received, the appropriate date is entered under "payment received date."

Continual tracking of outstanding payments also keeps information on cash flow current and allows for timely follow-up steps to collect past-due fees or other outstanding obligations.

Copyright © Volker E.H. Antoni
& Joel L. Hecker, Esq. 1983

Collecting

Having completed and delivered artwork that meets the buyer's specifications, it's quite natural to anticipate that payment will be made as agreed. Graphic artists who are not paid in a reasonable time will need to undertake additional efforts to collect outstanding fees, or to absorb losses of income and productive time personally.

Artists can often prevent payment problems in the first place by taking certain steps beforehand. The principal safeguard for artists is to outline payment and related terms clearly in a written and signed agreement right at the start of a job. Once the job has begun the artist's subsequent use of certain protective practices to deal with job changes and to provide proper billing will further encourage timely and full payment. This advance preparation gives artists something to fall back on and facilitates the collection of fees should non-payment occur.

Whether or not these preparatory steps have been taken, artists who do not receive timely payment for their work will want to implement appropriate and efficient collection strategies. This section looks at some of the collection resources available, how they work, what they entail and when they may be used. Background information is presented to guide graphic artists in their individual collection efforts.

Formulating a collection strategy

At the time payment becomes due but is not received in full, a collection process that has been planned in advance should be put into effect. Not taking such action immediately will only work to the artist's disadvantage, since invoices tend to get more difficult to collect as they get older. Both artist and buyer may lose or misplace important documents, experience memory lapses, or new events may complicate matters.

Any initial effort in a collection strategy starts with direct communication between artist and buyer. Insights into the nature of the problem and the buyer's attitude serve as the basis for determining subsequent action.

If a misunderstanding or error is involved, then a direct discussion between artist and buyer may solve the problem. If direct discussion is not sufficient, then artist and buyer could take advantage of arbitration, mediation or the support services of a local Guild grievance committee.

If the artist encounters an unreasonable or evasive buyer, more forceful measures may be required to collect outstanding fees. Artists may have to sue in small claims court or engage a collection agency or lawyer.

Direct negotiation

As noted, the first step in the collection process involves direct communication with the buyer to determine why payment has not been made. Unless complex legal matters or large amounts of money are at issue, direct negotiation is usually the most appropriate and simplest approach. The other resources to be discussed should be used only when direct negotiation is unsuccessful.

A discussion by phone or a personal visit may be most effective in resolving a payment problem. Alternately, the artist could write a brief business-like letter—with a copy of the original invoice attached and marked "Second Notice." The buyer should be reminded of and requested to provide the overdue payment immediately.

At this stage the artist usually can presume, until facts indicate otherwise, that human error or "red tape" was involved and that the call or letter will clear things up. These reminders often prove sufficient. There is, therefore, no need to alienate anyone, at least until it is clear that the non-payment is deliberate.

It is of course in the artist's best interest to act professionally at all times in dealing with the buyer or anyone else who may be contacted. Artists should be objective and realistic while conducting collection efforts.

When payment problems occur or are anticipated, letters and invoices should be sent by "Certified Mail Return Receipt Requested." At all times copies of correspondence between the parties should be retained. Documentation may prove to be crucial at a later stage.

Causes of non-payment

Artists usually learn why the payment has not been made from initial contacts with the buyer. The following is a look at some of the more common causes of non-payment and suggested strategies for responding to them. These basic negotiation concepts can be applied to other types of non-payment situations as well.

Buyer's error: Once the artwork is delivered, it's on to the next project for the buyer. Buyers or others may lose interest in processing the check. One purpose for providing an invoice is that it serves as a physical reminder. The buyer should not be expected to send the check automatically, nor are verbal requests for payment sufficient.

If the cause of non-payment is oversight, a new immediate due-date should be established and the buyer requested to follow up personally. The artist should send a letter confirming when payment will be made.

Artist's error: The artist may be the cause of the delay in payment. Perhaps an invoice was not provided or was forwarded to the wrong person, was incomplete, illegible, or possibly, did not document reimbursable expenses. In this situation the artist must correct the error in order to expedite the payment process.

Disputes over the agreement or professional standards

Not all disputes are the result of deliberate abuse; some are unintentional or caused by a lack of knowledge of professional standards. For example, buyers may have made a wrong assumption or may not have been aware of appropriate professional conduct in a particular situation.

Once it is clear why payment has not been made or other rights not respected, and the reason is contrary to the agreement or to professional standards, then the buyer should be informed of the correct position.

When contacting the buyer, reference should be to the written (or verbal) agreement. Well-negotiated agreements will usually cover the disputed issue and therefore specify either the obligations of the buyer or the rights of the artist.

Other provisions in the agreement providing alternatives or penalties in the event that the buyer does not act as originally agreed should also be brought to the buyer's attention. These provisions may provide additional negotiating leverage.

If necessary, the buyer's attention should be directed to appropriate professional standards. Such relevant sources include the industry's "Code of Fair Practice" and the Guild's *Pricing & Ethical Guidelines.*

The buyer should be asked to comply with the artist's request or to respond to the issue if further discussion appears appropriate.

Extension of payment time

A buyer may claim to be experiencing a "cash-flow problem," that is, not having sufficient funds on hand to pay. It is difficult to verify whether this is a legitimate reason or an evasive maneuver.

Nor is it unusual for the buyer to blame the late payment on the company's computer. Long intervals between programmed payments, however, are unreasonable. Exceptions to automatic payments can and are made all the time. In this case, the artist should insist that the buyer authorize a handwritten check within a specified number of days.

If the cause of the delay appears legitimate and future payment clearly will be made, the artist may wish to accommodate the buyer and grant a reasonable extension. If an extension is granted, the new payment deadline should be put in writing.

Granting extensions should be viewed as a professional courtesy on the part of the artist, not a right to be exercised by the buyer. To compensate the artist fairly for the delay, the buyer should be willing to pay a stated percentage on the balance due as a service fee. This practice should be used particularly when longer periods are granted.

Refusal to negotiate

After direct negotiating attempts, a buyer may still refuse to make payment. The buyer may not respond to the artist's letters and calls, provide unreasonable explanations, not address the issue at hand, or not make payment as promised according to newly negotiated terms.

Faced with this situation, and as a last effort before turning to other alternatives, the artist should send a "demand letter." This can be done either directly or through a lawyer. The basis of the artist's claim should be briefly restated with a demand for immediate payment of any outstanding balance.

The demand letter should also state that legal action will be taken unless payment is received. The buyer will then have to reconsider his position in view of the artist's determination to pursue his or her legal rights.

Planning ahead

Up to this point in the collection strategy, a number of reasonable efforts have been made and sufficient time has elapsed to allow the buyer to respond or pay the debt. The artist has also accumulated several documents to verify the continued indebtedness and the attempt made to collect, which may later prove helpful.

If the buyer does not make the payment as agreed or requested, fails to respond or acts evasively, the artist may reasonably presume that the buyer is intentionally avoiding payment or has excessively slipshod accounting procedures.

The artist must now select alternative recourses as a logical follow-up action. Various recourses are discussed individually in the following sections.

The Guild's grievance committee

The Guild has, from its formative years, included the support services of the Grievance Committee, which provides guidance and assistance to members in resolving their differences with their clients. An overview of the Committee and its various functions and objectives is provided on pages 39 to 40. Guild members requiring this service may contact the Grievance Committee of their local Guild chapter.

In order for the committee to make an objective assessment of a grievance and to be able to enter a dialogue with the client based on fact, specific information from the member is requested. The following elements need to be incorporated within the submitted grievance:

1. The member's full personal name and business name (if any), address(es) and phone number(s);

2. The member's current membership category and dues status;

3. The full name of the client, the name and title of the art buyer and the relevant address(es) and phone number(s);

4. The exact job description;

5. The nature of the grievance, including a chronological narration of facts and the respective positions of the parties;

6. The names of other agencies and persons contacted in regard to the grievance, and the result of such contacts;

7. Copies, *not originals,* of relevant documents substantiating the grievance; i.e. agreement forms or purchase orders, invoices, correspondence, receipts, and so on.

Members cannot claim support of the Grievance Committee until the committee has reviewed the case and has notified the member that the case has been taken on. The Grievance Committee cannot take on a case if the member has already begun formal litigation.

Submitted grievances are reviewed by the committee at its first opportunity. If it is determined that the grievance is justified, the committee will contact the member. A plan of action will be recommended and appropriate support or direct assistance will be provided. It is crucial that the member participate fully and keep the committee advised of subsequent developments.

The Grievance Committee cannot offer assistance in a dispute involving questionable professional conduct on the member's part, such as misrepresentation of talent, accepting work on speculation, plagiarism, or any violation of the Code of Fair Practice.

Arbitration and mediation

Arbitration and mediation are long-established processes for settling disputes privately and professionally. They involve the services of an impartial outside entity to bring about a resolution.

In arbitration, the arbitrator acts as a judge, reviewing the facts presented by both sides and then making a legally binding decision. In mediation, the mediator acts as an umpire, guiding both parties in working out their own resolution. A mediator cannot make a legally binding decision. If the parties do not reach an agreement they must then proceed to arbitration or court if they wish to obtain a binding determination.

Both parties must agree in order to use these services. Arbitrators and mediators cannot summon the parties. An arbitration provision in an artist's contract establishes the buyer's consent once the contract is signed. Should the buyer not appear for arbitration, a binding decision may be reached in the buyer's absence.

Arbitration and mediation are speedier and far less expensive than suing in formal court. Their conciliatory and private atmosphere may be more conducive to the artist who has had or anticipates a long business relationship with the buyer. These services may also be relevant when the artist's monetary claim is in excess of the small claims court's limit. Fees are usually moderate, consisting of a flat fee or a percentage of the monies claimed.

The Joint Ethics Committee, comprised of organizations representing artists, art buyers and agents, including the Guild, has provided these services to the metropolitan New York City area for over 20 years. The JEC is not a collection agency; it deals with ethical issues only. This independent organization is unique to the industry as its arbitrators and mediators are for the most part graphic art practitioners. A full discussion of the JEC appears on pages 14 to 16.

The American Arbitration Association is available in 24 cities around the country and services may be arranged for in other localities. Arbitration and mediation may also be sponsored by some of the volunteer arts-lawyer groups, including Volunteer Lawyers for the Arts in New York City and Bay Area Lawyers for the Arts in San Francisco.

Small claims court

Small claims courts give artists access to the legal system, while avoiding the usual encumbrance, costs and lengthy duration of formal courts. The small claims procedure is streamlined, speedy and available for a very minimal fee.

Artists can handle their own cases with a little preparation. Information can be obtained from flyers prepared by the court, "how-to" publications and, best, from local rules books. The court clerk, or a legal advisor in some localities, is often available to help with preparation.

Artists can bring claims in which a monetary judgment is sought before the court. Such claims could include non-payment for completed or cancelled artwork, as well as non-payment for the original art, subsequent re-uses, or for unreturned or damaged art.

Each court has a dollar limit for what it considers a "small claim." Amounts in excess of the limit would normally have to be brought to a formal court. However if the monies owed are only slightly in excess of the court's limit, a reduced amount that fits within the limit can be sued for. This claim must be made with the understanding that the balance above the court's limit is permanently forfeited. It may also be possible to split up larger amounts of owed monies into several smaller claims to be sued for individually. This can be done for distinctly separate legal claims.

Collection services

Collection alternatives, authorized by law, may be used by the artist who remains empty-handed despite a favorable arbitration or court decision. The failure to pay after the court has affirmed an arbitration award or rendered its decision makes the buyer liable for further legal action not previously available to the artist.

When the buyer fails to pay, the artist gains the right, within limitations, to place a lien on the buyer's funds and assets. Available funds, such as bank accounts or a portion of an individual's salary, can then be seized by a sheriff or marshal and turned over to the artist. Similarly the proceeds of property or cars sold at a public auction may be used to settle the debt.

Commercial collection agencies are available to seek payment on the artist's behalf before an arbitration decision or judgment is obtained. Their efforts involve escalated demands on the buyer through letters, phone calls or visits, or by using a lawyer.

Collection agencies' fees, in addition to their routine expenses, range from 20 percent to 50 percent of the monies actually recovered. If the agency engages a lawyer, an additional fee would most likely be required.

A signed agreement between the artist and the agency should be reviewed carefully for actions the agency will take and the attendant costs. Particular care should be taken in dealing with a commercial agency that may use practices that could be deemed unprofessional since they may reflect unfavorably on the artist.

Consulting or hiring a lawyer

The services of a lawyer can assist in a number of ways and at different stages in a collection strategy. Consulting with a lawyer about a problem at hand may provide sufficient information to continue individual collection efforts. The lawyer may be able to advise about available resources, chances for successful resolution, and legal matters to consider.

For simple payment-due problems a general practitioner or collection lawyer could be engaged. The lawyer's efforts would be similar to that of a collection agency. The psychological effect of receiving a lawyer's letter or call often produces quick resolutions or conclusions to disputes.

If the nature of the dispute involves the artist's legal rights in and economic control over artwork, then a lawyer specializing in art matters should be selected. It is important that the lawyer be familiar with the applicable laws as well as the business aspects of the artist's profession.

When a dispute must be cleared up before payment can be made, engaging a lawyer to negotiate with the buyer might be helpful. The lawyer may be able to take a more forceful role on the artist's behalf and may bring about a fairer and quicker settlement. A lawyer's presence and negotiation skills may also result in avoiding a lawsuit. When the problem is resolved, and it proves advisable, a lawyer could provide a written agreement to bring complex issues to a final and binding close.

Whether the problem relates to the nature of the rights involved or the amounts owed, the artist should, at the very least, arrange for an initial consultation. In this manner the artist can obtain a determination as to what the relevant law is and whether the artist's position is supportable under the law.

Lawyer's fees vary, and different arrangements exist, from flat fees to a percentage of the monies recovered. Initial one-time consultation fees are often lower. Artists with specified limited income may well be able to take advantage of volunteer arts-lawyer groups for their collection, as well as other legal needs. These exist in or near the cities where there are Guild chapters, as well as in other cities around the country.

Georgia Volunteer Lawyers for the Arts
32 Peachtree Street, N.W.
Atlanta, GA 30303
404/577-7378

Lawyers for the Creative Arts
220 South State Street
Chicago, IL 60604
312/987-0198

Lawyers Committee for the Arts
2700 Q Street, N.W., Suite 204
Washington, DC 20007
202/433-6777

Volunteer Lawyers and Accountants for the Arts
1540 Sul Ross
Houston, TX 77006
713/526-4876

Los Angeles Lawyers for the Arts
617 South Olive Street
Los Angeles, CA 90014
213/688-7404

Volunteer Lawyers for the Arts
1560 Broadway, Suite 711
New York, NY 10036
212/575-1150

Philadelphia Volunteer Lawyers for the Arts
260 South Broad Street
Broad & Spruce Streets
Philadelphia, PA 19102
215/545-3385

San Diego Lawyers for the Arts
7730 Herschel Avenue, Suite A
La Jolla, CA 92037
714/454-9696

Bay Area Lawyers for the Arts
Fort Mason Center, Bldg. 310
San Francisco, CA 94123
415/775-7200

Suing in formal court

Bringing a suit in formal court is not normally necessary to resolve a payment or other dispute. Various alternatives, as already noted, are available to the artist and buyer for providing workable means for resolving most disputes.

Formal court should only be considered as a last resort when the buyer refuses to negotiate or does so unrealistically, leaving the artist with no other choice.

Claims in excess of the small claims court limit must be brought to formal court. Similarly, non-monetary issues, such as copyright disputes or action required of the buyer, must also be taken to formal court.

The artist does not necessarily have to hire a lawyer in order to sue in formal court. The law provides for a person to appear as his or her own lawyer.

In disputes where the issue is clear, artists will usually not be prejudiced by representing themselves in court. In disputes not involving large sums of money, some lawyers will provide legal consultation to the artist on how to prepare the case. This alternative can benefit the artist by reducing legal costs.

Of course, when a great deal of money or complex legal issues are involved, it is prudent to hire a lawyer to handle the entire matter. In such event, the fees and expenses should be discussed with the lawyer at the outset. The artist will therefore be aware of the monetary commitment before using a formal court.

Putting it into perspective

Preparation for the possibility of non-payment of fees is best made right at the beginning of the job. Written agreements should establish clearly the buyer's payment obligations as well as any conditions that would go into effect when payment is not made as agreed.

The first step in fee collection should be direct contact with the buyer to ascertain the nature of the problem. This communication will also enable the artist, should it prove necessary, to determine which alternative recourses to pursue.

The services of an outside party, such as an arbitrator, (which should be provided for in the original agreement) or mediator, or the Guild's Grievance Committee, may assist the parties in achieving a resolution.

Should arbitration not be available or the buyer prove uncooperative, the artist may be required to use more forceful alternatives.

Small claims court can provide an inexpensive and speedy legal determination of claims within its jurisdiction.

When payment is refused despite a favorable arbitration decision or court judgment, the artist can use the services of a sheriff or marshal.

Lawyers may be engaged at any stage of the collection process, depending upon the issues involved, to provide advice or full representation.

Commercial collection agencies may also be used to seek payment of fees in the artist's behalf.

Establishing written safeguards early can prevent payment problems as well as provide the artist with practical alternatives. These alternatives protect the artist's rights and facilitate the collection of outstanding fees. And, *getting paid* is, of course, the just entitlement of professional artists.

On the Guild

in New York City. Local chapters of the Guild exist in California, Colorado, Florida, Georgia, Indiana, Massachusetts, New York, Western New York and Vermont.

National benefits and services

The national organization offers a wide range of benefits and services to members, whether they are attached to a specific chapter or are members at-large. These programs and services were developed as a direct result of members' expressed needs.

National newsletter

The National Newsletter is published and distributed monthly to all Guild members. It features important and timely information on industry trends, professional concerns, legislative developments and rights issues. The paper is directed by an editor-in-chief who also serves on the National Board of Directors.

Individual members, board members and chapters are encouraged to use the newsletter to share information about local activities and professional concerns; to foster dialogue about issues of mutual concern; to bring up ideas for the Guild's national policy agenda. This can be done through letters to the editor, contributing columns, and planning announcements.

Legal referral network

Because independent contractors often face legal questions particular to their type of business, the Guild has a referral system listing lawyers around the country who are familiar with artists' issues and who are willing to work with our members for reduced fees. Lawyers who are members of the referral network have been screened by the Guild's counsel, Eisner & Levy, to insure the appropriateness of their experience. This *member only* service is available throughout the country.

Areas for which members might consult lawyers include: contract review, bill collection, copyright and patent advice, incorporation and partnership, tax questions, and real estate, among others.

Chapters and individual members can recommend lawyers with whom they work for

The Graphic Artists Guild was formed in 1967 by artists concerned about improving their professional lives by affecting industry standards, ethics, professional practices and pricing. These artists had, in many instances, already attained a high degree of professionalism, experience and influence in the field. They sought to create an organization that would provide a voice for artists and a means of acting together based on members' concerns.

These founding members and the many who have become Guild members during the last 20 years have demonstrated that active membership in the Graphic Artists Guild is the way to ensure the advancement of their interests and equitable professional conditions.

Today, most graphic artists join the Guild to act together to protect their professional integrity and their art by sharing information, discussing problems in the industry and working to improve the profession. Guild members work together on contract issues, pricing and artists' rights legislation—communicating with each other to take advantage of the experiences of the group.

Guild members have established a strong track record of successful lobbying on behalf of artists on state and federal levels, developing groundbreaking publications on professional practices and pricing strategies, establishing educational seminars, and group health, life and disability insurance plans.

The Graphic Artists Guild is a national organization whose headquarters are located inclusion in the service by writing or calling the national office.

Insurance

The Guild offers group insurance to its members for health, life and disability coverage. All members, with the exception of students, are eligible to apply for these plans.

Professional education programs

This project arranges seminars and workshops on subjects such as negotiation, marketing, self-promotion, and financial planning for groups of artists around the country. Members can request these programs through their local chapter or by contacting National directly.

Another component of this project is curriculum development for art schools, in which teachers who are Guild members share information about teaching professional practices on the undergraduate level.

The Guild also sponsors courses and workshops in cooperation with art schools, undergraduate art departments and related organizations.

Professional practices monitoring

The national organization monitors problems that occur throughout the industry and tracks member complaints on issues concerning standards, practices and pricing. For those members in nonchapter areas, the national office will consider grievances with clients on issues such as late-payment, contract disputes, collections, return of original artwork, etc. Either through legal referral or action by the national board of directors, members can receive support for their rights when a case has been accepted.

Public policy and legislation

Artists are recognized as special contributors to our society and economy. As such, they are accorded special status within the U.S. Constitution and through the 1978 Copyright Law. The Guild has a legislation and public policy committee that monitors federal and state policy developments and works to protect artists' rights in local, state and federal arenas. Activities of the committee and legislative developments are reported regularly in the National Newsletter.

The Guild-authored Copyright Justice Act, which seeks to reform the work-for-hire provision of the Copyright Law, is pending in the U.S. Congress. The national organization is also the leader of a creators' coalition that includes writers, photographers, performing artists and visual artists who have joined in the effort for work-for-hire reform.

Other lobbying projects include Moral Rights, which protects an artist's original work from alteration, defacement or damage, even after reproduction rights are sold; Fair Practices, which clears up the ambiguity of ownership of the original work; Tax Equity, to insure that artists can claim full market-value deductions for works donated to charitable institutions; and creators' rights in light of the developments in new technologies.

Bills on Moral Rights and Fair Practices have been passed in New York, Massachusetts, Maryland, Oregon and California.

National board of directors

The national board of directors, which has oversight responsibility for the organization, is comprised of elected artist-members. Each local chapter has representatives on the national board and the full board meets twice a year to establish goals and priorities, share information on program development and approve the organization's budget. During the rest of the year, board meetings are held monthly in New York City to consider ongoing issues and programs.

Chapters

Each chapter of the Guild runs its own programs oriented to the needs of its region and members, under the direction of elected artist-members. The local chapters are the "lifeblood" of the Guild, where members' direct input influences services and programs. As the chapters identify needs and concerns, local programs are developed; if an issue becomes a concern for more than one chapter, or more than one group of members, it is then referred to the national board for assessment and action.

Local services and benefits

Newsletters

Each chapter publishes its own newsletter covering issues of regional interest, announcing meetings and programs, and reporting on members' activities. Most chapter newsletters are published on a quarterly basis.

Artist-to-artist hotline

Chapters across the country have established artist-to-artist hotlines that are staffed by member-volunteers. Members with questions about professional issues, such as pricing, contracts or negotiating, can call seasoned professionals in the Guild for help. Information received through the hotlines is often used in assessing markets and targeting problems in the field.

Discounts on supplies

Many chapters have developed discount programs with suppliers in their areas, where members can receive from 5 to 20 percent off on art supplies and services.

Grievance committees

Grievance procedures for members who are experiencing contractual or professional disputes with clients exist in most chapters. These committees help resolve disputes through informal contact with the client. If these disputes are not resolved through committee assistance, it may make recommendations for further action that the artist may take. These committees may also provide support letters for court cases.

Meetings and networks

Regular member meetings are features of all Guild chapters. At these meetings, programs on issues such as self-promotion, pricing, negotiating or resource-swaps are highlighted. Members are able to confer directly with peers on business issues, keep updated on the latest developments in their field and socialize.

Professional education programs

Local chapters may run in-depth seminars and workshops on subjects such as pricing, marketing and negotiation. Members are active in helping to develop the curricula for these programs, which are coordinated under the direction of the chapter boards and staff.

Chapters sometimes arrange cooperative programs with local art schools or art departments in colleges and universities, which attract wide audiences.

The Graphic Artists Guild Foundation

The Graphic Artists Guild Foundation was formed in 1983 to "foster, promote, and advance greater knowledge, appreciation and understanding of the graphic arts... by the presentation and creation of the graphic arts, activities designed to promote, aid and advance the study of existing work, and to promote the creation, presentation and dissemination of new works; to sponsor workshops, training sessions, symposia, lectures and other educational endeavors."

Further, the Foundation's constitution states among its goals, "to help monitor and establish rules governing industry practices and to contribute to modifying these when necessary."

The Foundation receives grants and donations to conduct studies whose information will benefit the industry, the public and the arts in general. It has recently concluded a two-year study, partially sponsored by the National Endowment for the Arts, of art contests and competitions. The study assessed the nature of contests and competitions and developed a set of ethical guidelines and standards for these events.

More Guild resources

Legal Guide for the Visual Artist Revised Edition by Tad Crawford

This highly acclaimed guide is updated and expanded to cover the enormous growth in the field of art law since its first publication in 1977. *Legal Guide for the Visual Artist* trains artists to think in a new way. It alerts them to issues that are likely to trap the unwary or uninformed. It opens doors to those who seek to better their business practices, increase their incomes and protect their artwork. Simply knowing when to consult a lawyer can be a great asset that will help artists to avoid time-consuming and expensive problems.

To Order: Send a check or money order for $16.95 per book, plus $2.25 postage and handling to:

Madison Square Press
10 E. 23rd Street
New York, NY 10010

Directory 5 sponsored by The Graphic Artists Guild

Published by Madison Square Press and sponsored by the Graphic Artists Guild, this advertising directory for illustrators offers discounted rates for guild members and will be distributed free to 16,000 art directors nation-wide. The publication date is Fall, 1988. For more information or to reserve pages in the directory, please contact Madison Square Press, 11 West 20 Street, New York, N.Y. 10011, (212) 475-1620.

The arts profession: What we know, what we don't know.

According to the Bureau of Labor Statistics (BLS), 313,000 artists were employed in 1982. The artist population increased by 9,000 in 1982, indicating a drop in growth compared with the last decade, when the number of persons in the arts professions nearly doubled.

Unemployment was up for artists and reached 6.6 percent, a figure comparable to the peak unemployment figures for the 1973-75 recession years. Unemployment among all professional and technical workers (including artists) was only 3.3 percent, so artists as a group had doubled the average unemployment rate.

Who are "artists"?

The Bureau of Labor Statistics uses the terms *commerical and graphic artists and designers* to include: illustrators, cartoonists, animators, designers, art directors, mechanical artists, industrial designers, fashion designers, textile designers, memorial designers and floral designers.

The BLS indicates that artists are employed by the advertising industry, the publishing industry, department stores and other retailers, durable goods manufacturing firms, motion pictures producers, government agencies, broadcast companies, manufacturing industries and services industries.

The BLS finds that most graphic artists are working in larger cities, with the largest concentration in New York, followed by Los Angeles and Chicago. They note that commercial and graphic artists are employed throughout the country, but believe that few are employed in small towns and rural areas.

Women artists

The percentage of women in the total artist labor force increased noticeably to 1/3 female, resulting from a great number of women entering the arts professions in the 1970s. Employment and unemployment

According to the BLS, the unemployment rate for the three groups of commercial artists averaged about 5.3 percent in 1982. The Bureau of Labor Statistics indicates that approximately 1/2 of all commercial artists are self-employed.

Job outlook

The BLS speculates that employment opportunities will grow for commercial and graphic artists through the mid-1990s. They believe that the growth will parallel or exceed the growth of other occupations, expanding with the economy. They also project that the supply of those entering the field will exceed the number of positions available. They note that designers tend to leave the field at a rate which exceeds that of other professional and technical employees.

The questions are the problem

Data collected on artists' occupations have some important limitations. Most important for us is that no specific figures are available for the number of people employed and unemployed in the graphic arts and related communications fields.

Survey questions, for example, identify only the primary occupation of an individual. We are all aware that artists often work simultaneously in other occupations to support their income and are, therefore, not counted in statistical studies as artists, unless more time was devoted to art than to the second occupation. Generally the figures do not reflect this high degree of self-employment.

Sometimes no occupational code exists for a certain discipline (i.e., photo-retoucher), therefore, no estimate for this population group can be ascertained.

The data from BLS does not include people with art skills who work for little or no pay in order to gain experience and it also does not include those not seeking active employment because of job market factors.

Graphic Artists Guild Membership Application

Please fill in all the information requested and mail completed application to the Graphic Artists Guild, 11 West 20 Street, New York, N.Y. 10011. Call (212) 463-7730 for any additional information.

NAME	
ADDRESS	APT OR FLOOR
CITY	STATE	ZIP
TELEPHONE (BUSINESS)	(HOME)

Membership Status
All professional graphic artists, or full-time graphic arts students are eligible for membership in the Graphic Artists Guild. Please check your appropriate category:

☐ *Sustaining Member*
A full-time graphic artist whose gross personal income derived from graphics is $30,000 or over per year.
Dues Rate: $175 per year.

☐ *Regular Member*
A full-time graphic artist whose gross personal income derived from graphics is $12,000 or over per year, but less than $30,000.
Dues Rate: $135 per year.

☐ *Provisional Member*
A full-time graphic artist whose gross personal income derived from graphics is less than $12,000 per year.
Dues Rate: $100 per year.

☐ *Student Member*
A full-time graphic arts student (list school and graduating year under "employment status" on the application). Members in this category are not eligible for the Guild's group insurance plans, since they are normally covered by school plans.
Dues Rate: $55 per year.

☐ *Associate Member*
Professionals who are active in a related field (i.e. teachers, artists' reps, etc.) and whose earnings are derived from ownership in or management of a business which profits from buying and selling others' artwork can become members of the Guild in this category. As associate members, professionals can take advantage of all Guild programs at members' rates, and participate in all Guild activities and services. Associate members *may not hold office or vote in elections*.
Dues Rate: $95 per year.

Employment Status
If you are on staff and do freelance work as well, please mark "1" for staff, and "2" for freelance.

☐ Staff   ☐ Student
School_____
Graduating year_____

☐ Freelance (business owner, partnership, corporation)

Discipline Area
Please mark "1" for the area in which you do most of your professional work. If there is another area in which you work, please mark "2," "3," in order of the amount of work you do.

____ Graphic Design
____ Production (mechanicals)
____ Illustration
____ Textile Design
____ Cartooning
____ Needleart Design
____ Instructor
____ Computer Arts
____ Artist Representative
____ Art Direction
____ Photography
____ Pre-Production Art
____ Other
*(please list)*_____

Method of Payment
All applications must be accompanied by payment in full of the $25.00 initiation fee, plus payment of your annual dues. You may make a partial payment of at least 50% of your annual dues, and we will bill you for the balance. If that balance is not paid within 120 days of joining the Guild, all services will be suspended. You will still be liable for the balance of your dues payment for the year. *Dues are not refundable.*

Please make your check or money order payable to Graphic Artists Guild.

Amount enclosed:

$_____ DUES
         PLUS $25.00 INITIATION FEE
$_____ TOTAL ENCLOSED

For office use only:

PEGS	MEMBERSHIP CARD
MAILING HOUSE	CODED

SIGNATURE   DATE

It takes about six weeks from the time we receive your application and appropriate dues payment until you receive your membership packet.* The membership packet includes your membership card, a copy of the most recent *Pricing and Ethical Guidelines* and other informational material on the Guild. You are eligible to take full advantage of Guild resources once your dues payment is registered with us.

*This membership packet is sent UPS. If you cannot receive UPS, please note that on your application form.

Membership Statement
My income is greater as a graphic artist than any income that I derive from any business which profits from the management of, the buying and/or selling of graphic artwork.[1]

I, the undersigned, agree to abide by the Constitution and by-laws[2] of the Graphic Artists Guild and do hereby authorize the Guild to act as my representative with regard to negotiating agreements, approved by the Guild membership, to improve pricing and ethical standards of the graphic arts profession.

I further understand that my membership in the Graphic Artists Guild is continuous and that I will be billed for membership dues annually on the date of my original application. If I wish to resign from the Graphic Artists Guild, I understand that I must resign in writing, and that I will be responsible for the payment of any dues owed prior to the date of my resignation.

Notes:
1. This statement does not apply to Associate Members, since they are not graphic artists.

2. These documents are on file at the National and Chapter Offices for inspection. They will be sent to you upon request and on receipt of $1.00 for postage and handling.

Glossary

accessories, clothing: Hat, gloves, shoes or slippers, jewelry, socks, belt, suspenders, necktie, collar, cuffs, scarf, umbrella, hair decorations, apron, handbag, tote, etc.

accessories, home furnishings: Floral arrangement, basket, lamp, coat hanger, storage box, garment bag, shoe organizer, drying towel, pot holder, shower curtain, tissue cover, toilet lid cover, bolster, pillow, cushion, door stop, book ends, frame, appliance cover, laundry bag, etc. (*Note:* Some home accessories can overlap as novelties.)

account executive: A representative of an advertising agency who handles specific accounts and acts as a client liaison to the art director, creative director, and others creating advertising for the account.

adult clothing: Clothing in sizes for teengirls, teenboys, misses', miss petite, junior, junior petite, women's, half-sizes, and men's.

advance: An amount paid prior to the commencement of work or in the course of work. It may be to cover expenses or it may be partial payment of the total fee. An advance as partial payment is common for a time-consuming project.

advance on royalties *or* **advance payment against royalties:** An amount paid prior to actual sales of the commissioned item or work; sometimes paid in installments. Advances are generally not expected to be returned, even if unearned in sales. Both the terms and the size of the advance are negotiable.

afghan: A small blanket, sometimes called a nap blanket, designed for use by one person. It can be formed in a variety of techniques, such as crochet, knitting, weaving, etc..

agreement: See *contract.*

all rights: The purchase of all rights of usage for reproduction of an artwork forever.

animator: An artist who is responsible for articulation on characters' movements.

applique *or* **applied work:** To apply or stitch one layer of fabric over another so that the applied pieces form a motif. See also *reverse applique.*

art director: One whose responsibilities include the selection of talent, purchase of visual work, and the supervision of the quality and character of visual work. Usually an employee of the advertising agency, publishing house, magazine, or other user of the graphic artist's work, although some organizations hire free-lance art directors to perform these duties.

art staff: A group of artists working for a company such as an advertising agency, publisher, magazine, or large design studio and under art director supervision.

artwork: Any finished work of a graphic artist.

assistant animator: Cleans up the animator's drawings according to a model sheet and does in-betweens. In some larger studios the assistants solely do the clean-up work.

author's alterations (AAs) *or* **author's corrections (ACs):** Alterations or corrections of type that has been set due to the client's errors, additions, or deletions. The typographer's or printer's changes for making AAs are usually passed on to the client. See also *printer's error.*

background: One who paints backgrounds which have already been designed.

bailment: An obligation on the part of the individual(s) with whom art is left to take reasonable care of it. This is a legal requirement and applies to situations such as leaving a portfolio for review.

basketry: The art of forming baskets from wood, reeds, yarns, etc., by weaving, braiding, coiling, or other techniques.

bedspread: The final or top cover for a bed of any size, primarily used for decorative purposes. See also *quilt.*

blanket: A layer of bedclothing placed over the top sheet and under the bedspread, used primarily for warmth. See also *quilt.*

bleed: A small extra area on the exterior dimensions of a page to allow for trimming. Also called "trim" area; the printing that runs into this area.

braiding: To plait together strands of yarn to strips of fabric to form a larger ply to be coiled and sewn together flat or dimensionally to make rugs, mats, baskets, etc.

camera-ready art *or* **camera copy:** Usually a mechanical or pasteup accompanied with finished art that is prepared for photographing for plate-making.

cancellation fee: When a project is terminated or not used by the client, this fee is paid as compensation for the artist's or studio's effort in developing the illustration of design.

cartoonist: A professional artist who creates art in a humorous and satirical style and/or as political commentary.

castoff: To provide a breakdown or estimate of length. In knitting, to put stitches on a knitting needle. In publishing, to estimate the typeset length or number of pages from manuscript or galley proof. In textiles, sometimes used as a synonym for knock-off; refers to a pattern or design that a company wishes to alter for a new pattern while retaining similarity to the original.

cel: Short for celluloid. A transparent sheet of celluloid on which the finished drawings are inked.

center truck: The center page spread in a magazine or newspaper which is a premium space for the placement of advertisements.

children's clothing: Sizes pertaining to boys and girls from toddlers to teens.

Chromalin proofs: A proprietary term for a color proof process employing a photosensitized clear plastic. Color separation film negatives are exposed to the plastic in such a way that process color will adhere to dots on the plastic. Four sheets (one for each process color) are exposed, treated with the separate process colors, placed in register, and then laminated. Such proofs are used for presentations and for checking register, obvious blemishes, and size. The color may be very accurate but is subject to a variation due to exposure and the application of the process color. Also *transfer key*. See also *Color Key* and *progressive proofs*.

chrome: See *transparency*.

cibachrome: A proprietary term for a full-color positive photographic print made from a transparency.

client accommodation: To work at fees below the normal rate in order to accommodate budgetary restrictions and to preserve a long-term working relationship.

Color Key: A proprietary term of the 3M Company; sometimes referred to as "3Ms." A method for obtaining separate film positives showing progressive color breakdown of the color separation negatives. Such proofs are useful for presentation and for checking register, obvious blemishes, and size; they are not a true indication of final printed color. *Chromalin* proofs are preferred for more accurate (though still not exact) color representation. *Progressive proofs* using process inks on press are the most accurate method for checking color. See also *Chromalin proofs* and *progressive proofs*.

color proofs: The first full-color printed pieces pulled off the press for approval before the press is considered ready to roll for the entire press run. Sometimes called *simple color proofs,* these proofs are useful for making corrections in color on press, particularly for those problems resulting from improper registration and the effects of overprinting. *Progressive proofs* are the preferred methods for accurately checking color.

commission (*n*) commission (*v*): Percentage of a fee paid by an artist to the artist's agent or gallery for service provided or business transacted. The act of giving an artist an assignment to create a work of art.

comprehensive *or* comp: A visualization of the idea for an illustration or design usually created for the client and artist to use as a guide for the finished art. *Tight comp* or *loose comp* refers to the degree of detail, rendering, and general accuracy used in the comprehensive.

confirmation form: A contract form that is used by an artist when no purchase order has been given or when the purchase order is incomplete with respect to important terms of the contract, such as amount of fee, rights transferred, etc.

contract: An agreement whether oral or written, whereby two parties bind themselves to perform certain obligations. Synonyms: *agreement* or *letter of agreement* (if the contract takes the form of a letter).

converter: A company that transfers designs onto printed or woven fabric.

copy: The text of an advertisement, editorial concern of a magazine or a newspaper, or the text of a book.

copyright: The right to copy or authorize the copying of creative work. Any freelance artist creating artwork automatically owns the right of that work unless provisions have been made prior to the commencement of the project to transfer the copyright to the buyer.

corners: A type of layout for specific textile designs in which a single layout of a complete corner is used for the repeated design on all four corners. Commonly used in home furnishings (e.g., the design for the corners of a tablecloth, napkin, or scarf).

C print *or* inter neg: A full-color positive print from a negative transparency.

creative director: Usually an employee or officer of an advertising agency whose responsibilities may include over all supervision of all aspects of the character and quality of the agency's work for its client. The creative director's background may be art, copy, or client contact.

crochet: A method of making a lace or a textile structure from any yarn, fabric strip, or stringy material with a hook, using the chain stitch or variations on the chain to form the textile.

croques: Rough sketches made by an artist, particularly by fashion illustrators.

design brief: An analysis of a project prepared either by the publisher or the designer. When the designer assumes this responsibility it should be reflected in the design fee. The design brief may include: (1) a copy of the manuscript, with a selection of representative copy for sample pages and a summary of all typographical problems, copy areas, code marks, etc.; (2) an outline of the publisher's manufacturing program for the book: compositor and composition method, printer and paper stock, binder and method of binding; (3) a description of the proposed physical characteristics of the book, such as trim size, page length, list price, quantity of first printing, and whether the book will print in one color or more than one. The publisher should so indicate whether any particular visual style is expected.

director: One who oversees the complete picture from conception to finish. Has complete control over all phases: Character design (which is usually supplied by an agency), layout, sound etc.

dummy: A book, brochure, or catalog idea in a roughly drawn form usually made up to contain the proper number of pages and used as a reference for positioning, pagination, and in position.

dye transfer: Similar in appearance to a color photograph but different in the important respect that it is produced from a transparency by printing continuous tones of color dyes.

embroidery: A general term referring to decorating the surface of any fabric with freeformed stitches that are based on plain sewing. For example: embroidery with wool or a wool-like yarn on fabric is called *crewel embroidery*. Stitches and fabric vary according to the will of the designer. also *counted embroidery:* The formation of regimented stitches on even-weave fabrics on needlepoint canvas known by various names which denote their style of stitches (e.g., hardanger, black work, drawn thread work). *Cross stitch embroidery:* Can be either freeformed embroidery over Xs printed on the fabric or counted embroidery worked on an even-weave fabric or canvas.

employee, freelance: Terms of freelance employment include: Work hours determined by assignment using one's own workspace and materials; freelancers generally provide their own benefits. The freelancer often collects state sales tax from clients and pays his or her own income taxes.

engineered design: A pattern specifically designed to fit certain size factors and to be repeated in a particular fashion (e.g., panel print to fit a Tressi blouse or dress design).

finished art: Usually an illustration, photograph, or mechanical that is prepared and ready for the engraver or printer.

first North American serial rights: The right to be the first magazine to publish art for use in one specific issue to be distributed in North America.

first rights: The right to be the first user of art for one-time use; frequently used to describe the right to publish art in a magazine serial or drawn from a book in which the art will appear.

floor covering: Any textile structure or painting technique that is used to cover a floor partially or completely for either decorative or functional purposes.

format: An arrangement of type and illustration that is used for many layouts; an arrangement used in a series.

Fortune double-500 company: The *Fortune* magazine's annual listing based on sales revenues of the 1000 largest corporations in the United States.

general apprentice: One who does a little of everything except camera work.

graphic artist: a visual artist working in a commercial area.

graphic designer: A professional graphic artist who works with the elements of typography, illustration, photography, and printing to create commercial communications tools such as brochures, advertising, signage, posters, slide shows, book jackets, and other forms of printed or graphic communications. A visual problem solver.

graphic film artist: One who is skilled in creating special effects on film by use of computerized stands, matted, and/or adding computerized movement to artwork (e.g., television logos with glows, set movement).

graphics: Visual communications.

Group head: Some advertising agencies divide their clients into groups under a group head who supervises the work of art directors on the various accounts.

guild: An association of like-minded professionals seeking to protect and better their status and/or skills. When employees are members in equal proportion to freelancers, such a guild qualifies with the United States government as a union. In this capacity, a guild may represent employees who are its members in collective bargaining.

gutter: The area in a magazine, newspaper, or book, where the left (verso) and right (recto) pages meet. Important elements are often not placed in this area because of the fold.

half-body garments: A garment that is worn either from the waist up or from the waist down, such as a vest, sweater, poncho, pants, skirt, etc..

hand letterer: A professional artist who creates letterforms for use in logotypes, alphabets, and specific titles or captions.

hard furniture: Any furniture that requires the designer to use a hard substance such as wood, metal, etc. for structural support or decorative purposes. It may also incorporate padding and a textile surface.

illustrator: A professional graphic artist who communicates a pictorial idea by creating a visual image using paint, pencil, pen, collage, or any other graphic technique except photography for a specific purpose.

image: A pictorial idea.

inbetweener: One who does the drawing in between the drawings that have been cleaned up by the assistant.

infant clothing: Refers to newborn and baby sizes up to toddler sizes.

inker: One who inks onto cells the lines of finished drawings.

invoice: A statement given to a client showing the amount due on an assignment. Usually submitted after work has been completed unless advance payments are to be made. When advance payments are made, the invoice should reflect these and show the balance due.

jacquard sketches: A sketch usually done on graph paper to be used on jacquard woven fabrics such as tablecloths, upholstery, and towels.

junior checker (paint and ink only): One who inspects cels for the proper and thorough application of the correct paint colors.

key line artist: A sometimes pejorative term for a mechanical or pasteup artist.

kickback: A sum of money or a large figure that is given to an artist by a supplier for the artist's part in passing on work such as printing. Kickbacks are illegal. Quite often the supplier's kickback costs are hidden in its invoices submitted to the client of work completed.

knitting: The method of forming a lace or a textile structure from any yarn, fabric strip, or stringy material with two or more eyeless needles, pegged tools, or sticks, etc. using various looped stitches to form the structure.

knock-off (*n*) **knock off** (*v*): A term most often

used in the textile design industry to identify a design that at the request of the client or stylist has been copied by a different artist than the one who created it. Broadly used to mean the copying of an artist's style or artwork when no creative input and/or significant changes are made by the artist in creating knock-off. Knock-offs are unethical and often illegal.

lace: A general term for any openwork or sheer fabric with holes formed by any technique, including knitting, crochet, bobbin lace, netting, hairpin lace, tatting, eyelet, needle lace, etc..

latch hook: A method of knotting short or long lengths of yarn over crosswise threads of a rug canvas with a latch hook tool. The technique is generally used for rug making, pillows, and wall hangings.

layette: A coordinated ensemble for the newborn consisting of a receiving blanket, cap, jacket, and booties.

Layout: The design, usually in sketch form, of the elements of an advertisement, magazine or book page, or any other graphic work (e.g., brochures, catalogs, etc.) intended for reproduction. Used as a guide and usually executed by an art director or illustration graphic designer.

layout: An artist who lays out and arranges backgrounds.

letterforms: Any forms that are made out of letters, numerals, or ampersands.

letter of agreement: See *contract.*

live area: The area on the camera copy of a page or a publication beyond which essential elements should not be positioned.

logo: A mark or symbol created for an individual, company, or product that translated the impression of the body it is representing into a graphic image.

Logotype: Any alphabetical configuration that is designed to identify by name a producer, company, publication, or individual.

lucey: One of several optical devices used to enlarge or reduce images.

macrame: A method of ornamental knotting for cords and yarns, generally used to form cringes, hammocks, wall hangings, plant holders, etc.

Markup (*n*) mark up (*v*): A service charge added to expense account items to reimburse the artist for the time to process the billing of such items to the client and the cost of advancing the money to pay such expenses; the process of adding such a charge.

Markers: Felt-tipped pens used in a technique for illustrating comprehensives or for sketching a rough in black-and-white or color. Proprietary synonyms: *Magic Markers, Stabilo.*

mechanical: Ruled and pasted flats or boards composed by a production artist for the printer to use in the printing and engraving process.

moonlighting: A freelance commission taken on by a salaried person to be completed in the person's spare time.

needlepoint *or* canvas work: The formation of regimented stitches over the meshes or threads of a special open-weave fabric called canvas.

novelties: A general term for gift or boutique-type items or for clever decorative or functional items such as eyeglass, comb, or mirror case; Christmas decorations (stockings, tree skirt, ornaments, etc.); calendar; clock; cosmetic bag; jewelry bag; typewriter cover; golf bag and club covers; exercise or beach mat, etc.. Also, wax transfer patterns for embroidery or applique motifs. (*Note:* some novelties can overlap as home accessories).

opaque projector: A projector that uses reflected light to project the image of a non-transparent object onto a canvas, board, or screen; the image is then used by an artist to copy or show work.

overhead: Nonbillable expenses such as rent, phone, insurance, secretarial and accounting services, and salaries.

page makeup: Assembling in sequence the typographic and/or illustrative elements of a brochure, catalog, book or similar item.

pasteup (*n*): Usually reproduction copy of galley type fastened in position with wax or glue by a production artist for the use of the engraver in the platemaking process. Also, *paste-up (adj.)* and *paste up (v.).*

patchwork: Piecing, sewing, or joining together pieces of fabric to form motifs or a complete fabric structure. Generally, the pieces are cut in planned shapes. When shapes are unplanned or take on a helter-skelter appearance, it is called *crazy patchwork* or *crazy quilt.*

per diem: A day rate given to a professional by a client to complete a day's assignment.

portfolio *or* artist's book: Reproductions and/or originals that represent the body of an artist's work.

preplanner/checker: One who checks that the animation is in sync and flows correctly (before camera).

printer's error (PE): A mistake made in the film negatives, platemaking, or printing that is not due to the client's error, addition, or deletion. These alterations are normally absorbed by the printer or typographer. See also *author's alterations.*
production artist: A professional artist who works with a designer in taking a layout through to mechanicals, pasteups, and often on through the printing process.

production coordinator: One who is responsible for making sure that everything is in order before it goes under the camera.

professional: One who strives for excellence in business and follows fair practices in every professional endeavor.

profit: The difference remaining (i.e., net income) after overhead, expenses, and taxes are subtracted from income received (gross income).

progressive proofs *or* **progs:** Proofs of color separation negatives that have been exposed to offset plates and printed using process inks. Presented in the sequence of printing, i.e., (1) yellow plate alone, (2) red alone, (3) yellow and red, (4) blue alone, (5) yellow, red, and blue, (6) black alone, and (7) yellow, red, blue, and black. The preferred way for checking the color of the separation negatives using the same inks, paper, ink densities, and color sequence as intended for the production run. See also *color proofs.*

proposal or estimate: A graphic designer's detailed analyses of the cost and components of a project. Used to firm up an agreement before commencing work on a project for a client.

punch needle: Refers to both a fine, delicate embroidery technique (fine yarns or threads and fine fabrics and needles) and to a heavy rug technique (using heavy yarns and coarse fabrics and needles) where loops of varying lengths are formed on the surface of the fabric by pushing a handled-needle through the fabric from the wrong side. Fine versions are generally used for decorations in clothing or home accessories; coarse versions for chair cushions, mats, rugs, and wall hangings.

purchase order: A form given by a client to an artist describing the details of an assignment and when signed by an authorized person, authorizing work to commence.

quilt: A bedcovering that functions as both a blanket and or a bedspread that consists of two fabric layers, one placed above and the other below a filling layer. The filling can be a non-woven layer of cotton or polyester batting or a woven layer of cotton or polyester batting of a woven fabric such as flannel. Small hand running stitches, machine stitches, or yarn tufts through all layers over the item produce the quilted structure and design. Also the quilted structure can be used as a technique to produce clothing and other decorative or functional items.

readers: Copies with type prepared for the author or client to proofread and mark corrections on. They are nonreproduction quality and their value is only in checking corrections.

ready-made: Refers to clothing or fabric that was purchased in a store or available to the designer at the stage when it could have been purchased at retail.

reel: A film or number of films spliced together.

reference file: File compiled by an illustrator or designer made up of clippings from newspapers, magazines, and other printed pieces that are referred to for ideas and inspiration as well as technical information.

repeat: The textile design process by which consecutive press impressions may be made to but together imperceptibly so that the textile will appear as one consecutive image and the process run may be continued indefinitely.

representative *or* **rep:** A professional agent who promotes specific talent in illustration, photography, or textile design and negotiates contracts for fees and commissions. Usually receives a percentage of the negotiated fee as payment for the services provided to the talent.

reprint rights: The right to print something that has been published elsewhere.

reproduction copy *or* **repro:** Proofs printed in the best possible quality for use as camera copy for reproduction. Also *reproduction proof.*

residuals: Payments received in addition to the original fee, usually for extended usage of a work. See also *royalty.*

retoucher: A professional artist who alters a photograph to improve or change it for reproduction. Usually working on transparencies, or color and black-and-white prints.

reverse applique *or* **cut through applique:** When two or more layers of fabric are handled together, with the upper layer(s) cut away and stitched separately in order to reveal the under layer(s) and thus form a motif.

roughs: Loosely drawn ideas, often done in pencil on tracing paper, by an illustrator or designer. Usually several roughs are sketched out before a comprehensive is developed from them.

royalty: Payments to the artist that are based on a percentage of the revenue generated through the quantity of items sold (e.g., books, cards, calendars). See also *advance on royalties.*

sales tax: Each state government establishes the rate of taxation of items sold. It varies between 4 and 8 percent of the amount billed the client, which the freelance graphic artist is often required to be licensed to charge, collect, and remit to the state on a quarterly basis.

second rights: The right to use art that has appeared elsewhere. Frequently applied to use by magazines of art that has appeared previously in a book or another magazine.

shoot (*v*): In advertising, a day's filming or a day's shooting of still photography.

simultaneous rights: The right to publish art at the same time as another publication. Normally used when the two publications have markets that do not overlap.

sizing: The process of marking an original with a percentage or a multiplier for reduction or enlargement on camera.

sketch: Design for textiles not done in repeat. See also *roughs.*

soft furniture: Any furniture that uses only a soft filling such as batting, foam pillows, etc. to form the inner structure.

soft sculpture: A decorative dimensional item formed from fabrics or in one of the many textile structures which is stuffed with a soft filling.

speculation: Accepting assignments without any guarantee of payment after work has been completed. Payment upon publication is also speculation.

spine: The area between the front and back book bindings and on which the author, title, and publisher are indicated.

spot: A small drawing or illustration used as an adjunct to other elements in an advertisement, editorial, or book page.

spot: A television commercial.

stenciling: A method of painting on a surface using a template and a stiff bristle brush with a blunt end.

storyboards: A series of sketches drawn by artists in small scale to a television screen and indicating camera angles, type of shot (e. g., close-up, extreme close-up), back grounds, etc.. Essentially a plan for shooting a commercial for television; often accompanied by announcer's script and actor's lines.

storyboards: Sketches of action for animation. Synonyms: *story* or *story sketches*.

studio: The place where an artist works. Also an organization offering a complete graphic service. In textile design, an agency representing designs by more than one textile designer.

style: A particular artist's unique form of expression; also referred to as "a look." In textile design referred to as "hand."

subsidiary rights: In publishing, those rights not granted to the publisher but which the publisher has the right to sell to third parties in which case the proceeds are shared with the artist.

tablewear: Functional items that are used at the dining room or kitchen table, such as placemat, napkin, napkin ring, runner, tea cozy, hot pad, tablecloth, coaster, etc..

talent: A group of artists represented by an agent or gallery.

technique: Refers to the particular media used by a graphic artist.

textbook: In book publishing, applies to any book that is to be sold through schools and used for educational purposes.

textile designer: A professional artist who creates art usually to be used in repeat on surfaces such as fabric, wallpaper, wovens, or ceramics.

thumbnail *or* **thumbnail sketch:** A very small, often sketchy visualization of an illustration or design. Usually several thumbnails are created together to show different approaches to the visual problem being solved.

trade book: In book publishing, applies to any book that is to be sold in bookstores to the general public.

transparency *or* **chrome:** A full-color translucent photographic film positive. Color slides are also referred to as transparencies

union: A group of people in the same profession and working to monitor and upgrade the business standards of their industry.

weaving: A method of interlacing yarns or any stringy material in both a lengthwise and crosswise manner simultaneously. A traditional loom is generally used to control the interlacing technique, but other devices may also be used.

whole-body garments: Any one-piece garment worn from the neck and stopping anywhere below mid-thigh, such as dresses, coats, capes, etc..

workbook: In book publishing, applies to any book accompanying a textbook, usually in the elementary school level, for students to complete exercises in by following written and pictorial instructions.

work-for-hire: For copyright purposes, "work-for-hire" or similar expressions such as "done-for-hire" or "for hire" signify that the commissioning party is the owner of the copyright in the artwork as if the commissioning party had, in fact, been the artist.

Index

N O T E S

NOTES

NOTES

NOTES

NOTES